HOLIDAY & CELEBRATIONS

IT'S TIME TO GATHER

Every season offers a reason to celebrate. This year more than ever, it's important to step away from life's obligatory to-do list and reconnect with the people we love. Whether you're a newly minted host, the best cook on the block or simply need a no-sweat, knock-out dish to pass at a potluck, this brand-new edition of *Taste of Home Holiday & Celebrations* is your ultimate guide for turning life's special moments into unforgettable occasions. In addition to 25 innovative party themes and over 300 delicious recipes, you'll find charming gifts, easy crafts, no-fuss table decor, and countless tips and ideas. From simple gatherings to classy dinners that pull out all the stops, fresh inspiration for creating the party of your dreams fills every page.

© 2021 RDA Enthusiast Brands, LLC.
1610 N. 2nd St., Suite 102,
Milwaukee, WI 53212-3906
All rights reserved. Taste of Home is a registered
trademark of RDA Enthusiast Brands, LLC.

Visit us at **tasteofhome.com** for other
Taste of Home books and products.

International Standard Book Number:
D 978-1-62145-761-9
U 978-1-62145-762-6
International Standard Serial Number:
1535-2781
Component Number:
D 118000104H
U 118000106H

Executive Editor: Mark Hagen
Senior Art Director: Raeann Thompson
Editor: Amy Glander
Art Director: Courtney Lovetere
Senior Designer: Jazmin Delgado
Deputy Editor, Copy Desk: Dulcie Shoener
Senior Copy Editor: Ann Walter
Senior Food Editor: Peggy Woodward, RDN

Cover:
Photographer: Mark Derse
Set Stylist: Melissa Franco
Food Stylists: Shannon Norris, Sarah Fischer

Pictured on front cover:
Refreshing Berry Wine, p. 122; Sidecar, p. 14;
Marinated Sausage Kabobs, p. 19; Cheese-Stuffed
Cherry Tomatoes, p. 197; Pineapple Cheese Ball,
p. 8; Crab Wonton Cups, p. 68; Shrimp Cocktail with
Homemade Dipping Sauce, p. 10

Printed in USA
1 3 5 7 9 10 8 6 4 2

TABLE OF CONTENTS

'TIS THE SEASON

GIVING THANKS

EASTER GATHERINGS

SPECIAL CELEBRATIONS

'TIS THE SEASON

Cue up the holiday tunes, light the candles and set the table. This year it's easier than ever to usher in the merriest season of the year with simple yet elegant gatherings that are sure to make a lasting impression. From mouthwatering main dishes and must-have sides to cookie masterpieces and party-perfect drinks, these recipes offer fresh and creative ways to create the quintessential Christmas experience.

RETRO HOLIDAY COCKTAIL PARTY

Fire up the fondue pot and grab the cocktail shaker! This Christmas, add some old-school class to a grown-up gathering with a lineup of 1960s appetizers and libations that would impress the likes of Don and Betty Draper. These easy, era-inspired recipes, tips and tricks are guaranteed to make your party swanky.

MAI TAI

PINEAPPLE CHEESE BALL
(PICTURED ON COVER)

Pineapple lends a fruity tang to this fun and tasty appetizer. Instead of forming one large cheese ball, you could also make two smaller balls—one to serve before a meal and one to take to a party.
—Anne Halfhill, Sunbury, OH

- -

Prep: 20 min. + chilling
Makes: 1 cheese ball (3 cups)

- 2 pkg. (8 oz. each) cream cheese, softened
- 1 can (8 oz.) unsweetened crushed pineapple, drained
- ¼ cup finely chopped green pepper
- 2 Tbsp. finely chopped onion
- 2 tsp. seasoned salt
- 1½ cups finely chopped walnuts
  Optional: Assorted crackers and fresh vegetables

In a small bowl, beat softened cream cheese, pineapple, green pepper, onion and seasoned salt until blended. Cover and refrigerate for 30 minutes. Shape into a ball (mixture will be soft); coat in walnuts. Cover and refrigerate overnight. Serve cheese ball with crackers and vegetables if desired.

2 Tbsp.: 87 cal., 8g fat (2g sat. fat), 10mg chol., 155mg sod., 3g carb. (1g sugars, 1g fiber), 3g pro.

MAI TAI

This party favorite has been around for quite some time. It's not overly fruity and features a good blend of sweet and sour. For a splash of color, garnish with strawberries and lime.
—Taste of Home *Test Kitchen*

- -

Takes: 5 min. • **Makes:** 1 serving

- 1½ to 2 cups ice cubes
- 2 oz. light rum
- ¾ oz. Triple Sec
- ½ oz. lemon juice
- 1½ tsp. lime juice
- 1½ tsp. amaretto
  Optional garnish: Lime slice, lime twist, edible flowers and fresh pineapple

1. Fill a shaker three-fourths full with ice. Place remaining ice in a rocks glass; set aside.
2. Add rum, Triple Sec, juices and amaretto to shaker; cover and shake for 10-15 seconds or until condensation forms on outside of shaker. Strain mixture into prepared glass. Garnish as desired.

⅔ cup: 241 cal., 0 fat (0 sat. fat), 0 chol., 7mg sod., 15g carb. (13g sugars, 0 fiber), 0 pro.

TOM COLLINS

This cocktail has been popular for a long time, but the origin of the name is still up for debate. Some think it was named after a sweet gin called Old Tom, and others believe the drink was named for the bartender who invented it.
—Taste of Home *Test Kitchen*

- -

Takes: 5 min. • **Makes:** 1 serving

- 1½ to 2 cups ice cubes, divided
- 2 oz. gin
- 1½ oz. sour mix
- ½ cup club soda, chilled
  Optional: orange slice maraschino cherry

1. Fill a shaker three-fourths full with ice. Place remaining ice in a Collins or highball glass; set glass aside.
2. Add the gin and sour mix to shaker; cover and shake until condensation forms on outside of shaker, 10-15 seconds. Strain into prepared glass. Pour club soda into glass. If desired, garnish with orange slice and cherry.

1 serving: 213 cal., 0 fat (0 sat. fat), 0 chol., 29mg sod., 22g carb. (21g sugars, 0 fiber), 0 pro.

TEST KITCHEN TIP

To soften cream cheese quickly, cut an unwrapped block into 1-in. cubes. This creates more exposed surface area, allowing warm room temperature air to soften the cold cream cheese more quickly. Another easy trick is to place the sealed foil package in a bowl of warm water for about 20 minutes. Or simply pop a block of unwrapped cream cheese in the microwave for 15 seconds. Check for softness intermittently and reheat in 10-second increments until it has reached desired softness.

PINEAPPLE
CHEESE BALL

3. Arrange shrimp on a serving platter; serve with sauce. If desired, serve the shrimp with lemon wedges.

1 oz. cooked shrimp with about 2 tsp. sauce: 59 cal., 1g fat (0 sat. fat), 66mg chol., 555mg sod., 4g carb. (2g sugars, 0 fiber), 9g pro.

GOLDEN CHICKEN SALAD PUFFS

Stuffed with a chunky chicken salad, these pretty golden puffs are perfect for any holiday spread. Guests enjoy the subtle sweetness from the pineapple and the crunch of the celery and pecans.
—*Lola Pullen, Lakeland, FL*

- -

Prep: 20 min. • **Bake:** 15 min.
Makes: about 3½ dozen

1	cup water
½	cup butter, cubed
½	tsp. salt
1	cup all-purpose flour
4	large eggs, room temperature

FILLING

2	cups finely chopped cooked chicken
1	can (8 oz.) crushed pineapple, drained
½	cup mayonnaise
¼	cup chopped celery
¼	cup thinly sliced green onions
¼	cup chopped pecans
2	Tbsp. sweet pickle relish
¼	tsp. onion salt
¼	tsp. garlic salt
¼	tsp. paprika
	Salt and pepper to taste

1. In a large saucepan, bring water, butter and salt to a boil. Add flour all at once and stir until a smooth ball forms. Remove from the heat; let stand for 5 minutes. Add eggs, 1 at a time, beating well after each addition. Continue beating until smooth and shiny.

2. Drop by rounded teaspoonfuls 2 in. apart onto a greased baking sheet. Bake at 400° for 15-20 minutes or until golden brown. Remove to wire racks. Immediately cut a slit in each puff to allow steam to escape; cool.

3. Split puffs and set tops aside; remove soft dough form inside. In a large bowl, combine the filling ingredients. Fill puffs and replace tops. Chill until serving. Refrigerate leftovers.

2 puffs: 152 cal., 11g fat (4g sat. fat), 59mg chol., 200mg sod., 7g carb. (2g sugars, 0 fiber), 6g pro.

SHRIMP COCKTAIL WITH HOMEMADE DIPPING SAUCE

(PICTURED ON COVER)

During the '60s, shrimp cocktail was one of the most popular party foods around. And it's still a crowd favorite. It's the one appetizer I serve for every special occasion as well as small plate-style meals.
—*Peggy Allen, Pasadena, CA*

- -

Prep: 30 min. + chilling
Makes: about 6 dozen (1¼ cups sauce)

3	qt. water
1	small onion, sliced
½	medium lemon, sliced
2	sprigs fresh parsley
1	Tbsp. salt
5	whole peppercorns
1	bay leaf
¼	tsp. dried thyme
3	lbs. uncooked large shrimp, peeled and deveined (tails on)

SAUCE

1	cup chili sauce
2	Tbsp. lemon juice
2	Tbsp. prepared horseradish
4	tsp. Worcestershire sauce
½	tsp. salt
	Dash cayenne pepper
	Lemon wedges, optional

1. In a Dutch oven, combine the first 8 ingredients; bring to a boil. Add shrimp. Reduce heat; simmer, uncovered, until shrimp turn pink, 4-5 minutes.

2. Drain shrimp and immediately rinse in cold water. Refrigerate until cold, 2-3 hours. In a small bowl, combine the sauce ingredients. Refrigerate until serving.

FROZEN BLUE LAGOON MARGARITAS

A special toast to anyone who mixes up a frosty batch of blue lagoon margaritas for a soiree. Guests will swoon over the citrusy sweet tang and electrifying shade of blue.
—*Willie DeWaard, Coralville, IA*

- -

Takes: 15 min. • **Makes:** 4 servings

- 4   lime slices
- 3   Tbsp. coarse sugar
- ½   cup chilled lemon-lime soda
- ½   cup tequila
- ½   cup blue curacao
- ⅓   cup partially thawed frozen limeade concentrate
- 2   cups ice cubes

1. Using lime slices, moisten the rims of four margarita or cocktail glasses. Set aside lime slices for garnish. Sprinkle sugar on a plate; hold each glass upside down and dip rim into sugar. Set aside. Discard remaining sugar on the plate.
2. In a blender, combine the remaining ingredients; cover and process until blended. Pour into prepared glasses. Garnish with reserved lime slices. Serve immediately.
1 cup: 205 cal., 0 fat (0 sat. fat), 0 chol., 5mg sod., 26g carb. (22g sugars, 1g fiber), 0 pro.

PLANTER'S PUNCH

A real taste of the Caribbean, this rum punch would be great at a tropical holiday party. Add lemon-lime soda if the drink is too strong.
—Taste of Home *Test Kitchen*

- -

Takes: 10 min. • **Makes:** 4 servings

- 7   cups ice cubes
- 1   cup dark rum
- 1   cup orange juice
- ½   cup unsweetened pineapple juice
- 2   oz. amaretto
- 2   oz. grenadine syrup

GARNISH
    Orange slices and maraschino cherries

Place the ice in a pitcher. Pour in the rum, juices, amaretto and grenadine; stir. Serve in hurricane or highball glasses. Garnish drinks as desired.
1½ cups: 257 cal., 0 fat (0 sat. fat), 0 chol., 5mg sod., 24g carb. (22g sugars, 1g fiber), 0 pro.

FROZEN BLUE LAGOON MARGARITAS

Christmas Quiz

It's the most musical time of the year. How many of these classic holiday songs will make your party playlist? Answers on page 14.

1. Written in 1942, it made the Billboard 100 every year until 1963.
   A. "I'll Be Home for Christmas"
   B. "Silver Bells"
   C. "White Christmas"

2. Co-written by crooner Mel Torme, this was a hit for another beloved singer.
   A. "Sleigh Ride"
   B. "Frosty the Snowman"
   C. "The Christmas Song"

3. This novelty hit in 1952 was performed by a 13-year-old singer.
   A. "I Want a Hippopotamus for Christmas"
   B. "I Saw Mommy Kissing Santa Claus"
   C. "Grandma Got Run Over by a Reindeer"

4. This jazzy 1953 hit was from the singer who later played Catwoman.
   A. "Here Comes Santa Claus"
   B. "Santa Baby"
   C. "Must Be Santa"

5. This is considered the first rock 'n' roll holiday hit.
   A. "Jingle Bell Rock"
   B. "Baby, It's Cold Outside"
   C. "Let It Snow"

6. It was on Elvis' first Christmas album in 1957.
   A. "Jingle Bells"
   B. "Winter Wonderland"
   C. "Blue Christmas"

7. It didn't chart until two years after Brenda Lee recorded it.
   A. "Santa Claus Is Coming to Town"
   B. "Rockin' Around the Christmas Tree"
   C. "Deck the Halls"

8. This one's a country favorite from Buck Owens.
   A. "Santa Claus Is Back in Town"
   B. "Thinking About Drinking for Christmas"
   C. "Santa Looked a Lot Like Daddy"

TEQUILA SUNRISE

TEQUILA SUNRISE

Everyone loves the pretty sunset-colored layers in this refreshing cocktail classic. It's like a mini vacation in a glass!
—Taste of Home *Test Kitchen*

- -

Takes: 5 min. • **Makes:** 1 serving

1   to 1¼ cups ice cubes
1½ oz. tequila
4½ oz. orange juice
1½ tsp. grenadine syrup
GARNISH
   Orange slice and maraschino cherry

Place ice in a Collins or highball glass. Pour the tequila and orange juice into the glass. Slowly pour grenadine over a bar spoon into the center of the drink. Garnish as desired.
¾ cup: 184 cal., 0 fat (0 sat. fat), 0 chol., 0 sod., 17g carb. (15g sugars, 0 fiber), 1g pro.

CHOCOLATE RUM BALLS

Roll these truffle-like rum balls in crushed Oreos to get the right amount of crunch. I've been known to stock them in freezer for those times a chocolate craving calls.
—Dauna Harwood, Elkhart, IN

- -

Prep: 30 min. + chilling
Makes: about 3 dozen

1   tsp. instant coffee granules
¼   cup dark rum, warmed
4   oz. cream cheese, softened
1   cup confectioners' sugar
1   cup ground almonds
3   oz. unsweetened chocolate, melted
8   Oreo cookies, finely crushed

1. Dissolve coffee granules in warm rum. Beat cream cheese, confectioners' sugar, almonds and rum mixture until blended. Stir in melted chocolate. Refrigerate until firm enough to roll, about 1 hour.
2. Shape mixture into 1-in. balls; roll in the crushed cookies. Store in an airtight container in the refrigerator, separating the layers with waxed paper.
1 rum ball: 70 cal., 4g fat (2g sat. fat), 3mg chol., 21mg sod., 7g carb. (5g sugars, 1g fiber), 1g pro.
Make ahead: Rum balls can be made 3 days in advance. Store in an airtight container in the refrigerator.

CLASSIC SWISS CHEESE FONDUE

This rich and fancy fondue is a great appetizer for a throwback party. Or, let it warm you up on a cold and blustery day. Don't be surprised when the pot is scraped clean.
—Taste of Home *Test Kitchen*

- -

Takes: 30 min. • **Makes:** about 4 cups

1   garlic clove, halved
2   cups white wine, chicken broth or unsweetened apple juice, divided
¼   tsp. ground nutmeg
7   cups shredded Swiss cheese
2   Tbsp. cornstarch
   Optional: Cubed bread and assorted fresh vegetables

1. Rub garlic clove over the bottom and sides of a fondue pot; discard garlic and set fondue pot aside. In a large saucepan over medium-low heat, bring 1¾ cups wine and nutmeg to a simmer. Gradually add cheese, stirring after each addition until cheese is melted (cheese will separate from wine).
2. Combine cornstarch and remaining wine until smooth; gradually stir into the cheese mixture. Cook and stir until thickened and mixture is blended and smooth. Transfer to prepared fondue pot and keep warm. Serve with bread cubes and vegetables.
¼ cup: 214 cal., 15g fat (9g sat. fat), 44mg chol., 90mg sod., 2g carb. (0 sugars, 0 fiber), 13g pro.

SIDECAR

(PICTURED ON COVER)
Welcome guests in from the cold with this sunny, tart citrus delight.
—Taste of Home *Test Kitchen*

Takes: 5 min. • **Makes:** 1 serving

      Ice cubes
1   oz. brandy
⅔   oz. (4 tsp.) Triple Sec
1½ to 3 tsp. lemon juice
GARNISH
      Lemon twist

1. Fill a shaker three-fourths full with ice. Add the brandy, Triple Sec and lemon juice. Cover shaker and shake for 15-20 seconds or until condensation forms on outside of shaker. Strain into a chilled cocktail glass. Garnish as desired.

1 serving: 137 cal., 0 fat (0 sat. fat), 0 chol., 2mg sod., 10g carb. (8g sugars, 0 fiber), 0 pro.

To make a thin citrus spiral to garnish a cocktail, the best tool to use is a channel knife, which cuts a thin rope from the peel. Roll the cut peel into a twist, or gently wrap the peel around a straw to create a twist shape. Use a paring knife to make a wider twist.

LIME DIVINE TARTS

Winter is prime time for limes, so why not showcase them at your holiday party? These cute cups are impressive but easy to make.
—Ann Yri, Lewisville, TX

Prep: 30 min. + chilling
Bake: 15 min. + cooling
Makes: 2 dozen

2   large eggs
1   large egg yolk
½   cup sugar
¼   cup lime juice
1   tsp. grated lime zest
¼   cup unsalted butter, cubed
TART SHELLS
½   cup unsalted butter, softened
3   oz. cream cheese, softened
1   cup all-purpose flour
      White chocolate curls and lime zest strips

1. In a small heavy saucepan over medium heat, whisk eggs, egg yolk, sugar, lime juice and zest until blended. Add the butter; cook, whisking constantly, until mixture is thickened and coats the back of a spoon. Transfer to a small bowl; cool. Cover and refrigerate the mixture until chilled.
2. In a small bowl, cream butter and cream cheese until smooth. Gradually add flour; mix well. Cover and refrigerate 1 hour or until easy to handle.
3. Preheat oven to 375°. Shape dough into 1-in. balls; press onto the bottom and up sides of 24 ungreased miniature muffin cups. Prick bottoms with a fork. Bake 15-17 minutes or until golden brown. Cool shells for 5 minutes before removing from pans to wire racks to cool completely.
4. Fill the shells with lime mixture. Garnish with chocolate curls and lime zest strips. Refrigerate leftovers.
1 tart: 107 cal., 8g fat (5g sat. fat), 45mg chol., 18mg sod., 9g carb. (4g sugars, 0 fiber), 2g pro.

COCONUT SHRIMP

Jumbo shrimp is the perfect vehicle for crunchy, tropical coconut flakes. The fruity salsa is delightful as a dip for this island-inspired appetizer.
—Marie Hattrup, Sonoma, CA

Prep: 20 min. • **Cook:** 5 min./batch
Makes: 6 servings

18   uncooked jumbo shrimp (about 1 lb.)
⅓   cup cornstarch
¾   tsp. salt
½   tsp. cayenne pepper
3   large egg whites
2   cups sweetened shredded coconut
      Oil for deep-fat frying
APRICOT-PINEAPPLE SALSA
1   cup diced pineapple
½   cup finely chopped red onion
½   cup apricot preserves
½   cup minced fresh cilantro
2   Tbsp. lime juice
1   jalapeno pepper, seeded and chopped
      Salt and pepper to taste
      Lime wedges, optional

1. Peel and devein shrimp, leaving tails intact. Make a slit down inner curve of each shrimp, starting with the tail; press lightly to flatten. In a shallow dish, combine the cornstarch, salt and cayenne; set aside. In a bowl, beat egg whites until stiff peaks form. Place coconut in another shallow dish. Coat the shrimp with cornstarch mixture; dip into egg whites, then coat with coconut.
2. In an electric skillet or deep-fat fryer, heat oil to 375°. Fry the shrimp, a few at a time, 1-1½ minutes on each side or until golden brown. Drain on paper towels.
3. In a bowl, combine salsa ingredients. Serve shrimp with salsa and, if desired, lime wedges.
Note: Wear disposable gloves when cutting hot peppers; the oils can burn skin. Avoid touching your face.
3 shrimp with 3 Tbsp. salsa: 1513 cal., 37g fat (14g sat. fat), 1655mg chol., 2031mg sod., 58g carb. (33g sugars, 2g fiber), 224g pro.

Christmas music quiz answers: 1-C; 2-C; 3-B; 4-B; 5-A; 6-C; 7-B; 8-C.

COCONUT
SHRIMP

A FAMILY-STYLE CHRISTMAS

There's no place like home for the holidays. Start here for all the right ingredients to cook up happy Yuletide memories you'll cherish forever. Get inspired and enjoy effortless entertaining with a menu that's casual, family-friendly and brimming with all the flavor and comfort you'd expect in a festive feast to share with those you love most.

Winning Cranberry Glazed Ham (p. 23)
Buttery Crescent Rolls (p. 21) **Pimiento Green Beans** (p. 21)

Christmas Day Countdown

It's the most wonderful day of the year! Many of the dishes in this menu can be prepared in advance, while others are best to make the day of. Use this timeline as your guide to get a jump on all the festivities.

A FEW WEEKS BEFORE

☐ Prepare two grocery lists—one for nonperishable items to buy now and one for perishable items to buy a few days before Christmas.

☐ Prepare and bake the cake layers for the Favorite Italian Cake, but do not assemble or frost. Place layers in airtight container and store them in the freezer.

TWO DAYS BEFORE

☐ Buy remaining grocery items.

☐ Wash china, stemware and table linens.

THE DAY BEFORE

☐ Bake the Buttery Crescent Rolls. Let rolls cool and store in an airtight container.

☐ Prepare the marinade for the Winning Cranberry Glazed Ham. Add the marinade to ham in a 2-gal. resealable bag. Seal bag and place in the refrigerator to chill overnight.

☐ Prepare and bake the Mixed Nut Bars. Cut and store bars in an airtight container.

☐ Prepare and bake the Dark Chocolate Cream Pie. Cover and refrigerate overnight.

☐ Set the table.

CHRISTMAS DAY

☐ In the morning, take the cake layers for the out of the freezer to thaw. Prepare the cream cheese frosting; assemble and frost cake. Cover and place in the refrigerator until ready to serve.

☐ About 4 hours before dinner, prepare the marinade for the Marinated Sausage Kabobs. Add cheese, olives, salami and peppers to the marinade; refrigerate for at least 4 hours.

☐ About 3 hours before dinner, remove ham from the refrigerator. Bake ham and keep warm until dinnertime.

☐ About 1 hour before guests arrive, prepare the Artichoke Nibbles and Crab-Stuffed Mushrooms. Cover and keep warm until serving.

☐ About 30 minutes before dinner, prepare the Four-Cheese Macaroni. Cover and keep warm until serving.

☐ About 30 minutes before dinner, prepare the Wassail Punch and Pimiento Green Beans. Keep warm until ready to serve.

RIGHT BEFORE DINNER

☐ Right before guests arrive, bring out the Artichoke Nibbles and Crab-Stuffed Mushrooms. Thread kabob ingredients onto skewers. Set up appetizers on buffet table.

☐ As guests arrive, prepare individual servings of Sparkling Pom-Berry Splash. Serve splash and wassail with appetizers.

☐ Warm the remaining cranberry mixture in a small saucepan on the stovetop; serve with ham.

☐ Warm crescent rolls in the oven just before serving.

☐ Following dinner, remove the chocolate pie and Italian cake from the refrigerator. Slice cake and pie. Serve desserts alongside Mixed Nut Bars.

ARTICHOKE NIBBLES

My mother-in-law gave me the recipe for these cheesy appetizers when I married her son. I've been making them for holidays and special occasions ever since.
—*Karen Brown, Trenton, MI*

Prep: 15 min. • **Bake:** 25 min. + cooling
Makes: about 3½ dozen

- 1 small onion, chopped
- 1 garlic clove, minced
- 1 tsp. canola oil
- 2 jars (6½ oz. each) marinated artichoke hearts, drained and chopped
- 4 large eggs
- 2 Tbsp. minced fresh parsley
- ¼ tsp. salt
- ⅛ tsp. pepper
- ⅛ tsp. dried oregano
- ⅛ tsp. hot pepper sauce
- 2 cups shredded cheddar cheese
- ⅓ cup crushed saltines (about 10 crackers)

1. Preheat the oven to 325°. In a small skillet, saute onion and garlic in oil until tender. Stir in artichokes. Remove from heat; set aside. In a large bowl, whisk the eggs, parsley, salt, pepper, oregano and hot pepper sauce. Stir in the cheddar cheese, cracker crumbs and artichoke mixture.

2. Pour into a greased 11x7-in. baking dish. Bake, uncovered, until a thermometer reads 160°, 25-30 minutes. Cool for 10-15 minutes before cutting. Serve warm.

1 piece: 44 cal., 4g fat (1g sat. fat), 23mg chol., 105mg sod., 1g carb. (0 sugars, 1g fiber), 2g pro.

SPARKLING POM-BERRY SPLASH

Add a splash of color to cocktail hour with this lovely red beverage. Garnish with lime slices and blueberries for extra flair.
—*Shirley Warren, Thiensville, WI*

Takes: 5 min. • **Makes:** 1 serving

- 2 oz. pomegranate blueberry juice, chilled
- 1 tsp. lime juice
- ⅓ cup sparkling moscato wine, chilled

Pour pomegranate blueberry and lime juices into a champagne flute; top with wine.

1 serving: 92 cal., 0 fat (0 sat. fat), 0 chol., 11mg sod., 10g carb. (9g sugars, 0 fiber), 0 pro.

MIXED NUT BARS

One pan of these bars goes a long way. They get a nice flavor from butterscotch chips.
—*Bobbi Brown, Waupaca, WI*

Prep: 10 min. • **Bake:** 20 min. + cooling
Makes: 3½ dozen

- 1½ cups all-purpose flour
- ¾ cup packed brown sugar
- ¼ tsp. salt
- ½ cup plus 2 Tbsp. cold butter, divided
- 1 cup butterscotch chips
- ½ cup light corn syrup
- 1 can (11½ oz.) mixed nuts

1. Preheat the oven to 350°. In a small bowl, combine flour, brown sugar and salt. Cut in ½ cup butter until mixture resembles coarse crumbs. Press into a greased 13x9-in. baking pan. Bake for 10 minutes.
2. Meanwhile, in a microwave, melt the butterscotch chips and remaining butter; stir until smooth. Stir in corn syrup.
3. Sprinkle nuts over crust; top with the butterscotch mixture. Bake until set, about 10 minutes. Cool on a wire rack. Cut into bars.
1 serving: 143 cal., 8g fat (4g sat. fat), 8mg chol., 104mg sod., 16g carb. (10g sugars, 1g fiber), 2g pro.

Merry & Bright

Bring holiday cheer to the table with festive place settings. Tie a satin napkin into a big chunky knot and adorn it with a holiday tag, jingle bell and a sprig of pine.

MARINATED
SAUSAGE KABOBS

MARINATED
SAUSAGE KABOBS
(PICTURED ON COVER)

These flavorful and colorful appetizers are so fun they'll be the talk of the party. And they're so easy. Simply assemble the day before and forget about them! Your guests will love the marinade flavor.
—*Joanne Boone, Danville, OH*

Prep: 20 min. + marinating • **Makes:** 3 dozen

- ¼ cup olive oil
- 1 Tbsp. white vinegar
- ½ tsp. minced garlic
- ½ tsp. dried basil
- ½ tsp. dried oregano
- 8 oz. cheddar cheese, cut into ¾-in. cubes
- 1 can (6 oz.) pitted ripe olives, drained
- 8 oz. hard salami, cut into ¾-in. cubes
- 1 medium sweet red pepper, cut into ¾-in. pieces
- 1 medium green pepper, cut into ¾-in. pieces

1. In a large shallow dish, combine the first 5 ingredients; add the remaining ingredients. Stir to coat; refrigerate at least 4 hours. Drain, discarding marinade.
2. For kabobs, thread cheese, olives, salami and peppers onto toothpicks.
1 kabob: 69 cal., 6g fat (2g sat. fat), 12mg chol., 165mg sod., 1g carb. (0 sugars, 0 fiber), 3g pro.

BUTTERY
CRESCENT ROLLS

BUTTERY CRESCENT ROLLS

I double the recipe for these rolls because they never last long. I roll them into crescents, but you can shape them any way you'd like.
—*Kelly Kirby, Mill Bay, BC*

Prep: 35 min. + rising • **Bake:** 10 min.
Makes: 2 dozen

- 1 Tbsp. active dry yeast
- 1 tsp. plus ⅓ cup sugar
- ½ cup warm water (110° to 115°)
- ½ cup butter, softened
- ½ cup warm 2% milk (110° to 115°)
- 1 large egg, room temperature
- ¾ tsp. salt
- 4 cups all-purpose flour

1. In a large bowl, dissolve yeast and 1 tsp. sugar in warm water. Add butter, milk, egg, salt, remaining sugar and 2 cups flour. Beat until smooth. Stir in enough remaining flour to form a soft dough.
2. Turn onto a floured surface; knead until smooth and elastic, 6-8 minutes. Place in a greased bowl, turning once to grease the top. Cover and let rise in a warm place until doubled, about 1 hour.
3. Punch the dough down. Turn onto a lightly floured surface; divide in half. Roll each dough portion into a 12-in. circle; cut each circle into 12 wedges. Roll up the wedges from the wide end and place point side down 2 in. apart on greased baking sheets. Curve ends to form crescents. Cover and let rise in a warm place until doubled, about 30 minutes.
4. Preheat oven to 350°. Bake until golden brown, 10-12 minutes. Remove from pans to wire racks.
1 roll: 128 cal., 4g fat (3g sat. fat), 19mg chol., 107mg sod., 19g carb. (4g sugars, 1g fiber), 3g pro.

> **TEST KITCHEN TIP**
>
> To make golden brown rolls that are very soft and tender, use milk as the liquid, which adds tenderness to the dough and forms a soft crust. Brush the tops of the rolls with melted butter after baking to produce a pretty sheen.

PIMIENTO GREEN BEANS

PIMIENTO GREEN BEANS

Here's an easy way to turn everyday green beans into a special side dish. Pimientos, Parmesan cheese and chicken broth add savory flavor and a dash of color.
—*Lynn McAllister, Mt. Ulla, NC*

Prep: 5 min. • **Cook:** 10 min.
Makes: 10 servings

- 2 lbs. fresh green beans, cut into 2-in. pieces
- 1 can (14½ oz.) chicken broth
- ½ cup chopped onion
- 1 jar (2 oz.) chopped pimientos, drained
- ½ tsp. salt
- ⅛ to ¼ tsp. pepper
- ¼ cup shredded Parmesan cheese

In a large saucepan, bring beans, broth and onion to a boil. Reduce heat; cover and cook for 10-15 minutes or until crisp-tender. Drain. Stir in pimientos, salt and pepper. Sprinkle with Parmesan cheese.
¾ cup: 44 cal., 1g fat (0 sat. fat), 2mg chol., 336mg sod., 8g carb. (3g sugars, 3g fiber), 3g pro. **Diabetic exchanges:** 1 vegetable

WASSAIL PUNCH

Cloves and cinnamon dress up a blend of fruit juices for special occasions. The spicy, warm drink is sure to help you forget about any nip in the air.
—*Dorothy Anderson, Ottawa, KS*

Takes: 25 min.
Makes: 14 servings (about 3½ qt.)

- 2 qt. apple cider
- 2 cups orange juice
- 2 cups pineapple juice
- ½ cup sugar
- ½ cup lemon juice
- 12 whole cloves
- 4 cinnamon sticks (3 to 4 in.) Optional: Orange slices and cranberries

1. In a large Dutch oven, bring the first 7 ingredients to a boil. Reduce the heat; simmer, uncovered, until flavors are blended, 10-15 minutes.
2. Strain and discard cinnamon and cloves. If desired, garnish with orange slices and cranberries. Serve warm.
1 cup: 134 cal., 0 fat (0 sat. fat), 0 chol., 15mg sod., 34g carb. (30g sugars, 0 fiber), 0 pro.

CRAB-STUFFED MUSHROOMS

Mushroom caps plump with a crabmeat filling make a wonderful appetizer for entertaining. You can also use the recipe as a light entree, served on salad greens or with pasta.
—*Tonya Farmer, Iowa City, IA*

Prep: 25 min. • **Bake:** 15 min.
Makes: 2½ dozen

 1 medium tomato, seeded and diced
 ½ cup soft bread crumbs
 2 Tbsp. mayonnaise
 1 Tbsp. minced fresh parsley
 1 garlic clove, minced
 ¼ tsp. salt
   Dash cayenne pepper
 1 can (6 oz.) crabmeat, drained, flaked and cartilage removed
 30 medium fresh mushrooms
 1 Tbsp. olive oil
 ¼ cup shredded Parmesan cheese

1. Preheat oven to 400°. In a large bowl, combine the first 7 ingredients. Fold in crabmeat; set aside.
2. Remove and discard mushroom stems. Brush inside of mushroom caps with oil. Spoon 1-2 tsp. of crab mixture into each cap; sprinkle with Parmesan cheese.
3. Place in a 15x10x1-in. baking pan coated with cooking spray. Bake until mushrooms are tender and the filling is lightly browned, 15-20 minutes.

1 mushroom: 24 cal., 1g fat (0 sat. fat), 6mg chol., 72mg sod., 1g carb. (0 sugars, 0 fiber), 2g pro.

TEST KITCHEN TIP

We recommend using button or cremini mushrooms for this recipe. Buttons, the most common mushrooms, account for 90 percent of the United States mushroom intake annually according to the United States Department of Agriculture. Cremini mushrooms, sometimes mistaken for baby portobellos, are really just a more mature button mushroom with a deeper flavor profile and color and a meatier cap.

FOUR-CHEESE MACARONI

I adapted this recipe from one a friend gave me. It has a distinctive blue cheese taste and is very filling. Add cooked cubed chicken or crumbled bacon to make it even heartier.
—*Darlene Marturano, West Suffield, CT*

Takes: 20 min. • **Makes:** 8 servings

 1 pkg. (16 oz.) elbow macaroni
 ¼ cup butter, cubed
 ¼ cup all-purpose flour
 ½ tsp. salt
 ⅛ tsp. pepper
 3 cups 2% milk
 2 cups shredded cheddar cheese
 1½ cups shredded Swiss cheese
 ½ cup crumbled blue cheese
 ½ cup grated Parmesan cheese

1. Cook macaroni according to the package directions. Meanwhile, in a Dutch oven, melt butter over medium heat. Stir in flour, salt and pepper until smooth; gradually whisk in milk. Bring to a boil, stirring constantly; cook and stir 2 minutes or until thickened.
2. Reduce heat to low; stir in cheeses until melted. Drain macaroni; add to cheese sauce and stir until coated.

1 cup: 508 cal., 23g fat (13g sat. fat), 65mg chol., 603mg sod., 51g carb. (6g sugars, 2g fiber), 26g pro.

WINNING CRANBERRY GLAZED HAM

A dear friend gave me the recipe for this tender ham. I've served it for brunch and dinner at reunions, weddings, graduations, baptisms, holiday gatherings and more. It's a delicious way to please a crowd.
—*Sue Seymour, Valatie, NY*

Prep: 15 min. + marinating • **Bake:** 1¾ hours
Makes: 16 servings

- 2 cans (16 oz. each) whole-berry cranberry sauce
- 1 cup orange juice
- ⅓ cup steak sauce
- 2 Tbsp. canola oil
- 2 Tbsp. prepared mustard
- 2 Tbsp. brown sugar
- 1 fully cooked bone-in ham (7 to 9 lbs.)

1. In a large bowl, combine the cranberry sauce, orange juice, steak sauce, oil, mustard and brown sugar. Score the surface of the ham with shallow diagonal cuts, making diamond shapes.
2. Place ham in a 2-gal. resealable bag. Add half of cranberry mixture; seal bag and turn to coat. Cover and refrigerate for 8 hours or overnight, turning several times. Cover and refrigerate remaining cranberry mixture.
3. Preheat oven to 325°. Drain the ham, discarding marinade. Place ham on a rack in a foil-lined roasting pan; cover with foil. Bake for 1¾ hours.
4. Place reserved cranberry mixture in a small saucepan; heat through. Uncover ham; brush with cranberry mixture.
5. Bake until a thermometer reads 140°, 45-60 minutes longer, brushing with the cranberry mixture every 15 minutes. Warm remaining cranberry mixture; serve with ham.
4 oz.: 264 cal., 7g fat (2g sat. fat), 87mg chol., 1164mg sod., 22g carb. (15g sugars, 1g fiber), 29g pro.

WINNING CRANBERRY GLAZED HAM

DARK CHOCOLATE
CREAM PIE

DARK CHOCOLATE CREAM PIE

Even though I'm not a fan of chocolate, this wonderful pie is one of my favorite desserts to make for my chocolate-loving friends. The filling is simple to make and begins to set up in the crust right away.
—*Kezia Sullivan, Sackets Harbor, NY*

- -

Prep: 30 min. + chilling • **Makes:** 8 servings

Dough for single-crust pie
1¼ cups sugar
¼ cup cornstarch
¼ tsp. salt
3 cups whole milk
3 oz. unsweetened chocolate, chopped
4 egg yolks, lightly beaten
3 Tbsp. butter
1½ tsp. vanilla extract
Optional: Whipped cream and grated chocolate

1. On a lightly floured surface, roll dough to a ⅛-in.-thick circle; transfer to a 9-in. pie plate. Trim crust to ½ in. beyond rim of plate; flute edge. Refrigerate 30 minutes. Preheat oven to 425°. Line crust with a double thickness of foil. Fill crust with pie weights, dried beans or uncooked rice. Bake on a lower oven rack until edge is golden brown, 20-25 minutes. Remove foil and weights; bake until bottom is golden brown, 3-6 minutes longer. Cool on a wire rack.
2. In a large saucepan, combine sugar, cornstarch and salt. Stir in milk and chocolate. Cook and stir over medium-high heat until thickened and bubbly. Reduce heat; cook and stir 2 minutes longer. Remove from the heat.
3. Stir a small amount of hot filling into egg yolks; return all to the pan, stirring constantly. Bring to a gentle boil; cook and stir 2 minutes longer. Remove from the heat.
4. Gently stir in butter and vanilla until butter is melted. Spoon into the crust. Cool on a wire rack. Cover and chill pie for at least 3 hours. If desired, serve the pie with whipped cream and grated chocolate.
1 piece: 390 cal., 19g fat (10g sat. fat), 128mg chol., 218mg sod., 52g carb. (37g sugars, 2g fiber), 7g pro.
Dough for single-crust pie (9 in.): Combine 1¼ cups all-purpose flour and ¼ tsp. salt; cut in ½ cup cold butter until crumbly. Gradually add 3-5 Tbsp. ice water, tossing with a fork until dough holds together when pressed. Cover and refrigerate 1 hour before using.
Note: Let pie weights cool completely before storing. Beans and rice may be reused for pie weights, but not for cooking or eating.

Bottle Brush Trees Display

Dress up your holiday table with a whimsical display of bottle brush trees. If you're feeling crafty, make your own trees using sisal rope. Look online for easy tutorials. Or, purchase the trees from *Amazon.com* or craft and decor retailers. Set the trees inside festive mugs and surround them with ornaments or other small baubles.

FAVORITE ITALIAN CAKE

Here's a scrumptious cake that will melt in your mouth and make you say, *Mil a Grazi!* (Thanks a million!) Pecan lovers will eagerly accept a second slice.
—*Marilyn Morel, Keene, NH*

- -

Prep: 40 min. • **Bake:** 20 min. + cooling
Makes: 16 servings

½ cup butter, softened
½ cup shortening
2 cups sugar
5 large eggs, room temperature
1 tsp. vanilla extract
2 cups all-purpose flour
1 tsp. baking soda
¼ tsp. salt
1 cup buttermilk
1 cup chopped pecans
½ cup sweetened shredded coconut
CREAM CHEESE FROSTING
11 oz. cream cheese, softened
½ cup butter, softened
3¾ cups confectioners' sugar
1 tsp. vanilla extract
1 cup coarsely chopped pecans

1. Preheat oven to 350°. Grease and flour three 9-in. round baking pans. Cream the butter, shortening and sugar until light and fluffy, 5-7 minutes. Add eggs, 1 at a time, beating well after each addition. Beat in the vanilla. Combine flour, baking soda and salt; add to creamed mixture alternately with buttermilk, beating well after each addition. Fold in pecans and coconut.
2. Pour into prepared pans. Bake until a toothpick inserted in center comes out clean, 20-25 minutes. Cool for 10 minutes before removing cake layers from pans to wire racks to cool completely.
3. For frosting, beat cream cheese and butter until fluffy. Add confectioners' sugar and vanilla; beat until smooth. Spread frosting between layers and over top and sides of cake. Press pecans onto sides of cake. Refrigerate.
1 piece: 628 cal., 37g fat (15g sat. fat), 109mg chol., 328mg sod., 70g carb. (56g sugars, 2g fiber), 7g pro.

GIFTS FROM THE KITCHEN

Who doesn't love a homemade treat? Look here for fudge, gumdrops, jelly, cookie mix and other festive goodies you can package up beautifully and give to someone special. Whether you want to make edible gifts for Christmas or need a heartfelt way to say thank you, your friends and neighbors will be thrilled with these sweet surprises!

GINGERBREAD
SPICE JELLY

CREAMY CARAMELS

I discovered the recipe for these soft buttery caramels in a local newspaper years ago and have made them ever since. I make them for Christmas, picnics and charity auctions. They are so much better than any kind you find in the stores.
—*Marcie Wolfe, Williamsburg, VA*

Prep: 10 min. • **Cook:** 30 min. + cooling
Makes: 64 servings (2½ lbs.)

- 1   tsp. plus 1 cup butter, divided
- 1   cup sugar
- 1   cup dark corn syrup
- 1   can (14 oz.) sweetened condensed milk
- 1   tsp. vanilla extract

1. Line an 8-in. square pan with foil; grease the foil with 1 tsp. butter and set aside.
2. In a large heavy saucepan, combine sugar, corn syrup and remaining butter; bring to a boil over medium heat, stirring constantly. Boil slowly for 4 minutes without stirring.
3. Remove from the heat; stir in milk. Reduce heat to medium-low and cook until a candy thermometer reads 238° (soft-ball stage), stirring constantly. Remove from the heat; stir in vanilla.
4. Pour into prepared pan (do not scrape saucepan). Cool. Using foil, lift candy out of pan. Discard foil; cut candy into 1-in. squares. Wrap individually in waxed paper; twist ends.
Note: We recommend you test your candy thermometer before each use by bringing water to a boil; the thermometer should read 212°. Adjust your recipe temperature up or down based on your test.
1 piece: 72 cal., 3g fat (2g sat. fat), 10mg chol., 45mg sod., 10g carb. (8g sugars, 0 fiber), 1g pro.

GINGERBREAD SPICE JELLY

I've made batches of this simple jelly, a winner at our county fair, to give as gifts for many years. When the jars are empty, people return them for a refill.
—*Robin Nagel, Whitehall, MT*

Prep: 15 min. + standing
Process: 10 min.
Makes: 5 half-pints

- 2½   cups water
- 18   gingerbread spice tea bags
- 4½   cups sugar
- ½   cup unsweetened apple juice
- 2   tsp. butter
- 2   pouches (3 oz. each) liquid fruit pectin

1. In a large saucepan, bring water to a boil. Remove from heat; add tea bags. Cover and steep 30 minutes.
2. Discard tea bags. Stir in the sugar, apple juice and butter. Bring to a full rolling boil over high heat, stirring constantly. Stir in pectin. Continue to boil 1 minute, stirring constantly.
3. Remove from heat; skim off foam. Ladle hot mixture into 5 hot half-pint jars, leaving ¼-in. headspace. Wipe rims. Center lids on jars; screw on bands until fingertip tight.
4. Place jars into canner with simmering water, ensuring that they are completely covered with water. Bring to a boil; process for 10 minutes. Remove jars and cool. (Jelly may take up to 2 weeks to set.)
2 Tbsp.: 91 cal., 0 fat (0 sat. fat), 1mg chol., 2mg sod., 23g carb. (23g sugars, 0 fiber), 0 pro.

TEST KITCHEN TIP

If your caramel becomes gritty or grainy, the sugar probably crystallized. If the melting sugar splashes up onto the sides of the pan, it quickly loses its moisture content and forms back into crystals. That can set off a chain reaction that can cause caramel to seize up, ruining the entire batch. Instead, gently swirl the pan as you go and use a wet pastry brush to wipe down any sugar that sticks to the sides of the pot.

CREAMY
CARAMELS

CRANBERRY EGGNOG BRAID

Whether at Thanksgiving, Christmas or New Year's, this is a good party bread. You can't beat it as a gift, either.
—*Mary Lindow, Florence, WI*

Prep: 25 min. + rising
Bake: 25 min. + cooling
Makes: 1 loaf (12 pieces)

- 3 to 3½ cups all-purpose flour, divided
- ¼ cup sugar
- ½ tsp. salt
- 1 pkg. (¼ oz.) active dry yeast
- ½ tsp. ground nutmeg
- 1¼ cups eggnog
- ¼ cup butter
- ½ cup dried cranberries

GLAZE
- 1 cup confectioners' sugar
- 1 to 2 Tbsp. eggnog
- ¼ tsp. vanilla extract
  Dash nutmeg

1. In a bowl, combine 1½ cups of flour, sugar, salt, yeast and nutmeg; set aside. In a saucepan, heat eggnog and butter to 120°-130° (the butter does not need to melt); add to flour mixture. Beat on low until moistened; beat on medium for 3 minutes.

2. Stir in cranberries and enough remaining flour to make a soft dough. Turn onto a floured surface; knead until smooth and elastic, 6-8 minutes. Place in a greased bowl, turning once to grease top. Cover and let rise in a warm place until doubled, about 1 hour.

3. Punch dough down; divide into thirds. Shape each third into a 16-in. rope. Braid ropes on a greased baking sheet; seal ends. Cover and let rise until nearly doubled, about 30 minutes.

4. Bake at 350° for 25-30 minutes or until golden. Immediately remove from pan to a wire rack to cool completely. Combine the first 3 glaze ingredients; drizzle over braid. Dust with nutmeg.

1 piece: 257 cal., 6g fat (4g sat. fat), 27mg chol., 153mg sod., 46g carb. (21g sugars, 1g fiber), 5g pro.

ORNAMENT
POPCORN BALLS

ORNAMENT POPCORN BALLS

Classic popcorn strung on the tree is lovely, but these ornament balls take that idea up a notch. And they're a yummy treat for the family, too. Wrap the snowmen in cellophane bags and tie with a ribbon for gifting.
—*Deirdre Cox, Kansas City, MO*

Takes: 30 min. • **Makes:** 1 dozen

- 10 cups popped popcorn
- 1 pkg. (10 oz.) large marshmallows
- ¼ cup butter, cubed
- ¼ tsp. salt
  Optional: Candy canes, black pearl sprinkles, orange licorice pastels and white Smarties

1. Place the popcorn in a large bowl. In a large saucepan, combine the marshmallows, butter and salt. Cook and stir over medium-low heat until melted. Pour over popcorn; mix well. Cool slightly.
2. With greased hands, shape mixture into 12 popcorn balls, about ¾ cup each. Place on waxed paper. Decorate as desired; let stand until set.

1 popcorn ball: 162 cal., 8g fat (3g sat. fat), 10mg chol., 184mg sod., 23g carb. (13g sugars, 1g fiber), 1g pro.

HOMEMADE ORANGE GUMDROPS

I get nothing but rave reviews when I make these gumdrops—I usually have to prepare three batches! The refreshing orange flavor is a nice change from chocolate candies.
—*Becky Burch, Marceline, MO*

Prep: 10 min. • **Cook:** 10 min. + standing
Makes: about 6 dozen

- 1 tsp. plus 1 Tbsp. butter, softened, divided
- 1 cup sugar
- 1 cup light corn syrup
- ¾ cup water
- 1 pkg. (1¾ oz.) powdered fruit pectin
- ½ tsp. baking soda
- 1½ tsp. orange extract
- 1 tsp. grated orange zest
- 4 drops yellow food coloring
- 1 drop red food coloring
  Additional sugar, optional

1. Line the bottom and sides of a 9x5-in. loaf pan with foil. Grease the foil with 1 tsp. butter; set aside.
2. Grease the bottom and sides of a large heavy saucepan with the remaining butter; add sugar and corn syrup. Cook and stir over medium heat until mixture comes to a boil, about 9 minutes. Cook over medium-high heat until a candy thermometer reads 280° (soft-crack stage), stirring occasionally.
3. Meanwhile, in another large saucepan, combine the water, pectin and baking soda (mixture will foam slightly). Cook and stir over high heat until mixture boils, about 2 minutes. Remove from the heat; set aside.
4. When corn syrup mixture reaches 280° (soft-crack stage), remove from the heat. Return pectin mixture to medium-high heat; cook until mixture begins to simmer. Carefully and slowly ladle corn syrup mixture in a very thin stream into pectin mixture, stirring constantly. Cook and stir 1 minute longer.
5. Remove from the heat; stir in the extract, zest and food coloring. Transfer to prepared pan. Let stand until firm, about 2 hours. Cut into squares. If desired, roll in additional sugar.

1 gumdrop: 30 cal., 0 fat (0 sat. fat), 1mg chol., 16mg sod., 7g carb. (6g sugars, 0 fiber), 0 pro.

SPICY OATMEAL COOKIE MIX

Brown sugar and spice and everything nice—like cinnamon, coconut, oats and chips—are layered together in pretty jars for yummy, ready-to-bake cookies. Remember to include prep and baking instructions along with a list of any additional ingredients the recipient will need for baking.
—Taste of Home *Test Kitchen*

Prep: 15 min. • **Bake:** 10 min./batch
Makes: about 3½ dozen

- 1 cup all-purpose flour
- 1 tsp. ground cinnamon
- ¾ tsp. baking soda
- ¼ tsp. salt
- ⅛ tsp. ground nutmeg
- ½ cup packed brown sugar
- ½ cup sugar
- 1 cup old-fashioned oats
- ½ cup milk chocolate chips
- ½ cup butterscotch chips
- ½ cup sweetened shredded coconut

ADDITIONAL INGREDIENTS
- ½ cup butter, softened
- 1 large egg, room temperature
- ¾ tsp. vanilla extract

1. In a small bowl, combine first 5 ingredients. In a 1-qt. glass jar, layer flour mixture, brown sugar, sugar, oats, chips and coconut, packing well between each layer. Cover and store in a cool, dry place up to 6 months. Yield: 1 batch (4 cups).

To prepare cookies: Preheat oven to 350°. In a large bowl, beat butter, egg and vanilla. Add cookie mix and mix well. Drop by rounded teaspoonfuls 2 in. apart onto ungreased baking sheets. Bake cookies for 9-11 minutes or until golden brown. Cool the cookies for 2 minutes before removing to wire racks.

1 cookie: 90 cal., 4g fat (3g sat. fat), 11mg chol., 63mg sod., 12g carb. (8g sugars, 0 fiber), 1g pro.

ROSEMARY WHEAT CRACKERS

These delightful rosemary scented crackers will delight all your snackers. Pair them with a premium cheese and a jar of homemade jam.
—Nancy Mueller, Menomonee Falls, WI

Prep: 20 min.
Bake: 10 min./batch + cooling
Makes: 4 dozen

- 1¼ cups all-purpose flour
- ¾ cup whole wheat flour
- 1 tsp. sugar
- ½ tsp. salt
- ½ tsp. dried rosemary, crushed
- ¼ cup olive oil
- ½ cup 2% milk
- 1½ tsp. kosher salt, divided

1. In a small bowl, combine the flours, sugar, salt and rosemary. Gradually add oil, tossing with a fork to combine. Add milk; toss with a fork until mixture forms a ball. Turn onto a lightly floured surface; knead 8-10 times.
2. Divide dough into 3 equal portions. On a greased baking sheet, roll out 1 dough portion into a 9x8-in. rectangle, about 1/16 in. thick. Sprinkle with ½ tsp. kosher salt. Using rolling pin, gently press salt into dough. Prick holes in dough with a fork. Score dough into 16 pieces. Repeat with remaining dough.
3. Bake at 400° until the edges are lightly browned, 9-11 minutes. Immediately cut along the scored lines. Cool completely on baking sheets. Store in an airtight container.

1 cracker: 30 cal., 1g fat (0 sat. fat), 0 chol., 85mg sod., 4g carb. (0 sugars, 0 fiber), 1g pro.

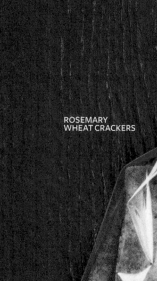

ROSEMARY WHEAT CRACKERS

Food Packaging Ideas

You've already taken the time to make something yummy. Wrap your treats in an equally beautiful package!

Make a cookie decorating kit: If the recipient has children, give them a homemade cookie decorating kit. Pack up plain baked cutout cookies along with sprinkles, candies and a tub of frosting.

Stack your tins: Elevate plain tins by stacking them. Choose decorative foil tins from the craft store or traditional cookie tins. Make them a bit more special with paint—simple colors like white and gold are especially elegant.

Upcycle containers: An oatmeal or cornmeal container makes a handy gift box. Or, to present a neat row of treats—such as gumdrops, caramels or fudge—use scissors or a utility knife to remove the teeth from an empty plastic wrap or aluminum foil box. Paint the container or dress it up with pretty paper. Line it with waxed paper, then fill it with treats.

Decorate a plain box: A simple brown box lets beautiful goodies shine. Tie up the box with ribbon or baker's twine to add a little color and flair. To go further, place three boxes containing different items on a wooden tray and give the entire package as a gift.

Attach a cookie cutter: If you're giving cookies or a homemade cookie mix, add an extra gift. After you place the cookies or mix inside a jar, loop a festive ribbon through a holiday-themed cookie cutter and attach it to the jar. Your baker friends are sure to love the sweet surprise!

GREAT
GRANOLA

GREAT GRANOLA

Oats, nuts and dried fruit make a crunchy homemade granola. It's a delicious way to top yogurt or to just eat it by the handful. Add a jar of honey to give the gift of an easy breakfast.
—*Johnna Johnson, Scottsdale, AZ*

Prep: 25 min. • **Bake:** 25 min. + cooling
Makes: 7 cups

- 2   cups old-fashioned oats
- ½   cup chopped almonds
- ½   cup salted pumpkin seeds or pepitas
- ½   cup chopped walnuts
- ¼   cup chopped pecans
- ¼   cup sesame seeds
- ¼   cup sunflower kernels
- ⅓   cup honey
- ¼   cup packed brown sugar
- ¼   cup maple syrup
- 2   Tbsp. toasted wheat germ
- 2   Tbsp. canola oil
- 1   tsp. ground cinnamon
- 1   tsp. vanilla extract
- 7   oz. mixed dried fruit (about 1⅓ cups)

1. In a large bowl, combine first 7 ingredients; set aside.

2. In a small saucepan, combine the honey, brown sugar, syrup, wheat germ, oil and cinnamon. Cook and stir over medium heat until smooth, 4-5 minutes. Remove from the heat; stir in vanilla. Pour over the oat mixture and toss to coat.

3. Transfer to a greased 15x10x1-in. baking pan. Bake at 350° until golden brown, stirring occasionally, 22-27 minutes. Cool completely on a wire rack. Stir in dried fruit. Store in an airtight container.

½ cup: 290 cal., 14g fat (2g sat. fat), 0 chol., 49mg sod., 38g carb. (25g sugars, 4g fiber), 6g pro.

CRISPY PEANUT BUTTER BALLS

I make over 40 different types of treats during the holidays for friends and family. These crispy no-bake peanut butter balls are one of my favorite candies to give away as gifts.
—*Liz David, St. Catharines, ON*

Prep: 40 min. + chilling • **Makes:** 6 dozen

- 2 cups creamy peanut butter
- ½ cup butter, softened
- 3¾ cups confectioners' sugar
- 3 cups crisp rice cereal
- 4 cups semisweet chocolate chips
- ¼ cup plus 1 tsp. shortening, divided
- ⅓ cup white baking chips

1. In a large bowl, beat peanut butter and butter until blended; gradually beat in the confectioners' sugar until smooth. Stir in cereal. Shape into 1-in. balls. Refrigerate until chilled.
2. In a microwave, melt chocolate chips and ¼ cup shortening; stir until smooth. Dip balls into chocolate; allow excess to drip off. Place on a waxed paper-lined pan. Let balls stand until set.
3. In a microwave, melt the white baking chips and remaining shortening. Stir until smooth. Drizzle over candies. Refrigerate until set.
1 piece: 133 cal., 8g fat (3g sat. fat), 3mg chol., 54mg sod., 14g carb. (12g sugars, 1g fiber), 2g pro.

PECAN KRINGLE STICKS

My family loves that the kringle is flaky and not too sweet—it just melts in your mouth. This makes a beautiful presentation on a cookie platter along with other holiday sweets.
—*Connie Vjestica, Brookfield, IL*

Prep: 40 min. + chilling • **Bake:** 20 min.
Makes: 4 kringles (6 servings each)

- 2 cups all-purpose flour
- 1 cup cold butter, cubed
- 1 cup sour cream
- FILLING
- 1 large egg white, room temperature
- 1 tsp. vanilla extract
- ½ cup sugar
- 1 cup chopped pecans
- ICING
- 1¼ cups confectioners' sugar
- 2 Tbsp. 2% milk

1. Place flour in a large bowl; cut in butter until crumbly. Stir in sour cream. Shape into a disk (mixture will be crumbly). Wrap and refrigerate overnight.
2. In a small bowl, beat egg white and vanilla on medium speed until soft peaks form. Gradually beat in sugar on high until stiff peaks form. Fold in pecans.
3. Divide the dough into 4 portions. Roll 1 portion into a 12x6-in. rectangle; place on an ungreased rimmed baking sheet (keep remaining dough refrigerated). Spread a fourth of the filling lengthwise down the center. Fold in sides of pastry to meet in the center; pinch seam to seal. Repeat with remaining dough and filling.
4. Bake at 375° for 18-22 minutes or until lightly browned. Combine confectioners' sugar and milk; drizzle over warm pastries.
1 piece: 201 cal., 13g fat (6g sat. fat), 27mg chol., 60mg sod., 19g carb. (11g sugars, 1g fiber), 2g pro.

CINNAMON TOASTED ALMONDS

Crunchy cinnamon almonds are a spectacular treat to bring to a party or gathering. They taste just like the cinnamon roasted almonds you find at county fairs.
—*Janice Thompson, Stacy, MN*

Prep: 15 min. • **Bake:** 25 min. + cooling
Makes: about 4 cups

- 2 large egg whites
- 6 tsp. vanilla extract
- 4 cups unblanched almonds
- ⅓ cup sugar
- ⅓ cup packed brown sugar
- 1 tsp. salt
- ½ tsp. ground cinnamon

1. In a large bowl, beat egg whites until frothy; beat in vanilla. Add the almonds; stir gently to coat. Combine the sugars, salt and cinnamon; add to nut mixture and stir gently to coat.
2. Spread evenly in 2 greased 15x10x1-in. baking pans. Bake at 300° for 25-30 minutes or until almonds are crisp, stirring once. Cool. Store in an airtight container.
¼ cup: 250 cal., 18g fat (1g sat. fat), 0 chol., 166mg sod., 16g carb. (10g sugars, 4g fiber), 8g pro.

COFFEE SHOP FUDGE

This smooth fudge has an irresistible crunch from pecans. The coffee and cinnamon blend nicely to provide subtle flavor. Package the fudge in a tin filled with decorative parchment paper and adorned with a ribbon.
—*Beth Osborne Skinner, Bristol, TN*

Prep: 15 min. + chilling
Makes: 2 lbs. (64 pieces)

- 1 tsp. butter, softened
- 1 cup chopped pecans
- 3 cups semisweet chocolate chips
- 1 can (14 oz.) sweetened condensed milk
- 2 Tbsp. strong brewed coffee, room temperature
- 1 tsp. ground cinnamon
- ⅛ tsp. salt
- 1 tsp. vanilla extract

1. Line an 8-in. square pan with foil; butter the foil and set aside. Place the pecans in a microwave-safe pie plate. Microwave, uncovered, on high for 3 minutes, stirring after each minute; set aside.
2. In a 2-qt. microwave-safe bowl, combine the chocolate chips, milk, coffee, cinnamon and salt. Microwave, uncovered, on high for 1 minute. Stir until smooth. Stir in vanilla and pecans. Immediately spread mixture into the prepared pan.
3. Cover and refrigerate until fudge is firm, about 2 hours. Remove from pan; cut into 1-in. squares. Cover and store at room temperature (70°-80°).
1 piece: 77 cal., 4g fat (2g sat. fat), 3mg chol., 16mg sod., 10g carb. (9g sugars, 1g fiber), 1g pro.

COZY CHRISTMAS FOR TWO

If this year's festivities are a small-scale affair, don't fret over getting stuck with a fridge full of leftovers. Creating a cozy, intimate meal for you and your sweetheart, or a friend or family member, is easy when you have these perfectly portioned recipes at your fingertips. Find small-batch versions of your favorite holiday favorites, designed just for two.

Honey-Dijon Salmon & Asparagus (p. 41) **Mushroom Rice Pilaf** (p. 39)

TENDER STUFFED
PORK TENDERLOIN

TENDER STUFFED PORK TENDERLOIN

My grandmother often prepared this dish for Sunday dinner. She loved to cook and eat, especially when she had someone to share her food with.
—*Mary Ann Marino, West Pittsburgh, PA*

Prep: 20 min. • **Bake:** 50 min.
Makes: 2 servings

- 1 pork tenderloin (¾ to 1 lb.)
- ½ cup chopped onion
- 2 Tbsp. butter
- 1 cup soft bread crumbs
- ¼ cup minced fresh parsley
- ¼ tsp. rubbed sage
- ¼ tsp. dried rosemary, crushed
- ¼ tsp. salt
- ⅛ tsp. pepper
- 1 large egg, lightly beaten
- 1 bacon strip

1. Make a lengthwise slit about three-fourths of the way through the pork tenderloin; open the tenderloin so it lies flat. Flatten to ¼-in. thickness; set aside.
2. In a small skillet, saute onion in butter until tender. Add bread crumbs; saute until crumbs are golden brown. Remove from the heat. Stir in the parsley, sage, rosemary, salt, pepper and enough egg to moisten the ingredients.
3. Spread the stuffing on 1 long side of the tenderloin to within ¼ in. of edges. Close meat and place the bacon on top; tie with kitchen string. Place tenderloin on a rack in a shallow roasting pan.
4. Bake, uncovered, at 350° for 50-60 minutes or until a thermometer reads 160°. Let stand for 5 minutes before slicing.
8 oz. cooked stuffed pork: 476 cal., 27g fat (12g sat. fat), 239mg chol., 719mg sod., 16g carb. (4g sugars, 2g fiber), 41g pro.

TEST KITCHEN TIP

Pork tenderloin (also called pork filet or pork tender) is long and skinny, and it's always sold as a boneless cut. Because each tenderloin only weighs about a pound, you'll usually find them packaged in pairs. The tenderloin contains very little fat, so one of the best ways to identify it is to look for the cut without a fat cap or intramuscular fat marbling. Pork tenderloin is a delicate muscle that runs along the spine. It isn't used for movement, so it's one of the most tender cuts of pork.

MUSHROOM RICE PILAF

MUSHROOM RICE PILAF

This speedy side dish complements almost any main dish. It's just the right amount for my husband and me, but also easy to double for a larger group.
—*Norma Jean Koelmel, Shattuc, IL*

Takes: 30 min. • **Makes:** 2 servings

- ¼ cup each chopped onion, celery and green pepper
- 1 Tbsp. butter
- ½ cup hot water
- 1 jar (4½ oz.) sliced mushrooms, drained
- ⅓ cup uncooked instant rice
- 1½ tsp. chicken bouillon granules

1. In a 1-qt. microwave-safe dish, combine the onion, celery, green pepper and butter. Microwave, uncovered, on high until the vegetables are crisp-tender, 2-4 minutes.
2. Stir in the remaining ingredients. Cook on high for 7-10 minutes or until rice is tender.
1 cup: 145 cal., 6g fat (4g sat. fat), 16mg chol., 960mg sod., 20g carb. (3g sugars, 3g fiber), 3g pro.

GRILLED SHRIMP WITH APRICOT SAUCE FOR 2

Succulent, bacon-wrapped shrimp get a flavor boost from sweet-hot sauce. Served on skewers, they make a fabulous addition to a festive menu.
—*Carole Resnick, Cleveland, OH*

Takes: 20 min.
Makes: 2 skewers (⅓ cup sauce)

- ¼ cup apricot preserves
- 1 Tbsp. apricot nectar
- ⅛ tsp. ground chipotle powder
- 6 uncooked large shrimp, peeled and deveined
- 3 slices Canadian bacon, halved

1. In a small bowl, combine the preserves, apricot nectar and chipotle powder. Chill until serving.
2. Thread shrimp and bacon onto 2 metal or soaked wooden skewers. Grill, covered, over medium heat for 3-4 minutes on each side or until shrimp turn pink. Serve with sauce.
1 serving: 208 cal., 4g fat (1g sat. fat), 80mg chol., 613mg sod., 28g carb. (16g sugars, 0 fiber), 17g pro.

COUNTRY GRAVY

- 2 Tbsp. all-purpose flour
- 1¼ cups 2% milk
- ¼ tsp. salt
- ¼ tsp. white pepper

1. Flatten steak to ¼-in. thickness. Cut into 2 serving-size pieces. Place flour and bread crumbs in separate shallow bowls. In another shallow bowl, whisk egg and water. Coat the steaks with flour, then dip into egg mixture and coat with crumbs.

2. In a large skillet, cook the steaks in oil over medium heat for 1-2 minutes on each side or until meat reaches desired doneness. Remove and keep warm.

3. For gravy, stir flour into pan drippings until blended, loosening browned bits. Gradually stir in milk. Bring to a boil over medium heat; cook and stir for 2 minutes or until thickened. Season the gravy with salt and pepper. Serve with steaks.

1 serving: 596 cal., 33g fat (6g sat. fat), 188mg chol., 600mg sod., 37g carb. (0 sugars, 1g fiber), 37g pro.

CANDIED SWEET POTATOES WITH PECANS

This traditional side dish is sized perfectly for two. The touch of pineapple juice adds a sweet flavor, and the pecans add a nice crunch.
—*Ruby Williams, Bogalusa, LA*

Prep: 40 min. • **Bake:** 15 min.
Makes: 2 servings

- 1 large sweet potato
- ¼ cup packed brown sugar
- 2 Tbsp. chopped pecans
- 1 Tbsp. unsweetened pineapple or orange juice
- 1 tsp. lemon juice
- ¼ tsp. ground cinnamon
- 1 Tbsp. butter

1. Place sweet potato in a small saucepan; cover with water. Bring to a boil. Reduce heat; cover and simmer for 30-40 minutes or just until tender. Drain.

2. When cool enough to handle, peel and cut into ¼-in. slices. Place in a greased shallow 2-cup baking dish.

3. In a small bowl, combine the brown sugar, pecans, pineapple juice, lemon juice and cinnamon; sprinkle over sweet potato slices. Dot with butter.

4. Bake, uncovered, at 350° for 15 minutes or until bubbly and heated through.

¾ cup: 385 cal., 11g fat (4g sat. fat), 15mg chol., 71mg sod., 71g carb. (45g sugars, 6g fiber), 4g pro.

GRAPEFRUIT LETTUCE SALAD

A light vinaigrette flavored with cilantro and grapefruit juice drapes this tangy salad. The dressing keeps well in the refrigerator, so feel free to make it ahead to save time. Then just assemble the salad right before dinner.
—*Vivian Haen, Menomonee Falls, WI*

Takes: 15 min. • **Makes:** 2 servings

- 2 Tbsp. pink grapefruit juice
- 1 Tbsp. olive oil
- 1½ tsp. red wine vinegar
- ½ tsp. honey
- 1½ tsp. minced fresh cilantro
- 2 cups torn Bibb or Boston lettuce
- 1 medium pink grapefruit, peeled and sectioned
  Optional: Sliced fennel bulb, fennel fronds and pistachios

In a small bowl, whisk the grapefruit juice, oil, vinegar and honey; stir in cilantro. In a salad bowl, toss lettuce and grapefruit. If desired, add the sliced fennel bulb, fennel fronds and pistachios. Drizzle with dressing; gently toss to coat.

1 cup: 120 cal., 7g fat (1g sat. fat), 0 chol., 5mg sod., 14g carb. (0 sugars, 2g fiber), 1g pro. **Diabetic exchanges:** 2 vegetable, 1½ fat.

SIRLOIN FRIED STEAK

I've been the chief cook ever since I moved in with my father. With its crispy coating, this southern specialty is his favorite meal. He loves it with mashed potatoes.
—*Judy Yackey, Kalispell, MT*

Takes: 25 min. • **Makes:** 2 servings

- ½ lb. beef top sirloin steak (½ in. thick)
- ¼ cup all-purpose flour
- ¼ cup seasoned bread crumbs
- 1 large egg
- 2 tsp. water
- 3 Tbsp. canola oil

HONEY-DIJON SALMON & ASPARAGUS

Here's our favorite salmon recipe. It's easy, nutritious and delicious. The best part is that cleanup is a snap!
—*Betty Stewart, Leola, PA*

Takes: 25 min. • **Makes:** 2 servings

- 1½ tsp. cornstarch
- 2¼ tsp. butter, melted
- 1 tsp. Worcestershire sauce
- 2 Tbsp. honey
- 1 Tbsp. Dijon mustard
  Dash white pepper
- 2 salmon fillets (4 oz. each)
- ¼ cup chopped walnuts
- ½ lb. fresh asparagus, trimmed

1. In a small bowl, combine cornstarch, butter and Worcestershire sauce until smooth. Stir in the honey, mustard and pepper.
2. Place salmon fillets on a double thickness of heavy-duty foil (about 18x12 in.). Drizzle with honey mixture and sprinkle with the walnuts. Place asparagus around the salmon. Fold foil around salmon and seal tightly. Grill, covered, over medium heat for 15-20 minutes or until fish flakes easily with a fork.
1 serving: 437 cal., 26g fat (6g sat. fat), 78mg chol., 335mg sod., 25g carb. (17g sugars, 2g fiber), 28g pro.

SAUSAGE-STUFFED SHELLS

I wanted to make traditional manicotti one day but was out of the noodles. So I used jumbo shells instead. They're easier to stuff and make a comforting small-yield entree for Christmas.
—*Lori Daniels, Beverly, WV*

Prep: 25 min. • **Bake:** 20 min.
Makes: 2 servings

- ⅓ lb. bulk Italian sausage
- 1 can (8 oz.) tomato sauce
- ¼ cup tomato paste
- 2 Tbsp. water
- 1 tsp. brown sugar
- ½ tsp. Italian seasoning
- ⅓ cup 4% cottage cheese
- ¾ cup shredded part-skim mozzarella cheese, divided
- 2 Tbsp. beaten egg
- ½ tsp. minced fresh parsley
- 6 jumbo pasta shells, cooked and drained
  Grated Parmesan cheese, optional

1. In a small saucepan, cook sausage over medium heat until no longer pink; drain. Set half of the sausage aside for filling. Add the tomato sauce, tomato paste, water, brown sugar and Italian seasoning to the sausage in the pan. Bring to a boil. Reduce the heat; simmer the meat sauce, uncovered, for 15 minutes, stirring occasionally.
2. In a small bowl, combine the cottage cheese, ½ cup mozzarella cheese, egg, parsley and reserved sausage. Stuff into shells. Spread ¼ cup meat sauce in an ungreased 1-qt. shallow baking dish. Place stuffed shells in dish; drizzle with remaining meat sauce.
3. Sprinkle with remaining mozzarella cheese and, if desired, Parmesan cheese. Bake shells, uncovered, at 350° for 20-25 minutes or until filling reaches 160°.
3 stuffed shells: 437 cal., 14g fat (7g sat. fat), 67mg chol., 1371mg sod., 40g carb. (13g sugars, 4g fiber), 36g pro.

VANILLA CUSTARD CUPS

My mother loved custard, so I'd make this old-fashioned dessert each week while I was living with her. Without leftovers, there's no chance of getting tired of this treat!
—*Billie Bohannan, Imperial, CA*

Prep: 10 min. • **Bake:** 30 min.
Makes: 2 servings

- 1 large egg
- 1 cup whole milk
- 3 Tbsp. brown sugar
- ¾ tsp. vanilla extract
- ⅛ tsp. salt, optional
- ⅛ tsp. ground nutmeg

1. In a small bowl, beat the egg, milk, brown sugar, vanilla and salt if desired until blended. Pour into two ungreased 6-oz. custard cups. Sprinkle with nutmeg.
2. Place the cups in a 9-in. square baking pan. Fill pan with hot water to a depth of 1 in. Bake, uncovered, at 350° for 30-35 minutes or until a knife inserted in the center comes out clean.
1 serving: 75 cal., 1g fat, 3mg chol., 119mg sod., 6g carb., 0 fiber), 8g pro.

POINSETTIA

Mix cranberry juice, Triple Sec and champagne for a festive holiday cocktail. Garnish with a few fresh berries for extra flair.
—*Taste of Home Test Kitchen*

Takes: 5 min. • **Makes:** 1 serving

- 1 oz. cranberry juice
- ½ oz. Triple Sec, optional
- 4 oz. chilled champagne or other sparkling wine

GARNISH

- 3 fresh cranberries

Pour cranberry juice into a champagne flute or wine glass. Add Triple Sec if desired. Top with champagne. Garnish as desired.
1 serving: 95 cal., 0 fat (0 sat. fat), 0 chol., 1mg sod., 5g carb. (4g sugars, 0 fiber), 0 pro.

To make a batch of Poinsettias (6 servings), slowly pour 1 bottle (750 ml) chilled champagne into a pitcher. Stir in ¾ cup cranberry juice and 3 oz. Triple Sec if desired.

MALTED CHOCOLATE CHEESECAKE

With an impressive presentation and classic malt flavor, this downsized dessert will make anyone feel special.
—*Anna Ginsberg, Chicago, IL*

- -

Prep: 30 min. • **Bake:** 40 min. + cooling
Makes: 2 servings

- 4 portions refrigerated ready-to-bake sugar cookie dough
- 4 oz. cream cheese, softened
- ½ cup dark chocolate chips, melted
- 2 Tbsp. sugar
- 1 large egg white, room temperature
- ½ tsp. vanilla extract

TOPPING
- 4½ tsp. cream cheese, softened
- 2 tsp. sugar
- 1 tsp. malted milk powder
- 1 tsp. baking cocoa
- ⅔ cup whipped topping
- 1 Tbsp. chocolate syrup

1. Line a 5¾x3x2-in. loaf pan with foil. Press cookie dough onto bottom of pan. Bake at 325° for 15-20 minutes or until golden brown. Cool on a wire rack.

2. In a small bowl, beat cream cheese, melted chocolate and sugar until smooth. Add egg white; beat on low speed just until combined. Stir in vanilla. Pour over crust.

3. Place loaf pan in a baking pan; add 1 in. of hot water to larger pan. Bake at 325° for 40-45 minutes or until center is just set and top appears dull.

4. Remove loaf pan from water bath. Cool on a wire rack for 10 minutes. Carefully run a knife around edge of pan to loosen; cool 1 hour longer.

5. Refrigerate overnight. For the topping, in a small bowl, beat the cream cheese, sugar, milk powder and baking cocoa until smooth. Fold in whipped topping. Spread over cheesecake. Cover and refrigerate for 1 hour.

6. Using foil, lift cheesecake out of pan. Cut in half. Drizzle chocolate syrup over each piece. Refrigerate leftovers.

1 piece: 934 cal., 58g fat (34g sat. fat), 74mg chol., 350mg sod., 92g carb. (68g sugars, 0 fiber), 14g pro.

MERINGUES WITH FRESH BERRIES

Juicy ripe berries and a dollop of light cream fill these cloudlike meringue desserts. When I double this recipe to serve friends, they always rave about it.
—*Agnes Ward, Stratford, ON*

Prep: 20 min. + standing
Bake: 1 hour + standing • **Makes:** 2 servings

- 2 large egg whites
- ⅛ tsp. cream of tartar
  Dash salt
- ¼ cup sugar
- ¼ tsp. vanilla extract
- 1 cup mixed fresh berries
- ½ tsp. sugar, optional
- ⅓ cup sour cream
- ⅛ to ¼ tsp. rum extract

1. Place egg whites in a small bowl; let stand at room temperature for 30 minutes. Add cream of tartar and salt; beat on medium speed until soft peaks form. Gradually beat in the sugar, 1 Tbsp. at a time, on high until stiff peaks form. Beat in vanilla.
2. Drop the meringue into 2 mounds on a parchment-lined baking sheet. Shape into 3½-in. cups with the back of a spoon.
3. Bake at 225° until set and dry, 1-1¼ hours. Turn oven off; leave meringues in the oven for 1 hour. Remove to wire racks to cool.
4. In a small bowl, combine the berries and, if desired, sugar; let stand for 5 minutes. Combine the sour cream and extract; spoon into meringue shells. Top with berries.
1 serving: 222 cal., 7g fat (5g sat. fat), 27mg chol., 149mg sod., 33g carb. (30g sugars, 2g fiber), 5g pro.

TEST KITCHEN TIP

For the strongest and most stable meringue, cream of tartar is added before beating. Cream of tartar is an acid that stabilizes the egg white. For this recipe, if you don't have any on hand, use ¼ tsp. lemon juice instead. (Or if you happen to have a copper-lined bowl, that'll produce the same effect.) It's also best to make meringues on a dry day. On humid or rainy days, they can absorb moisture and become limp or sticky.

MERINGUES WITH FRESH BERRIES

1

2

How to Make Meringue Cups

1. Line a baking sheet with parchment paper. Drop meringue into mounds on the paper. Using the back of a spoon, make a well in the center of each mound to form a 3-in. cup.

2. Bake as the recipe directs. After drying in the oven, remove meringues to cool completely. Once cooled, store in an airtight container at room temperature for up to 2 days.

MILK &
CHRISTMAS
COOKIES

To dunk or not to dunk? There is no question—of course, we dunk! After the clouds of flour and sugar have settled from your holiday baking extravaganza, take a moment to sit by the fire and enjoy the timeless pairing of a sweet, crispy cookie dipped in a glass of milk. Whether the milk is warm or cold and the cookies are studded with nuts or drizzled with icing, this match-made-in-heaven is sure to become your new favorite tradition.

Grandma's Spritz Cookies (p. 49) Double-Chocolate Pretzel Turtle Cookies (p. 46) Crisp Candy Cane Cookies (p. 51)

How to Freeze Cookies

Cookies freeze well once they're baked, as well as in dough form. This makes them a convenient snack to always have on hand. It's also is a timesaver when it comes to baking for the holidays or for other special occasions and get-togethers.

Theoretically, you can put any type of cookies in the freezer, but some varieties definitely hold up better than others. Avoid freezing any overly delicate treats, such as meringues. The best cookies to freeze are sturdy and simple—drop cookies, undecorated cutout cookies or cookie-type bars.

As for decorated cookies, whether it's a cutout cookie decorated with royal icing or a cookie with frosting or glaze, always freeze the cookies bare and decorate them when you're ready to use them. Make sure the cookies are thawed before decorating, since they will release moisture as they thaw.

Once your cookies are baked and completely cool, arrange them in a single layer on a baking sheet. Place the sheet in the freezer for 30 minutes or until the cookies are frozen solid. Then, layer frozen cookies in airtight containers, with a piece of parchment separating each layer. This will help prevent the cookies from sticking to each other.

Repeat until all of the cookies are packed, then freeze the containers for up to 3 months. Let the cookies thaw at room temperature or heat them in the microwave for a few seconds before serving.

FROSTED EGGNOG COOKIES

If you're a fan of eggnog, you'll definitely love that this recipe features it in both the cookie and the frosting.
—Amanda Taylor, Glen Ewen, SK

Prep: 30 min. + chilling
Bake: 10 min./batch + cooling
Makes: 13½ dozen

- 1 cup butter, softened
- 2 cups sugar
- 1 cup eggnog
- 5½ cups all-purpose flour
- 1 tsp. baking soda
- ¾ tsp. ground nutmeg

ICING

- ¼ cup butter, softened
- 3 cups confectioners' sugar
- ⅓ cup eggnog

1. In a large bowl, cream butter and sugar until light and fluffy, 5-7 minutes. Beat in eggnog. Combine flour, baking soda and nutmeg; gradually add to the creamed mixture and mix well. Shape into four 10-in. rolls. Wrap each in waxed paper. Refrigerate overnight.
2. Preheat oven to 375°. Unwrap; cut into ¼-in. slices. Place 1 in. apart on ungreased baking sheets. Bake until set, 8-10 minutes. Remove to wire racks to cool.
3. For icing, in a large bowl, beat butter until fluffy. Add confectioners' sugar and eggnog; beat until smooth. Frost cookies. Store in an airtight container.
1 cookie: 48 cal., 2g fat (1g sat. fat), 5mg chol., 20mg sod., 8g carb. (5g sugars, 0 fiber), 1g pro.

LARA'S TENDER GINGERSNAPS

Soft gingersnaps embody the tastes and smells of the Christmas season but are perfect for any fall or winter gathering. I enjoy the flavors of cloves, cinnamon and ginger blended into one delicious cookie.
—Lara Pennell, Mauldin, SC

Prep: 15 min. + chilling • **Bake:** 10 min./batch
Makes: 3 dozen

- 1 cup packed brown sugar
- ¾ cup butter, melted
- 1 large egg, room temperature
- ¼ cup molasses
- 2¼ cups all-purpose flour
- 1½ tsp. ground ginger
- 1 tsp. baking soda
- 1 tsp. ground cinnamon
- ½ tsp. ground cloves
- ¼ cup sugar

1. In a large bowl, beat brown sugar and butter until blended. Beat in the egg and molasses. Combine the flour, ginger, baking soda, cinnamon and cloves; gradually add to brown sugar mixture and mix well (dough will be stiff). Cover and refrigerate for at least 2 hours.
2. Preheat oven to 350°. Shape dough into 1-in. balls. Roll in sugar. Place 2 in. apart on greased baking sheets.
3. Bake until set, 9-11 minutes. Cool for 1 minute before removing from pans to wire racks.
1 cookie: 100 cal., 4g fat (2g sat. fat), 15mg chol., 70mg sod., 15g carb. (9g sugars, 0 fiber), 1g pro.

DOUBLE-CHOCOLATE PRETZEL TURTLE COOKIES

My father loves turtles, so I decided to turn a turtle into a cookie. The generous size makes them wonderful for gift-giving, and they're always the first to go at potlucks.
—Melissa Keenan, Larchmont, NY

Prep: 15 min. • **Bake:** 15 min./batch
Makes: 1 dozen

- ½ cup butter, softened
- ½ cup packed brown sugar
- ⅓ cup sugar
- 1 large egg, room temperature
- 1 tsp. vanilla extract
- 1 cup all-purpose flour
- ⅔ cup baking cocoa
- ½ tsp. baking powder
- ½ tsp. baking soda
- ½ tsp. salt
- 1 cup (6 oz.) Rolo candies, halved
- ½ cup coarsely crushed pretzels
- ½ cup coarsely chopped pecans

1. Preheat oven to 350°. In a large bowl, cream butter and sugars until light and fluffy, 5-7 minutes. Beat in the egg and vanilla. In another bowl, whisk flour, cocoa, baking powder, baking soda and salt; gradually beat into creamed mixture. Stir in Rolos, pretzels and pecans.
2. Drop dough by ¼ cupfuls 2 in. apart onto parchment-lined baking sheets. Bake until cookies look crackled, 12-14 minutes.
3. Allow cookies to cool completely on pans. Store between pieces of waxed paper in an airtight container.
1 cookie: 295 cal., 15g fat (7g sat. fat), 38mg chol., 321mg sod., 38g carb. (24g sugars, 2g fiber), 4g pro.

DOUBLE-CHOCOLATE
PRETZEL TURTLE COOKIES

BROWNIE BISCOTTI

Daintily drizzled with white chocolate, these eye-catching biscotti have serious dunkability! Dip them in white or chocolate milk, or include them in a holiday gift basket with an assortment of hot chocolate and teas.
—*Amber Sumner, Congress, AZ*

- -

Prep: 20 min. • **Bake:** 50 min. + cooling
Makes: 3 dozen

- ½ cup butter, melted
- 3 large eggs, room temperature
- 2 tsp. vanilla extract
- 2½ cups all-purpose flour
- 1⅓ cups sugar
- ¾ cup baking cocoa
- 2 tsp. baking powder
- ½ tsp. baking soda
- 1 cup unblanched almonds, toasted and coarsely chopped
- ½ cup miniature semisweet chocolate chips

DRIZZLE
- ½ cup white baking chips
- 1½ tsp. shortening

1. Preheat oven to 325°. In a large bowl, combine the butter, eggs and vanilla until well blended. Combine flour, sugar, cocoa, baking powder and baking soda; gradually add to butter mixture just until combined (dough will be crumbly).

2. Turn dough onto a lightly floured surface; knead in almonds and chocolate chips. Divide dough in half. On an ungreased baking sheet, shape each portion into a 12x3-in. log, leaving 3 in. between the logs.

3. Bake until set and the tops are cracked, 30-35 minutes. Cool 15 minutes. Carefully transfer to a cutting board; cut diagonally with a serrated knife into ½-in. slices.

4. Place cut side down on ungreased baking sheets. Bake until firm and dry, 20-25 minutes. Remove to wire racks to cool.

5. For the drizzle, in a microwave, melt white baking chips and shortening at 70% power for 1 minute; stir. Microwave at additional 10- to 20-second intervals, stirring until smooth. Drizzle over biscotti.

1 cookie: 144 cal., 7g fat (3g sat. fat), 23mg chol., 74mg sod., 19g carb. (10g sugars, 1g fiber), 3g pro.

Biscotti's dry, crunchy texture makes it perfect for dunking in milk, either warm or cold. You can also pair it with tea, coffee, cappuccino, cocoa or other hot drinks. Or do as they do in Tuscany and dunk it into a glass of sweet red wine.

GRANDMA'S
SPRITZ COOKIES

GRANDMA'S SPRITZ COOKIES

I use my grandmother's antique cookie press to make these festive cookies. I'm the only one in the family that can still get it to work!
—*Suzanne Kern, Louisville, KY*

Prep: 15 min. • **Bake:** 10 min./batch
Makes: 6½ dozen

- 1 **cup shortening**
- ¾ **cup sugar**
- 1 **large egg, room temperature**
- 1 **tsp. almond extract**
- 2¼ **cups all-purpose flour**
- ½ **tsp. baking powder**
  Dash salt
  Optional: Assorted sprinkles and colored sugar

1. Preheat oven to 400°. In a large mixing bowl, cream shortening and sugar until light and fluffy, 5-7 minutes. Add egg and almond extract; mix well. Combine the flour, baking powder and salt; add to creamed mixture until blended.
2. Using a cookie press fitted with the disk of your choice, press dough 2 in. apart onto ungreased baking sheets. Sprinkle with toppings if desired. Bake until set (do not brown), 7-8 minutes.
1 cookie: 44 cal., 3g fat (1g sat. fat), 2mg chol., 6mg sod., 5g carb. (2g sugars, 0 fiber), 0 pro.

MINI CINNAMON ROLL COOKIES

Intense cinnamon flavor fills this yummy cross between a snickerdoodle and a cinnamon roll. Try one with a cup of freshly brewed coffee.
—*Mary Gauntt, Denton, TX*

Prep: 1 hour • **Bake:** 10 min./batch + cooling
Makes: 2½ dozen

- 1 **cup butter, softened**
- 1¾ **cups sugar, divided**
- 3 **large egg yolks, room temperature**
- 1 **Tbsp. plus 1 tsp. honey, divided**
- 1 **tsp. vanilla extract**
- 2½ **cups all-purpose flour**
- 1 **tsp. baking powder**
- ½ **tsp. salt**
- ½ **tsp. cream of tartar**
- 1 **Tbsp. ground cinnamon**
- 8 **oz. white baking chocolate, chopped**

1. Preheat oven to 350°. In a large bowl, cream butter and 1¼ cups sugar until light and fluffy, 5-7 minutes. Beat in egg yolks, 1 Tbsp. honey and vanilla. Combine flour, baking powder, salt and cream of tartar; gradually add to creamed mixture. Mix well.

2. Shape a heaping tablespoonful of dough into a 6-in. log. In a shallow bowl, combine cinnamon and remaining sugar; roll log in cinnamon sugar. Loosely coil log into a spiral shape and place on a greased baking sheet. Repeat, placing cookies 1 in. apart. Sprinkle with remaining cinnamon sugar.
3. Bake until set, 8-10 minutes. Remove to wire racks to cool completely. In a small bowl, melt baking chocolate with remaining honey; stir until smooth. Drizzle over cookies. Let stand until set. Store in an airtight container.
1 cookie: 185 cal., 9g fat (6g sat. fat), 35mg chol., 111mg sod., 26g carb. (17g sugars, 0 fiber), 2g pro.

CANDY BAR COOKIES

These cookies are hard to resist if you love candy, because every bite is like finding a hidden treasure. They are fun to make and even more fun to eat. Be sure to have a glass of milk for dunking!
—*Deirdre Cox, Kansas City, MO*

Prep: 30 min. + chilling
Bake: 10 min./batch + standing
Makes: 6 dozen

- 1 **cup butter, softened**
- 1 **cup creamy peanut butter**
- 1 **cup sugar**
- 1 **cup packed brown sugar**
- 2 **large eggs, room temperature**
- 1 **tsp. vanilla extract**
- 2½ **cups all-purpose flour**
- 1 **tsp. baking soda**
- 3 **Butterfinger candy bars (2.1 oz. each), finely crushed**
- 1 **milk chocolate candy bar (3½ oz.)**

1. Cream the butter, peanut butter and sugars in a large bowl until light and fluffy, 5-7 minutes. Beat in the eggs and vanilla. Combine flour and baking soda; gradually add to creamed mixture and mix well. Refrigerate for 30 minutes.
2. Preheat oven to 350°. Shape dough into 1-in. balls; roll in crushed Butterfinger bars. Place 2 in. apart on parchment-lined baking sheets. Bake until set, 8-10 minutes. Cool for 2 minutes before removing from pans to wire racks.
3. Melt the chocolate candy bar; drizzle over cooled cookies. Let stand until set. Store in an airtight container.
1 cookie: 103 cal., 5g fat (3g sat. fat), 12mg chol., 63mg sod., 13g carb. (8g sugars, 0 fiber), 2g pro.

CHOCOLATE-PEANUT BUTTER TOPPERS

BANANAS FOSTER COOKIES

I was in a Christmas baking frenzy, trying to decide what to make next. My roommate suggested something with bananas and walnuts, so I created this fun twist on the classic southern dessert. Rolling the dough in brown sugar adds a nice caramel touch.
—*Elizabeth Smith, Arnold, PA*

Prep: 30 min. • **Bake:** 10 min./batch
Makes: about 5½ dozen

- ½ cup butter, softened
- 4 oz. cream cheese, softened
- 1 cup packed brown sugar
- ½ cup sugar
- 2 large eggs, room temperature
- 1 cup mashed ripe bananas (about 2 medium)
- 1 Tbsp. rum
- 2 tsp. vanilla extract
- 3 cups all-purpose flour
- 2 tsp. ground cinnamon
- 1½ tsp. baking powder
- 1 tsp. salt
- 1 tsp. baking soda
- 2 cups old-fashioned oats
- 1 cup chopped walnuts
- ½ cup packed brown sugar

1. Preheat oven to 350°. In a large bowl, cream butter, cream cheese and sugars until blended. Beat in eggs, bananas, rum and vanilla. In another bowl, whisk the flour, cinnamon, baking powder, salt and baking soda; gradually beat into creamed mixture. Stir in oats and walnuts.
2. Shape rounded teaspoons of dough into balls; roll in additional brown sugar. Place 1 in. apart on ungreased baking sheets. Bake until edges begin to brown, 10-12 minutes. Remove from pans to wire racks to cool. Store in airtight containers.
1 cookie: 85 cal., 4g fat (1g sat. fat), 11mg chol., 86mg sod., 12g carb. (5g sugars, 1g fiber), 2g pro.

CHOCOLATE-PEANUT BUTTER TOPPERS

My mother-in-law had special Sunday dinners, which sometimes included these cookies. She always enjoyed baking and even worked in a bakery to help put her sons through college. Her cookies were always picture-perfect.
—*Cathy Pawlowski, Naperville, IL*

Prep: 30 min. • **Bake:** 15 min./batch + cooling
Makes: 5 dozen

- 1 cup butter, softened
- ½ cup sugar
- 2 tsp. vanilla extract
- 2 cups all-purpose flour
  Additional sugar

PEANUT BUTTER TOPPING
- ⅓ cup packed brown sugar
- ⅓ cup creamy peanut butter
- ¼ cup butter, softened

CHOCOLATE GLAZE
- ½ cup semisweet chocolate chips, melted
- ⅓ cup confectioners' sugar
- 2 Tbsp. 2% milk

1. Preheat oven to 325°. In a large bowl, cream butter and sugar until light and fluffy, 5-7 minutes. Beat in vanilla. Gradually add flour to creamed mixture and mix well.
2. Shape into ¾-in. balls. Coat the bottom of a glass with cooking spray, then dip it in sugar. Flatten cookies with prepared glass, redipping glass in sugar as needed. Place on baking sheets. Bake until set, 12-15 minutes. Cool on a wire rack.
3. In a small bowl, beat the brown sugar, peanut butter and butter until smooth. Spread 1 tsp. over each cookie. Combine glaze ingredients; gently spread ¾ tsp. over each peanut butter layer. Store in a single layer in airtight containers.
1 cookie: 157 cal., 10g fat (6g sat. fat), 20mg chol., 75mg sod., 16g carb. (9g sugars, 1g fiber), 2g pro.

CRISP CANDY CANE
COOKIES

CRISP CANDY CANE COOKIES

Every Christmas my family gets together
to make all kinds of desserts. These cookies
are fun for the kids to shape and are delicious,
too! I add red food coloring to my dough for
a festive look.
—*Amy Johnson, Leesburg, VA*

Prep: 25 min. + chilling • **Bake:** 10 min./batch
Makes: 3 dozen

½ cup butter, softened
⅓ cup sugar
⅓ cup packed brown sugar
1 large egg, room temperature
1 tsp. vanilla extract
1¼ cups all-purpose flour
1 tsp. baking powder
¼ tsp. salt
5 candy canes, crushed
½ cup white chocolate chips, melted

1. Cream butter and sugars in a large bowl
until light and fluffy, 5-7 minutes. Beat in egg
and vanilla. Combine flour, baking powder
and salt; gradually add to creamed mixture
and mix well. Stir in crushed candy canes.
Cover and refrigerate for 30 minutes.
2. Preheat oven to 375°. Divide dough into
36 pieces; shape each into a 4-in. rope. Place
2 in. apart on greased baking sheets; curve
the top of each cookie to form a candy cane.
3. Bake until edges are lightly browned,
8-10 minutes. Cool for 2 minutes before
removing to wire racks to cool completely.
Drizzle with melted white chocolate and
additional crushed candy canes, if desired.
Let set before serving.
1 cookie: 66 cal., 3g fat (2g sat. fat), 12mg
chol., 54mg sod., 10g carb. (6g sugars,
0 fiber), 1g pro.

Secrets for Successful Cookies

Follow these easy tips to bake
the perfect cookies every time!

• Use butter, stick margarine (with
  at least 80% vegetable oil) or
  shortening. Whipped, tub, soft, liquid
  or reduced-fat products contain air
  and water and will produce flat and
  tough cookies.

• Avoid overmixing the batter. If it's
  handled too much, the gluten in the
  flour will be developed and cookies
  will be tough.

• For even baking, make cookies the
  same size and thickness.

• Preheat oven for 10-15 minutes.

• Use heavy-gauge dull aluminum
  baking sheets with 1 or 2 low sides.
  When a recipe calls for greased
  baking sheets, use shortening or
  cooking spray. Dark finishes may
  cause cookies to overbrown.

• Unless the recipe states otherwise,
  place cookie dough 2-3 in. apart on
  a cool baking sheet.

• Leave at least 2 in. between the baking
  sheet and the oven walls for good
  heat circulation. For best results, bake
  only 1 sheet of cookies at a time. If you
  need to bake 2 sheets at once, switch
  the position of baking sheets halfway
  through baking time.

• Let baking sheets cool before
  placing the next batch of cookie
  dough on them. The heat from
  warm baking sheets will soften the
  dough and cause it to spread.

• Use a kitchen timer. Check the
  cookies when the minimum baking
  time has been reached, baking longer
  if needed. Follow doneness tests
  given in individual recipes.

• Unless otherwise directed, let
  cookies cool for 1 minute on the
  baking sheet before removing
  to a wire rack. Cool completely
  before storing.

ALMOND SUGAR COOKIES

It's a tradition in our house to start baking cookies early in the season so we can try some new recipes each year. These nutty, melt-in-your-mouth treats are one of our favorites.
—*Lisa Hummell, Phillipsburg, NJ*

Takes: 30 min. • **Makes:** about 4½ dozen

- 1 cup butter, softened
- ¾ cup sugar
- 1 tsp. almond extract
- 2 cups all-purpose flour
- ½ tsp. baking powder
- ¼ tsp. salt
  Additional sugar

GLAZE
- 1 cup confectioners' sugar
- 1½ tsp. almond extract
- 2 to 3 tsp. water
  Green food coloring, optional
  Sliced almonds, toasted

1. Preheat oven to 400°. In a large bowl, cream butter and sugar until light and fluffy, 5-7 minutes. Beat in almond extract. Combine the flour, baking powder and salt; gradually add to creamed mixture and mix well. Roll into 1-in. balls.

2. Place 2 in. apart on ungreased baking sheets. Coat bottom of a glass with cooking spray; dip it in sugar. Flatten cookies with prepared glass, dipping glass in sugar again as needed.

3. Bake until edges are lightly browned, 7-9 minutes. Cool for 1 minute before removing to wire racks.

4. In a small bowl, whisk together the confectioners' sugar, almond extract and enough water to achieve glaze consistency. Tint with food coloring if desired; drizzle over cookies. Sprinkle with almonds.

1 cookie: 67 cal., 3g fat (2g sat. fat), 9mg chol., 43mg sod., 9g carb. (5g sugars, 0 fiber), 1g pro.

RED VELVET COOKIES

My mother made these unique cookies when I was little, and now I often bake a batch for my own family.
—*Mindy Young, Hanover, PA*

Prep: 30 min. • **Bake:** 15 min./batch + cooling
Makes: 7½ dozen

- 1 cup shortening
- 1 cup sugar
- ¾ cup packed brown sugar
- 3 large eggs, separated, room temperature
- 2 tsp. red food coloring
- 4 cups all-purpose flour
- 3 Tbsp. baking cocoa
- 3 tsp. baking powder
- 1 tsp. salt
- 1 cup buttermilk
- 2 cups semisweet chocolate chips

FROSTING
- 1½ cups butter, softened
- 3¾ cups confectioners' sugar
- ⅛ tsp. salt
- 3 to 4 Tbsp. 2% milk

1. Preheat oven to 350°. In a large bowl, cream shortening and sugars until light and fluffy, 5-7 minutes. Beat in egg yolks and food coloring.

2. Combine flour, cocoa, baking powder and salt. Add to creamed mixture alternately with the buttermilk, beating well after each addition.

3. In another bowl with clean beaters, beat egg whites until stiff peaks form; fold into batter. Fold in chocolate chips.

4. Drop batter by tablespoonfuls 2 in. apart onto greased baking sheets. Bake until set, 12-14 minutes. Remove to wire racks to cool completely.

5. In a large bowl, beat butter, confectioners' sugar and salt until blended. Add enough milk to achieve desired consistency. Crumble 8 cookies and set aside.

6. Frost remaining cookies; sprinkle with the cookie crumbs. Store in an airtight container.

1 cookie: 124 cal., 7g fat (3g sat. fat), 14mg chol., 79mg sod., 16g carb. (11g sugars, 0 fiber), 1g pro.

Nondairy Milk Alternatives

If you're not able to consume dairy, or choose not to, there are lots of plant-based milk alternatives. Almond, cashew, coconut, flax, hazelnut, oat, macadamia, rice and soy are just a few of the nondairy milks on the market. When browsing, give at least a couple of products a try. Once you find a nondairy milk you like, experiment with different flavors and sweetened vs. unsweetened.

HORN WALNUT COOKIES

It takes only a few ingredients to create these elegant and delicious horns. This is a terrific make-ahead recipe because the dough can be made in advance and refrigerated for up to seven days.
—*Loretta Stokes, Philadelphia, PA*

Prep: 40 min. • **Bake:** 35 min./batch
Makes: 4 dozen

- 1 cup plus 1 tsp. butter, softened, divided
- 1 pkg. (8 oz.) cream cheese, softened
- 3 cups all-purpose flour
- 4 cups ground walnuts
- 1¼ cups sugar, divided
- ½ cup 2% milk
- 1 tsp. vanilla extract
- ⅛ tsp. salt

1. Preheat oven to 325°. In a large bowl, beat 1 cup butter and the cream cheese until light and fluffy, 5-7 minutes. Gradually add flour, beating until mixture forms a ball. Divide dough into 4 portions. On a lightly floured surface, roll each portion into a 12-in. circle.
2. Melt the remaining 1 tsp. butter. In a large bowl, combine walnuts, ¾ cup sugar, milk, vanilla, salt and melted butter. Spread over circles. Cut each into 12 wedges. Roll up wedges, starting from the wide ends.
3. Place point side down on greased baking sheets. Curve ends to form crescents. Bake until lightly browned, 35-40 minutes. Remove to wire racks.
4. Place remaining sugar in a small shallow bowl. Roll warm cookies in sugar.
1 cookie: 145 cal., 10g fat (4g sat. fat), 15mg chol., 54mg sod., 13g carb. (6g sugars, 1g fiber), 2g pro.

When making shaped cookies, refrigerate the dough until it is chilled for easier handling. If there is a high butter content in the dough, the heat from your hands can soften the butter in the dough, making it harder to shape. Dust your hands lightly with flour to prevent dough from sticking while shaping it.

HALF-HOMEMADE HOLIDAY PLEASERS

Getting a fantastic holiday meal on the table has never been quicker or easier! These irresistible recipes are made with at-the-ready convenience foods—packaged doughs, mixes, pre-cut veggies, canned ingredients and other shortcuts—to make unbeatable dishes in a dash.

Festive Tossed Salad with Feta (p. 56) **Ranch Pork Roast** (p. 59) **Garlic Knots** (p. 56)

FESTIVE
TOSSED SALAD
WITH FETA

GARLIC KNOTS

Here's a handy bread that can be made in no time flat. Refrigerated biscuits make preparation simple. The classic Italian flavors complement a variety of meals.
—*Jane Paschke, University Park, FL*

Takes: 30 min. • **Makes:** 2½ dozen

- 1 tube (12 oz.) refrigerated buttermilk biscuits
- ¼ cup canola oil
- 3 Tbsp. grated Parmesan cheese
- 1 tsp. garlic powder
- 1 tsp. dried oregano
- 1 tsp. dried parsley flakes

1. Preheat oven to 400°. Cut each biscuit into thirds. Roll each piece into a 4-in. rope and tie into a knot; tuck ends under. Place 2 in. apart on a greased baking sheet. Bake until golden brown, 8-10 minutes.
2. In a large bowl, combine the remaining ingredients; add the warm knots and gently toss to coat.
1 roll: 46 cal., 2g fat (0 sat. fat), 0 chol., 105mg sod., 6g carb. (0 sugars, 0 fiber), 1g pro.

SEAFOOD BUFFALO DIP

The holidays can be so hectic. I needed a go-to recipe that was a favorite but didn't keep me in the kitchen for a long period of time. This is a crowd pleaser that fills us with the indulgence of the holidays.
—*Kae Treadway, Taylorsville, NC*

Prep: 10 min. • **Bake:** 30 min.
Makes: 16 servings

- 1 pkg. (8 oz.) cream cheese, softened
- 1 cup shredded part-skim mozzarella cheese
- ½ cup mayonnaise
- ½ cup blue cheese salad dressing
- 2 Tbsp. Buffalo wing sauce
- 1 Tbsp. lemon juice
- 8 oz. frozen cooked salad shrimp, thawed and coarsely chopped
- 6 oz. imitation crabmeat, finely chopped
- 1 jar (4 oz.) diced pimientos, drained Baked pita chips

Preheat oven to 350°. Combine the first 6 ingredients; fold in the shrimp, crab and pimientos. Bake until bubbly, 30-35 minutes. Serve with pita chips.
¼ cup: 181 cal., 15g fat (5g sat. fat), 53mg chol., 425mg sod., 4g carb. (1g sugars, 0 fiber), 7g pro.

FESTIVE TOSSED SALAD WITH FETA

I serve this colorful salad when we have guests over for dinner because it goes with just about any main entree and is a snap to toss together with packaged greens. Dried cranberries and feta cheese add a delightful touch.
—*Kate Hilts, Fairbanks, AK*

Takes: 10 min. • **Makes:** 12 servings

- ½ cup olive oil
- ¼ cup balsamic vinegar
- 3 Tbsp. water
- 1 envelope Italian salad dressing mix
- 2 pkg. (10 oz. each) Italian-blend salad greens
- 2 medium tomatoes, seeded and chopped
- 1 small red onion, thinly sliced
- 1 cup (4 oz.) crumbled feta cheese
- ¾ cup dried cranberries

In a jar with a tight-fitting lid, combine the oil, vinegar, water and salad dressing mix; shake well. In a large bowl, combine the greens, tomatoes, onion, cheese and cranberries. Serve with dressing.
1 cup: 156 cal., 11g fat (2g sat. fat), 5mg chol., 344mg sod., 14g carb. (10g sugars, 2g fiber), 3g pro.

TEST KITCHEN TIP

Have you ever purchased packaged greens, only to have them go bad in just a few days? Try the paper towel trick. Wash the greens and dry them completely. Lay a dry paper towel on the bottom of the container or bag the greens came in, then add about half the greens. Lay down another paper towel and the rest of the greens, then top with one more paper towel. The paper towels will absorb moisture away from the greens, keeping them fresh in your fridge for a few days longer.

GARLIC KNOTS

Stocking Your Pantry

The key to the magic of being able to pull together a terrific meal quickly (and prevent an unexpected grocery run) is to have a well-stocked pantry. If you cover your bases, you'll always have items in the cupboard and fridge that will work well together. Here are some suggestions for a few basic ingredients to always have on hand.

- Stock or broth (chicken, beef and/or vegetable)
- Vinegar (red wine, white wine and/or balsamic)
- Eggs
- Milk
- Butter
- Condensed soup (cream of mushroom and/or chicken)
- Salsa
- All-purpose flour
- A selection of herbs and spices
- Lemons
- Garlic
- Pastas
- Tomato sauce or paste
- Canned tomatoes (diced)
- Canned beans (garbanzo beans, white beans, kidney beans and/or black beans)
- Bread or rolls
- Rice mixes
- Onions
- Shredded cheeses
- Frozen vegetables (mixed veggies, peas, broccoli, cauliflower, spinach)
- Bottled salad dressings
- Rice
- Bacon
- Honey
- Hot sauce
- Bread crumbs
- Prepared mustard

RANCH PORK ROAST

RANCH PORK ROAST

A simple pork roast goes from ordinary to extraordinary with a mild rub that's perfect for seasoned and newbie cooks alike. Any leftover meat is tender and flavorful enough to be used in countless recipes.
—Taste of Home *Test Kitchen*

- -

Prep: 10 min. • **Bake:** 50 min. + standing
Makes: 8 servings

- 1 boneless pork loin roast (2½ lbs.)
- 2 Tbsp. olive oil
- 1 Tbsp. ranch salad dressing mix
- 2 tsp. Dijon mustard
- 1 garlic clove, minced
- ½ tsp. pepper

1. Preheat oven to 350°. If desired, tie pork with kitchen string at 2-in. intervals to help roast hold its shape. Combine the next 5 ingredients; rub over roast. Place on a rack in a shallow roasting pan. Pour 1 cup water into pan.
2. Bake, uncovered, until a thermometer reads 145°, 50-55 minutes. Let roast stand for 10-15 minutes before slicing.
4 oz. cooked pork: 212 cal., 10g fat (3g sat. fat), 70mg chol., 248mg sod., 2g carb. (0 sugars, 0 fiber), 27g pro. **Diabetic exchanges:** 4 lean meat, ½ fat.

CRANBERRY TURKEY CROSTINI

I wasn't quite sure what to expect when I made these, but they are fabulous. The jalapenos balance out the other ingredients perfectly. If you don't have shaved deli turkey, shaved chicken works just as well.
—Bridgetta Ealy, Pontiac, MI

- -

Prep: 30 min. + chilling • **Makes:** 2½ dozen

- 1 pkg. (12 oz.) fresh or frozen cranberries
- 1 medium tangerine, peeled and seeded
- ½ cup red wine vinegar
- ¼ cup chopped shallots
- ½ cup sugar
- ¼ cup chopped seeded jalapeno peppers
- ¼ tsp. pepper
- 30 slices French bread (¼ in. thick) Cooking spray
- 1 pkg. (8 oz.) reduced-fat cream cheese
- ½ lb. shaved deli smoked turkey

1. Place cranberries and tangerine in a food processor; cover and process until coarsely chopped. Set aside.
2. In a small saucepan, bring vinegar and shallots to a boil. Reduce the heat; simmer, uncovered, for 5 minutes or until mixture is reduced to ⅓ cup, stirring occasionally. Stir in the sugar, jalapenos, pepper and reserved cranberry mixture. Cook for 5 minutes over medium heat, stirring frequently. Transfer to a small bowl; refrigerate until chilled.
3. Place bread slices on ungreased baking sheets; lightly spray bread on both sides with cooking spray. Broil 3-4 in. from heat for 1-2 minutes on each side or until lightly browned. Spread each slice with 1½ tsp. cream cheese; top with turkey and 1 Tbsp. cranberry mixture.
Note: Wear disposable gloves when cutting hot peppers; the oils can burn skin. Avoid touching your face.
1 piece: 79 cal., 3g fat (1g sat. fat), 8mg chol., 131mg sod., 11g carb. (5g sugars, 1g fiber), 3g pro.

EASY BROCCOLI-CAULIFLOWER CASSEROLE

When I was teaching, a student's mother gave me this broccoli casserole recipe. It's a keeper at our house. My granddaughter makes it for special occasions.
—Nancy Herzig, Geneva, NY

- -

Prep: 5 min. • **Bake:** 1 hour
Makes: 8 servings

- 1 pkg. (16 oz.) frozen chopped broccoli, thawed
- 1 pkg. (16 oz.) frozen cauliflower, thawed
- 1 can (10¾ oz.) condensed cream of mushroom soup, undiluted
- ¾ cup mayonnaise
- 2 large eggs
- ¼ tsp. onion salt
- 3 cups (12 oz.) shredded cheddar cheese, divided

In a large bowl, combine first 6 ingredients. Stir in 2 cups cheese. Transfer to a greased 8-in. square baking dish. Sprinkle with the remaining cheese. Bake at 350° for 60-65 minutes or until bubbly.
¾ cup: 384 cal., 33g fat (11g sat. fat), 92mg chol., 759mg sod., 10g carb. (3g sugars, 4g fiber), 14g pro.

EASY REINDEER COOKIES

One year my son Eric wanted to give all the kids in his class a present. I suggested we bake them a holiday treat instead. We made these festive cookies using a cookie mix, pretzels, chocolate chips and Red Hots.
—Gretchen Vandenberghe, Toledo, OH

Prep: 15 min. + chilling • **Bake:** 20 min.
Makes: 2 dozen

- 1   pkg. (17½ oz.) peanut butter cookie mix
- ⅓   cup canola oil
- 1   large egg
- 30 miniature pretzels, halved
- ⅓   cup semisweet chocolate chips, melted
- 60 candy eyes
- 30 red milk chocolate M&M's

1. In a large bowl, beat cookie mix, oil and egg until well combined. Shape into a 7½-in. roll; securely wrap roll in waxed paper. Refrigerate for 1 hour. Unwrap and cut into ¼-in. slices.
2. Preheat oven to 350°. Place 2 in. apart on ungreased baking sheets. Using thumb and forefinger, squeeze each cookie slice at the equator, making a slight indentation on each side of the cookie. Press in miniature pretzel halves for antlers.
3. Bake until light brown, 9-11 minutes. Remove to wire racks to cool. Place melted chocolate chips in a piping bag or resealable bag; cut a small opening at corner. Adhere eyes and noses to cookies using small amount of the melted chocolate. Pipe mouth and eyebrows using melted chocolate; allow chocolate to set before serving.
1 cookie: 129 cal., 7g fat (2g sat. fat), 6mg chol., 134mg sod., 16g carb. (2g sugars, 0 fiber), 2g pro.

BLACK FOREST CHEESECAKE

I have taken this popular cheesecake to every gathering since I created the recipe about 15 years ago. My family asks for the dessert all the time, and I'm happy to make it.
—Christine Ooyen, Winnebago, IL

Prep: 20 min. + chilling • **Makes:** 8 servings

- 1   pkg. (8 oz.) cream cheese, softened
- ⅓   cup sugar
- 1   cup sour cream
- 2   tsp. vanilla extract
- 1   carton (8 oz.) frozen whipped topping, thawed
- 1   chocolate crumb crust (9 in.)
- ¼   cup baking cocoa
- 1   Tbsp. confectioners' sugar
- 1   can (21 oz.) cherry pie filling

1. In a large bowl, beat cream cheese and sugar until smooth. Beat in sour cream and vanilla. Fold in whipped topping. Spread half the mixture evenly into crust. Fold cocoa and confectioners' sugar into remaining whipped topping mixture; carefully spread over cream cheese layer. Refrigerate at least 4 hours.
2. Cut into pieces; top each piece with cherry pie filling.
1 piece: 469 cal., 24g fat (15g sat. fat), 50mg chol., 213mg sod., 54g carb. (38g sugars, 2g fiber), 5g pro.

FRUITY SHERBET PUNCH

Everybody loves glasses of this sweet fruit punch. When entertaining, I start with a quart of sherbet, then I add more later so it all doesn't melt right away.
—Betty Eberly, Palmyra, PA

Takes: 15 min.
Makes: 20 servings (about 5 qt.)

- 4   cups unsweetened apple juice
- 4   cups unsweetened pineapple juice
- 4   cups orange juice
- 2   liters ginger ale, chilled
- 1   to 2 qt. orange or pineapple sherbet

In a large punch bowl, combine juices. Stir in the ginger ale; top with sherbet. Serve punch immediately.
1 cup: 149 cal., 1g fat (0 sat. fat), 2mg chol., 23mg sod., 36g carb. (33g sugars, 0 fiber), 1g pro.

HARVEY WALLBANGER CAKE

This treat is from my Aunt Martha, who lived to the age of 94. She found clever ways to substitute vodka or rum for the water in almost any cake. The recipe for this deliciously moist Harvey Wallbanger cake was taped to her kitchen cabinet.
—Lynda Szczepanik, Highland Park, IL

Prep: 20 min. • **Bake:** 45 min. + cooling
Makes: 12 servings

- 1   pkg. orange cake mix (regular size)
- 1   pkg. (3.4 oz.) instant vanilla pudding mix
- 4   large eggs
- ½   cup canola oil
- ¾   cup orange juice
- ¼   cup vodka
- ¼   cup Galliano liqueur
GLAZE
- 2½ cups confectioners' sugar
- 4   Tbsp. orange juice
- 2   Tbsp. butter, melted
- ¼   tsp. vanilla extract
     Optional: Assorted white sprinkles and citrus fruit segments

1. Preheat oven to 350°. Grease and flour a 10-in. tube pan.
2. In large bowl, combine first 7 ingredients; beat on low speed 30 seconds. Beat on medium 2 minutes. Transfer the batter to prepared pan.
3. Bake until top springs back when lightly touched, 45-50 minutes. Cool in pan 10 minutes before removing to a wire rack to cool completely.
4. In small bowl, mix glaze ingredients until smooth. Pour over cake. If desired, top with white sprinkles and serve with segmented citrus fruit.
1 slice: 447 cal., 16g fat (3g sat. fat), 67mg chol., 370mg sod., 71g carb. (53g sugars, 0 fiber), 4g pro.

TEST KITCHEN TIP

A Harvey Wallbanger cake is a retro, boozy fluted tube pan cake inspired by the cocktail of the same name that became popular in the 1970s. These throwback cakes are typically made with an orange cake mix (or yellow if you can't find orange) and are spiked with the same ingredients in the cocktail—vodka, orange juice and Galliano liqueur.

HARVEY
WALLBANGER
CAKE

GIVING THANKS

When the temperatures tumble and the days become shorter, our appetites grow heartier, and suddenly our hands are busy kneading bread, simmering up soups and baking pies. Welcome this season of cool, crisp weather with a bounty of autumn-meets-winter fare the whole family will love. Whether you're hosting a laid-back dinner with all the fixings or simply seeking a new spin on stuffing or dessert, these festive ideas have all the right ingredients for a cozy, heartwarming meal.

A CLASSIC THANKSGIVING FEAST

A special kind of magic happens when people gather to share in a meal of thanksgiving and celebration. The delicious food, lively conversation and good company compel folks to linger a little longer and savor each bite. Look here for everything you need for a classic meal with a touch of elegance. From a roast turkey bathed in a flavorful herb brine to decadent sides and indulgent desserts, these enticing recipes are sure to impress.

Herb-Brined Turkey (p. 73)

Thanksgiving Day Countdown

It's among the most joyous holidays of the year, but Thanksgiving is also one of the busiest in the kitchen. Refer to this timeline to help plan the big feast.

A FEW WEEKS BEFORE

☐ Prepare two grocery lists—one for nonperishable items to buy now and one for perishable items to buy a few days before Thanksgiving.

☐ Bake the cake layers for the Chocolate Truffle Cake, but do not assemble or decorate. Store layers in an airtight container in the freezer.

TWO DAYS BEFORE

☐ Buy remaining grocery items.

☐ Bake the Angel Rolls. Store in an airtight container.

☐ Wash china, stemware and table linens.

THE DAY BEFORE

☐ Prepare brine for the Herb-Brined Turkey and add to turkey. Cover and refrigerate for 12-24 hours.

☐ Remove the chocolate cake layers from the freezer. Allow cakes to thaw. Meanwhile, prepare the filling and ganache. Assemble and frost cake. Create chocolate leaves and add to outside of cake. Cover and store in the refrigerator.

☐ Bake the crusts for the Pumpkin Latte Cheesecake Pretzel Tarts. Place unfilled tarts in an airtight container.

☐ Prepare the Herbed Pecan Stuffing. Cover and place in the refrigerator.

☐ Prepare the Layered Cranberry Slices. Cover and store in the refrigerator until ready to serve.

☐ Prepare the Spiced Pineapple Cooler, but do not add the ginger ale or ice. Store in the refrigerator.

☐ Set the table.

THANKSGIVING DAY

☐ In the morning, bake the Orchard Pear Pie. Cover and store until ready to serve.

☐ About 4 hours before dinner, remove the Herb-Brined Turkey from the refrigerator. Discard brine and add herbed butter to turkey. Roast turkey as directed. Let stand 20 minutes before carving.

☐ About 2½ hours before dinner, prepare and bake the Creamed Spinach Twice-Baked Potatoes.

☐ About 1½ hours before dinner, remove the stuffing from the refrigerator. Bake as directed, increasing uncovered bake time as needed until lightly browned and heated through.

☐ About 1 hour before dinner, prepare the cheesecake filling for the tarts; place in the refrigerator.

☐ About 40 minutes before dinner, prepare the Cranberry-Fig Goat Cheese Crostini.

☐ About 30 minutes before dinner, prepare the Ginger Butternut Squash, Crab Wonton Cups and the Olive Artichoke Dip. Keep warm until serving.

RIGHT BEFORE DINNER

☐ As guests arrive, set the Cranberry-Fig Goat Cheese Crostini, Crab Wonton Cups and Olive Artichoke Dip on the buffet table.

☐ As guests arrive, add ginger ale to Spiced Pineapple Cooler. Serve individual servings over ice.

☐ After dinner, fill pretzel tarts with the refrigerated cheesecake filling; garnish with toffee bits. Serve the tarts, cake and pie with whipped cream or ice cream if desired.

CRANBERRY-FIG
GOAT CHEESE
CROSTINI

CRANBERRY-FIG GOAT CHEESE CROSTINI

The blend of flavors in the crostini makes an absolutely scrumptious appetizer.
—*Barbara Estabrook, Appleton, WI*

- -

Prep: 25 min. • **Cook:** 10 min.
Makes: 2 dozen

  ½ **cup balsamic vinegar**
  1 **Tbsp. honey**
CROSTINI
  24 **French bread baguette slices**
      (½ in. thick)
  3 **Tbsp. olive oil**
CRANBERRY-FIG TOPPING
  ½ **cup coarsely chopped dried**
      cranberries
  ⅓ **cup coarsely chopped dried figs**
  ⅓ **cup coarsely chopped unblanched**
      almonds
  ⅓ **cup coarsely chopped pitted Greek**
      olives
  1 **Tbsp. olive oil**
  2 **tsp. balsamic vinegar**
  ⅛ **tsp. freshly ground pepper**
CHEESE SPREAD
  2 **logs (4 oz. each) spreadable**
      goat cheese
  1 **tsp. grated lemon zest**
      Dash freshly ground pepper
      Minced fresh mint

1. In a small saucepan, combine vinegar and honey. Bring to a boil. Reduce heat; simmer, uncovered, until mixture is reduced by half, about 5 minutes. Set aside to cool.
2. Lightly brush both sides of baguette slices with oil; place on an ungreased baking sheet. Broil 3-4 in. from the heat 1-2 minutes on each side or until golden brown. Set aside.
3. In a small bowl, combine the topping ingredients; toss to coat. In another bowl, beat goat cheese, lemon zest and pepper until blended.
4. To serve, spread goat cheese mixture over toasts. Stir cranberry mixture; spoon over goat cheese. Drizzle with balsamic glaze and sprinkle with mint.
1 crostini: 109 cal., 6g fat (1g sat. fat), 7mg chol., 135mg sod., 10g carb. (5g sugars, 1g fiber), 3g pro.

CRAB WONTON CUPS
(PICTURED ON COVER)
Add these tasty little crab tarts to your list of holiday finger foods. They're excellent served warm and crispy from the oven.
—*Connie McDowell, Greenwood, DE*

Takes: 30 min. • **Makes:** 32 appetizers

- 32 wonton wrappers
      Cooking spray
- 1   pkg. (8 oz.) cream cheese, softened
- ½   cup heavy whipping cream
- 1   large egg, room temperature
- 1   Tbsp. Dijon mustard
- 1   tsp. Worcestershire sauce
- 5   drops hot pepper sauce
- 1   cup lump crabmeat, drained
- ¼   cup thinly sliced green onions
- ¼   cup finely chopped sweet red pepper
- 1   cup grated Parmesan cheese
      Minced chives, optional

1. Preheat oven to 350°. Press the wonton wrappers into miniature muffin cups coated with cooking spray. Spritz wrappers with cooking spray. Bake until lightly browned, 8-9 minutes.
2. Meanwhile, in a small bowl, beat cream cheese, cream, egg, mustard, Worcestershire sauce and pepper sauce until smooth. Stir in crab, green onions and red pepper; spoon into wonton cups. Sprinkle with the grated Parmesan cheese.
3. Bake 10-12 minutes or until filling is heated through. Serve warm. If desired, garnish with minced chives. Refrigerate leftovers.
1 wonton cup: 77 cal., 5g fat (3g sat. fat), 26mg chol., 153mg sod., 5g carb. (0 sugars, 0 fiber), 3g pro.

OLIVE ARTICHOKE DIP
All it takes is five easy ingredients to whip up a rich, savory dip your guests will go crazy for. We enjoy it warm on baguette slices.
—*Kathie Morris, Redmond, OR*

Takes: 25 min. • **Makes:** 3 cups

- 2   jars (6½ oz. each) marinated artichoke hearts, drained and diced
- ¾   cup grated Parmesan cheese
- 1   can (4 oz.) chopped green chiles
- 1   can (2¼ oz.) sliced ripe olives, drained
- 2   Tbsp. mayonnaise
      Sliced French bread or tortilla chips

Preheat oven to 350°. In a bowl, combine the first 5 ingredients. Transfer to an ungreased 1-qt. baking dish. Bake, uncovered, until bubbly, 20-25 minutes. Serve with bread or tortilla chips.
2 Tbsp.: 41 cal., 4g fat (1g sat. fat), 2mg chol., 166mg sod., 2g carb. (0 sugars, 1g fiber), 1g pro.

ANGEL ROLLS
Delight your family and friends with these soft, tender yeast rolls that come together in a jiffy, thanks to quick-rise yeast. My family especially likes them smothered with sausage gravy.
—*Debbie Graber, Eureka, NV*

Prep: 20 min. + standing
Bake: 15 min. • **Makes:** 14 rolls

- 3½ cups bread flour
- 2   Tbsp. sugar
- 1   pkg. (¼ oz.) quick-rise yeast
- 1¼ tsp. salt
- 1   tsp. baking powder
- ½   tsp. baking soda
- 1   cup buttermilk
- ½   cup canola oil
- ⅓   cup water
      Melted butter

1. Preheat oven to 400°. In a large bowl, combine 1½ cups flour, sugar, yeast, salt, baking powder and baking soda. In a small saucepan, heat the buttermilk, oil and water to 120°-130°. Add to dry ingredients; beat just until moistened. Stir in enough remaining flour to form a soft dough.
2. Turn onto a floured surface and knead until smooth and elastic, 4-6 minutes. Cover and let rest for 10 minutes.

3. Roll out dough to ½-in. thickness; cut with a floured 2½-in. biscuit cutter. Place rolls on a greased baking sheet.
4. Bake rolls until they're golden brown, 15-18 minutes. Brush the tops with butter. Remove from pan to a wire rack to cool.
1 roll: 184 cal., 8g fat (1g sat. fat), 1mg chol., 303mg sod., 25g carb. (3g sugars, 1g fiber), 5g pro.

GINGER BUTTERNUT SQUASH
It's nice to have a stovetop dish on your holiday menu so you don't have to worry about too many things going in the oven. Lightly seasoned with ginger, maple and nutmeg, this butternut squash is a favorite.
—*Joan Kane, Framingham, MA*

Takes: 30 min. • **Makes:** 8 servings

- 1   medium butternut squash (about 4 lbs.), peeled and cubed
- ½   cup butter, cubed
- 2   Tbsp. maple syrup
- ¼   cup finely chopped crystallized ginger
- 1¼ tsp. salt
- ½   tsp. pepper
- ½   tsp. ground nutmeg

In a large saucepan, bring 1 in. of water to a boil. Add squash; cover and cook until tender, 15-20 minutes. Drain. Mash the squash with remaining ingredients.
⅔ cup: 242 cal., 12g fat (7g sat. fat), 31mg chol., 474mg sod., 36g carb. (12g sugars, 8g fiber), 2g pro.

TEST KITCHEN TIP

Although it falls in the winter squash category, butternut squash is typically available year-round. Choose ones that are heavy and blemish-free. They don't need to go in the fridge, but store them in a cool, dry place.

GINGER
BUTTERNUT
SQUASH

HERBED PECAN STUFFING

I updated a basic stuffing recipe by using wholesome multigrain bread in place of customary white bread. It adds a hearty, crunchy taste.
—*Edie DeSpain, Logan, UT*

Prep: 35 min. • **Bake:** 45 min.
Makes: 12 servings

- 8 cups cubed day-old multigrain bread
- ¾ cup golden raisins
- ½ cup apple juice
- ¼ cup olive oil
- 4 celery ribs, diced
- 1 large onion, chopped
- 3 garlic cloves, minced
- 1 cup minced fresh parsley
- 1½ tsp. salt
- 1½ tsp. rubbed sage
- ¾ tsp. dried thyme
- ½ tsp. fennel seeds, crushed
- ¼ tsp. pepper
- 1 large egg
- 1½ to 2 cups chicken broth
- 1½ cups coarsely chopped pecans, toasted

1. Preheat oven to 225°. Place bread cubes in a single layer on an ungreased baking sheet. Bake until partially dried, tossing occasionally, 30-40 minutes. Set aside. Increase oven temperature to 325°.

2. Meanwhile, combine golden raisins and apple juice in a saucepan; bring to a boil. Remove from heat; let stand for 15 minutes. In a large skillet or Dutch oven, heat oil over medium-high heat. Add celery, onion and garlic; cook and stir until tender, 5-7 minutes. Stir in the parsley, salt, sage, thyme, fennel seeds and pepper; remove from the heat. Beat egg and broth; add to vegetable mixture with bread cubes and raisin mixture. Toss well. Stir in pecans. Transfer to a greased 13x9-in. baking dish.

3. Cover and bake for 30 minutes. Uncover; bake 15-20 minutes longer or until stuffing is lightly browned.

1 cup: 255 cal., 17g fat (2g sat. fat), 18mg chol., 564mg sod., 24g carb. (10g sugars, 4g fiber), 5g pro.

HERBED PECAN STUFFING

CREAMED SPINACH TWICE-BAKED POTATOES

This make-ahead side dish combines two of my favorite recipes: twice-baked potatoes and creamed spinach. It's a new take on potatoes and is easy for holiday potlucks.
—*Teri Rasey, Cadillac, MI*

Prep: 1 hour • **Cook:** 1½ hours
Makes: 12 servings

- 12 medium russet potatoes
- 4 Tbsp. butter, cubed
- 1¾ to 2 cups 2% milk, divided
- 2 tsp. salt, divided
- ¼ tsp. pepper
- 2 lbs. fresh spinach
- 2 Tbsp. olive oil
- 1 small onion, finely chopped
- 2 Tbsp. all-purpose flour
- ½ tsp. ground nutmeg

TOPPING
- ½ cup grated Parmesan cheese
- ½ cup dry bread crumbs
- ¼ cup butter, melted

1. Preheat oven to 400°. Scrub potatoes; pierce several times with a fork. Place in foil-lined 15x10x1-in. baking pans; bake until tender, 1¼-1½ hours.
2. When cool enough to handle, cut each potato lengthwise in half. Scoop out pulp, leaving ¼-in.-thick shells. In a large bowl, mash pulp with butter, ¼ to ½ cup milk, 1 tsp. salt and pepper; set aside. In a large Dutch oven, place steamer basket over 1 in. of water. Place one-fourth of the spinach in basket. Bring water to a boil. Reduce heat to maintain a low boil; steam, covered, 3-4 minutes or just until spinach is wilted. Transfer to a colander; rinse under cold water and drain. Repeat with remaining spinach; squeeze dry. Coarsely chop spinach.
3. In a large skillet, heat oil over medium heat. Add onion; cook and stir until tender. Stir in flour, nutmeg and remaining 1 tsp. salt until blended; gradually whisk in remaining 1½ cups milk. Bring to a boil, stirring constantly; cook and stir until thickened, 1-2 minutes. Stir in spinach; heat through.
4. Spoon mashed potato mixture into potato shells. Return to baking pans. Top with the spinach mixture. For the topping, combine Parmesan cheese, bread crumbs and melted butter; sprinkle over potatoes. Bake until heated through, 12-15 minutes.
2 stuffed potato halves: 303 cal., 10g fat (5g sat. fat), 21mg chol., 316mg sod., 46g carb. (4g sugars, 6g fiber), 8g pro.

SPICED PINEAPPLE COOLER

I enjoy cooking, especially when I'm preparing a dish that is different. That's definitely the case with this spicy, refreshing party punch.
—*Nancy Burford, Senatobia, MS*

Prep: 10 min. • **Cook:** 20 min. + chilling
Makes: 13 servings

- 1½ cups water
- ⅔ cup sugar
- 4 cinnamon sticks (3 in.)
- 12 whole cloves
- 1 can (46 oz.) unsweetened pineapple juice
- 1½ cups orange juice
- ½ cup lemon juice
- 1 can (12 oz.) ginger ale, chilled
  Ice cubes
  Additional cinnamon sticks, optional

1. In a small saucepan, bring water, sugar, cinnamon and cloves to a boil. Reduce heat; cover and simmer for 15 minutes. Strain. Cool to room temperature.
2. Pour into a large pitcher; stir in juices. Refrigerate until chilled. Just before serving, stir in ginger ale. Serve over ice. Garnish with additional cinnamon sticks if desired.
¾ cup: 119 cal., 0 fat (0 sat. fat), 0 chol., 4mg sod., 29g carb. (25g sugars, 0 fiber), 1g pro.

LAYERED CRANBERRY SLICES

My mom came up with this unique twist on jellied cranberry sauce for our holiday meals. It's a been a favorite on our family table for over 50 years.
—*Judy Hoggle, Demopolis, AL*

Takes: 15 min. • **Makes:** 14 servings

- 1 pkg. (8 oz.) cream cheese, softened
- 2 Tbsp. mayonnaise
- ½ cup chopped pecans, toasted
- 1 can (14 oz.) jellied cranberry sauce

In a small bowl, beat cream cheese and mayonnaise until blended; stir in pecans. Remove cranberry sauce from the can in 1 piece; cut into fourteen ¼-in. slices. Spread cream cheese mixture over half of the slices; top with remaining slices. Cut each in half. Cover and refrigerate until serving.
2 pieces: 137 cal., 10g fat (4g sat. fat), 17mg chol., 75mg sod., 12g carb. (8g sugars, 1g fiber), 1g pro.

HERB-BRINED
TURKEY

HERB-BRINED TURKEY

This roast turkey makes an impressive main course. The enticing aroma will have guests counting the minutes until carving time.
—*Stephan-Scott Rugh, Portland, OR*

Prep: 35 min. + marinating
Bake: 3¾ hours + standing
Makes: 14 servings

- 2 cups kosher salt
- 1 cup packed brown sugar
- 5 fresh sage leaves
- 1 fresh thyme sprig
- 1 fresh rosemary sprig
- 2 qt. water
- 2 qt. cold water
- 1 turkey (14 to 16 lbs.)

HERB BUTTER
- 2 cups butter, softened
- ½ cup olive oil
- 1 cup packed fresh parsley sprigs
- ⅓ cup fresh sage leaves
- ⅓ cup fresh rosemary leaves
- ¼ cup fresh thyme leaves
- 2 garlic cloves
- 1 tsp. salt
- 1 tsp. pepper

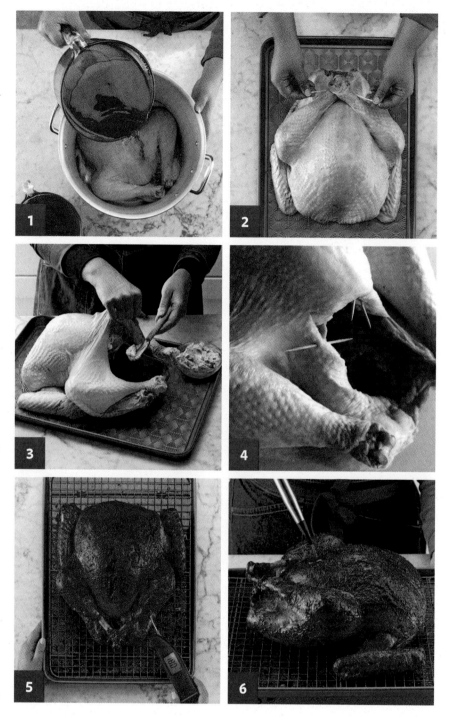

1. In a large stockpot, combine the salt, brown sugar, sage, thyme, rosemary and 2 qt. water. Bring to a boil. Cook and stir until the salt and sugar are dissolved. Remove from the heat. Add the cold water to cool the brine to room temperature. Pour brine into a large glass measuring cup or other pourable container.
2. In the same stockpot, place the turkey, breast side up. Add the cooled brine (Step #1). Add additional cool water as needed to ensure the turkey is completely submerged. Cover and refrigerate for 12-24 hours, turning occasionally.
3. Drain and discard brine; rinse turkey and pat dry. Tie drumsticks together (Step #2). Place the remaining ingredients in a food processor; cover and process until smooth. With fingers, carefully loosen skin from turkey breast; rub half of the butter mixture under skin (Step #3). Secure skin to underside of breast with toothpicks (Step #4). Rub the remaining butter mixture over skin.
4. Place turkey, breast side up, on a rack in a roasting pan. Bake at 450° for 30 minutes. Reduce the heat to 325°; bake 3¼-3¾ hours longer or until thermometer reads 180° (Step #5), basting twice during the last 30 minutes of cooking (Step #6). Cover loosely with foil if turkey browns too quickly.
5. Remove turkey to a serving platter; cover and let stand for 20 minutes before carving.
10 oz. cooked turkey: 834 cal., 58g fat (25g sat. fat), 314mg chol., 658mg sod., 1g carb. (0 sugars, 0 fiber), 73g pro.

↑

You can use 2 oven-sized roasting bags instead of a stockpot to brine your turkey. Place a turkey-sized oven roasting bag inside a second roasting bag; add turkey. Carefully pour cooled brine into bag. Squeeze out as much air as possible; seal bags and turn to coat. Place the turkey in a roasting pan. Follow the remaining steps in the recipe as directed.

CHOCOLATE
TRUFFLE CAKE

CHOCOLATE TRUFFLE CAKE

Love chocolate? Then this tender, luxurious layer cake is for you. With a ganache glaze and a fabulous bittersweet filling, the indulgence is so worth it.
—*JoAnn Koerkenmeier, Damiansville, IL*

Prep: 35 min. + chilling
Bake: 25 min. + cooling
Makes: 16 servings

2½ cups 2% milk
1 cup butter, cubed
8 oz. semisweet chocolate, chopped
3 large eggs, room temperature
2 tsp. vanilla extract
2⅔ cups all-purpose flour
2 cups sugar
1 tsp. baking soda
½ tsp. salt
FILLING
6 Tbsp. butter, cubed
4 oz. bittersweet chocolate, chopped
2½ cups confectioners' sugar
½ cup heavy whipping cream
GANACHE
10 oz. semisweet chocolate, chopped
⅔ cup heavy whipping cream

1. In a large saucepan, cook milk, butter and chocolate over low heat until melted. Remove from the heat; let stand for 10 minutes.
2. Preheat oven to 325°. In a large bowl, beat eggs and vanilla; stir in chocolate mixture until smooth. Combine flour, sugar, baking soda and salt; gradually add to chocolate mixture and mix well (batter will be thin).
3. Transfer to 3 greased and floured 9-in. round baking pans. Bake 25-30 minutes or until a toothpick inserted in center comes out clean. Cool 10 minutes before removing from pans to wire racks to cool completely.
4. For filling, in a small saucepan, melt butter and chocolate. Stir in confectioners' sugar and heavy whipping cream until smooth.
5. For ganache, place chocolate in a small bowl. In a small saucepan, bring cream just to a boil. Pour over chocolate; whisk until smooth. Cool, stirring occasionally, until ganache reaches a spreading consistency.
6. Place 1 cake layer on a serving plate; spread with half of the filling. Repeat layers. Top with the remaining cake layer. Spread ganache over top and sides of cake. Store in the refrigerator.

1 piece: 676 cal., 38g fat (22g sat. fat), 109mg chol., 299mg sod., 84g carb. (63g sugars, 3g fiber), 8g pro.

TEST KITCHEN TIP

To garnish with chocolate leaves, brush lemon leaves with 2 coats of melted milk chocolate, refrigerating until set between layers. Once the second coat is set, remove lemon leaves from chocolate and press chocolate leaves onto frosted cake. Lemon leaves can be found at most supermarket florists.

PUMPKIN LATTE CHEESECAKE PRETZEL TARTS

The flavor of the creamy filling in these pretzel cups reminds me of a pumpkin latte. Use extra toffee chips for a fun and yummy garnish.
—*Arlene Erlbach, Morton Grove, IL*

Prep: 25 min. + chilling
Bake: 10 min. + cooling
Makes: 2 dozen

- 2 cups finely crushed pretzels
- 3 Tbsp. light brown sugar
- 10 Tbsp. butter, melted
- 1 egg white, room temperature

FILLING
- 2 Tbsp. instant espresso powder
- 1 Tbsp. hot water
- 1 can (15 oz.) pumpkin
- 1 pkg. (8 oz.) cream cheese, softened
- ½ cup packed light brown sugar
- 1 Tbsp. pumpkin pie spice
- 1½ cups heavy whipping cream
- 1 cup brickle toffee bits

1. Preheat oven to 350°. In a small bowl, mix pretzels and brown sugar; stir in butter and egg white. Press onto bottoms and up the sides of greased muffin cups. Bake until firm and lightly browned, 10-12 minutes. Cool for 10 minutes before removing from pans to wire racks to cool completely.
2. For the filling, in a large bowl, dissolve the espresso powder in hot water. Beat in the pumpkin, cream cheese, brown sugar and pie spice until smooth. In another large bowl, beat the cream until stiff peaks form; reserve 1 cup for topping. Fold remaining whipped cream into pumpkin mixture; stir in toffee bits.
3. Spoon into pretzel cups. Top with reserved whipped cream. Refrigerate at least 1 hour before serving.
1 tart: 239 cal., 17g fat (10g sat. fat), 43mg chol., 240mg sod., 21g carb. (14g sugars, 1g fiber), 2g pro.

ORCHARD PEAR PIE

I made this pie using freshly picked Bartlett pears from the orchard. It's a lovely dessert to include in your holiday menu. You can also use canned pears if fresh are not available.
—*Mary Anne Thygesen, Portland, OR*

Prep: 30 min. + chilling
Bake: 30 min. + cooling
Makes: 8 servings

Dough for single-crust pie
- 1 large egg, room temperature
- ¾ cup sour cream
- ½ cup sugar
- ¼ cup all-purpose flour
- ¼ cup plain Greek yogurt
- 1 tsp. vanilla extract
- ¼ tsp. salt
- 4 large ripe pears, peeled and chopped (about 4 cups)

TOPPING
- ¾ cup all-purpose flour
- ¾ cup old-fashioned oats
- ½ cup packed brown sugar
- 2 Tbsp. chopped pecans
- ½ tsp. ground cardamom
- ½ cup cold butter

1. On a lightly floured surface, roll dough to a ⅛-in.-thick circle; transfer to a 9-in. pie plate. Trim to ½ in. beyond rim of plate; flute edge. Refrigerate 30 minutes. Preheat oven to 400°.
2. In a small bowl, whisk the egg, sour cream, sugar, flour, yogurt, vanilla and salt. Gently stir in pears. Pour into crust. Bake 15 minutes.
3. Meanwhile, for topping, in a small bowl, combine flour, oats, brown sugar, pecans and cardamom. Cut in cold butter until crumbly; sprinkle over pie.
4. Bake until a knife inserted in the center comes out clean and topping is golden brown, 15-20 minutes. If needed, cover the pie edge loosely with foil during the last 15 minutes of baking to prevent overbrowning. Remove foil. Cool completely on a wire rack. Store pie in the refrigerator.
1 piece: 599 cal., 31g fat (18g sat. fat), 91mg chol., 346mg sod., 77g carb. (39g sugars, 5g fiber), 7g pro.
Dough for single-crust pie (9 in.) Combine 1¼ cups all-purpose flour and ¼ tsp. salt; cut in ½ cup cold butter until crumbly. Gradually add 3-5 Tbsp. ice water, tossing with a fork until dough holds together when pressed. Cover and refrigerate 1 hour.

Secrets to a Successful Thanksgiving

Take it from our culinary crew and experienced editors: There are clever ways to make prepping and hosting Thanksgiving easier than ever.

PLAN EARLY
"Get in touch with your family early in the month to see if they want to contribute and what they like best to eat. It's good to have a sense of who is coming and what they'd like to bring as early as possible."
—*Maggie Knoebel, Culinary Assistant*

USE YOUR FREEZER
"Make and freeze dishes that can be prepared ahead of time. Place the item in a zip-top bag or freezer-safe container along with instructions for thawing and reheating."
—*Rashanda Cobbins, Food Editor*

ALWAYS GIVE YOURSELF MORE TIME THAN YOU THINK YOU NEED
"Overestimate how long it will take you to do everything. This way, if there is a monkey wrench that throws off your timing, you've got time to spare."
—*Peggy Woodward, Senior Food Editor*

OPT FOR SLOW COOKER SIDES
"Oven space is at a premium on Thanksgiving, so include at least one slow-cooker side dish that you can prep the night before and then just switch on the day of the feast."
—*Mark Hagen, Executive Editor*

SET UP A BEVERAGE STATION
"If you're hosting, the last thing you need to be doing is opening bottles of wine or mixing drinks. Instead, stock a self-serve beverage station and let it be known that guests are welcome to it."
—*Lisa Kaminski, Associate Editor*

KEEP NOTES
"I keep an entertaining journal. I write down the menu—including quantities, who attended and who brought what dish. I make notes of how new foods were received and what I should make more of the next year."
—*Julie Schnittka, Senior Editor*

ACCEPT HELP
"When a guest volunteers to do the dishes, always say YES!"
—*Lara Eucalano, Senior Editor*

SPOTLIGHT ON STUFFING

The turkey may be the centerpiece of the meal, but it's the side dishes that steal the show. Whether you call it stuffing or dressing, you're guaranteed to be inspired by these delicious recipes. With variations that include sausage, apples, nuts, squash and more, each one puts a tasty spin on the must-have Thanksgiving dish.

Cranberry Pecan Stuffing (p. 83)

CORN & ONION STUFFING

1 tsp. pepper
6 thick-sliced bacon strips, chopped
1 lb. maple pork sausage
4 celery ribs, chopped
2 medium onions, chopped
2 medium carrots, shredded
6 cups seasoned stuffing cubes, divided
2 cups crushed multigrain Club Crackers (2½x1 in.) (about 40 crackers)
1 can (12 oz.) evaporated milk
1 can (10½ oz.) condensed cream of celery soup, undiluted
6 large eggs, lightly beaten
1 cup cooked long grain rice
1 cup sour cream
1 tsp. garlic powder
1 tsp. poultry seasoning
1 tsp. rubbed sage
½ tsp. celery salt
½ tsp. ground cumin
¼ tsp. cayenne pepper
½ cup butter, cubed

1. Preheat oven to 425°. Place the squash and apples on a rimmed baking sheet. Drizzle with oil; sprinkle with salt and pepper. Toss to coat. Roast until tender, about 25 minutes. Reduce oven setting to 375°.
2. Meanwhile, in a Dutch oven, cook the bacon over medium heat until crisp, stirring occasionally. Remove with a slotted spoon; drain on paper towels. Discard drippings.
3. Add sausage, celery, onions and carrots to pan; cook over medium-high heat until sausage is no longer pink and vegetables are tender, 10-12 minutes, breaking up sausage into crumbles; drain.
4. Transfer to a large bowl. Add 5 cups stuffing cubes, crackers, evaporated milk, soup, eggs, rice, sour cream, seasonings and reserved squash mixture and bacon; toss. Transfer to 2 greased 13x9-in. baking dishes. Lightly crush remaining 1 cup stuffing cubes. Sprinkle over tops; dot with butter.
5. Bake, covered, for 30 minutes. Uncover and bake 15-20 minutes longer or until bubbly and lightly browned.
¾ cup: 401 cal., 26g fat (10g sat. fat), 98mg chol., 793mg sod., 34g carb. (9g sugars, 5g fiber), 11g pro.

→

CORN & ONION STUFFING

I have an affinity for side dishes that offer something new and different, and this one does just that. This stuffing is perfect with pork, beef or poultry. You can leave it in the slow cooker until it's time to eat—or make it early, refrigerate it until almost serving time, and reheat it right before dinner.
—*Patricia Swart, Galloway, NJ*

- -

Prep: 10 min. • **Cook:** 3 hours
Makes: 8 servings

1 can (14¾ oz.) cream-style corn
1 pkg. (6 oz.) stuffing mix
1 small onion, chopped
1 celery rib, chopped
¼ cup water
2 large eggs
1 tsp. poultry seasoning
⅛ tsp. pepper
¼ cup butter, melted

Combine first 8 ingredients. Transfer to a greased 3-qt. slow cooker. Drizzle with butter. Cook, covered, on low until set, 3-4 hours.
½ cup: 192 cal., 8g fat (4g sat. fat), 63mg chol., 530mg sod., 26g carb. (4g sugars, 1g fiber), 5g pro.

APPLE, BUTTERNUT & SAUSAGE DRESSING

I combined four things I love into one dish: apples, butternut squash, bacon and maple sausage! Now, it's one of my most requested dishes during the holidays.
—*Brenda Crouch, Ansley, NE*

- -

Prep: 1¼ hours • **Bake:** 45 min.
Makes: 2 pans (10 servings each)

1 medium butternut squash (about 3 lbs.), peeled and cubed
3 medium tart apples, peeled and cubed
2 Tbsp. olive oil
1 tsp. kosher salt

To easily peel butternut squash, position the squash vertically upright on a cutting board. Next, use a vegetable peeler to remove the skin. If your peeler isn't getting the job done, use a sharp chef's knife to slice off the skin.

SAVORY ZUCCHINI
BREAD PUDDING

SAVORY ZUCCHINI BREAD PUDDING

I've been serving this vegetarian dish for years and always receive compliments on it. If you don't have day-old bread, slice fresh bread and bake it at 300° for 10 minutes before cubing it.
—*Mary Ann Dell, Phoenixville, PA*

Prep: 25 min. • **Bake:** 40 min.
Makes: 12 servings

- 1 small onion, chopped
- 1 celery rib, chopped
- 3 Tbsp. butter
- 1 cup all-purpose flour
- 2 Tbsp. sugar
- 1 tsp. baking powder
- 1 tsp. salt
- 1 tsp. ground cinnamon
- 1 tsp. poultry seasoning
- ½ cup canned pumpkin
- 2 large eggs
- ⅓ cup 2% milk
- ¼ cup butter, melted
- 4 cups day-old cubed bread
- 3 medium zucchini, chopped
- ½ cup shredded cheddar cheese

1. In a small skillet, saute onion and celery in butter until tender; set aside.
2. In a large bowl, combine the flour, sugar, baking powder, salt, cinnamon and poultry seasoning. In a small bowl, whisk the pumpkin, eggs, milk and butter; stir into dry ingredients just until moistened. Fold in the bread cubes, zucchini, cheese and onion mixture.
3. Transfer to a greased 13x9-in. baking dish. Cover and bake at 325° for 30 minutes. Uncover; bake 10-15 minutes longer or until lightly browned.
¾ cup: 182 cal., 10g fat (6g sat. fat), 58mg chol., 408mg sod., 20g carb. (5g sugars, 2g fiber), 5g pro.

TEST KITCHEN TIP

Despite its name, poultry seasoning is vegetarian and is perfectly fine to use in vegetarian dishes. You can find it in the spice aisle in grocery stores or make your own by combining ¾ tsp. rubbed sage and ¼ tsp. dried thyme or marjoram. This will yield 1 tsp. seasoning.

BACON & SAUSAGE STUFFING

This recipe was inspired by my mother's stuffing recipe. It smells like heaven while you're making it, and people can never seem to get enough.
—*Stephan-Scott Rugh, Portland, OR*

Prep: 25 min. • **Cook:** 4 hours + standing
Makes: 20 servings

- 1 lb. bulk pork sausage
- 1 lb. thick-sliced bacon strips, chopped
- ½ cup butter, cubed
- 1 large onion, chopped
- 3 celery ribs, sliced
- 10½ cups unseasoned stuffing cubes
- 1 cup sliced fresh mushrooms
- 1 cup chopped fresh parsley
- 4 tsp. dried sage leaves
- 4 tsp. dried thyme
- 6 large eggs
- 2 cans (10¾ oz. each) condensed cream of chicken soup, undiluted
- 1¼ cups chicken stock

1. In a large skillet, cook sausage over medium heat for 6-8 minutes or until no longer pink, breaking into crumbles. Remove the sausage with a slotted spoon; drain on paper towels. Discard the drippings.
2. Add bacon to pan; cook over medium heat until crisp. Remove to paper towels to drain. Discard drippings. Wipe out pan. In same pan, heat butter over medium-high heat. Add the onion and celery; cook and stir 6-8 minutes or until tender. Remove from heat.
3. In a large bowl, combine stuffing cubes, sausage, bacon, onion mixture, mushrooms, parsley, sage and thyme. In a small bowl, whisk eggs, soup and stock; pour over the stuffing mixture and toss to coat.
4. Transfer to a greased 6-qt. slow cooker. Cook, covered, on low 4-5 hours or until a thermometer reads 160°. Remove lid; let stand 15 minutes before serving.
¾ cup: 290 cal., 17g fat (6g sat. fat), 89mg chol., 823mg sod., 25g carb. (2g sugars, 2g fiber), 11g pro.

BADGER STATE STUFFING

Your family will love the contrasting sweet, savory and slightly tart flavors in this spin on a Thanksgiving classic. Feel free to use your favorite beer or dried fruit to make the dish your own.
—*Andrea Fetting, Franklin, WI*

Prep: 35 min. • **Bake:** 50 min. + standing
Makes: 8 servings

- ½ lb. bacon strips, diced
- ½ lb. sliced fresh mushrooms
- 1 medium onion, diced
- 1 cup chopped celery (about 3 stalks)
- 1 cup chopped carrot (about 4 medium carrots)
- 2 garlic cloves, minced
- 1 can (8 oz.) sauerkraut, rinsed and well drained
- ½ cup amber beer or chicken broth
- 5 cups cubed sourdough bread (½-in. cubes)
- 1 cup dried cherries or dried cranberries
- 1 large egg
- 1¼ cups chicken broth
- 3 Tbsp. minced fresh parsley
- 1 tsp. poultry seasoning
- ½ tsp. pepper

1. Preheat oven to 350°. In a large skillet, cook bacon over medium heat until crisp, stirring occasionally. Remove with a slotted spoon; drain on paper towels. Discard the drippings, reserving 3 Tbsp. in pan.
2. Add mushrooms, onion, celery and carrot to drippings; cook and stir over medium-high heat until tender, 8-10 minutes. Add garlic; cook 1 minute longer. Stir in sauerkraut and beer. Bring to a boil; cook, uncovered, until liquid is reduced by half.
3. In a large bowl, combine the bread cubes, cherries, bacon and sauerkraut mixture. In a small bowl, whisk egg, broth, parsley, poultry seasoning and pepper. Gradually stir into the bread mixture.
4. Transfer to a greased 2-qt. baking dish. Bake, covered, 20 minutes. Uncover; bake until lightly browned, 30-35 minutes longer. Let stand 10 minutes before serving.
1 cup: 271 cal., 11g fat (4g sat. fat), 39mg chol., 700mg sod., 35g carb. (18g sugars, 3g fiber), 9g pro.

PRESSURE-COOKER
DRESSING

SAUSAGE-HERB DRESSING

To make time for last-minute Thanksgiving essentials, I prep the sausage part of this recipe a day or two ahead of time, then finish the dressing in my slow cooker on the big day. It has stood the test two years running!
—*Judy Batson, Tampa, FL*

Prep: 20 min. • **Cook:** 2 hours
Makes: 10 servings

- 1   lb. bulk sage pork sausage
- 1   medium sweet onion, chopped (about 2 cups)
- 2   celery ribs, chopped
- ¼   cup brewed coffee
- ½   tsp. poultry seasoning
- ½   tsp. dried oregano
- ½   tsp. rubbed sage
- ½   tsp. dried thyme
- ½   tsp. pepper
- 1½ cups chicken or turkey broth
- 1   pkg. (12 oz.) seasoned stuffing cubes (8 cups)
     Chopped fresh parsley

1. In a 6-qt. stockpot, cook and crumble sausage with onion and celery over medium heat until no longer pink, 5-7 minutes; drain. Stir in coffee and seasonings; cook 3 minutes, stirring occasionally.
2. Add broth; bring to a boil. Remove from heat; stir in stuffing cubes. Transfer to a greased 4- or 5-qt. slow cooker.
3. Cook, covered, on low until heated through and edges are lightly browned, 2-2½ hours, stirring once. Sprinkle with parsley.
¾ cup: 254 cal., 11g fat (3g sat. fat), 25mg chol., 919mg sod., 29g carb. (4g sugars, 2g fiber), 9g pro.

TEST KITCHEN TIP

Don't be tempted to add more broth. The dressing will moisten as it cooks. Stir once during cooking so the mixture heats evenly.

PRESSURE-COOKER DRESSING

Here's an easy dish that's perfect for special get-togethers. Once everything is in the pressure cooker, you're free to turn your attention to other dishes.
—*Rita Nodland, Bismarck, ND*

Prep: 15 min. + standing
Cook: 10 min. + releasing
Makes: 8 servings

- 2   Tbsp. olive oil
- 1   medium celery rib, chopped
- 1   small onion, chopped
- 2   cups reduced-sodium chicken broth
- 1   tsp. poultry seasoning
- ¼   tsp. salt
- ¼   tsp. pepper
- 8   cups unseasoned stuffing cubes

1. Select saute setting on a 6-qt. electric pressure cooker. Adjust for medium heat; add oil. When oil is hot, cook and stir celery and onion until crisp-tender, 3-4 minutes. Press cancel. Stir in broth and seasonings. Gently stir in stuffing cubes; toss to combine. Transfer to a greased 1½-qt. baking dish.
2. Place trivet insert and 1 cup water in the pressure cooker. Cover baking dish with foil. Fold an 18x12-in. piece of foil lengthwise into thirds, making a sling. Use the sling to lower the dish onto the trivet.
3. Lock lid; close pressure-release valve. Adjust to pressure-cook on high 15 minutes. Let pressure release naturally 10 minutes; quick-release any remaining pressure. Using foil sling, carefully remove baking dish. Let stand 10 minutes.
½ cup: 225 cal., 5g fat (0 sat. fat), 0 chol., 634mg sod., 40g carb. (3g sugars, 3g fiber), 8g pro.

CRANBERRY PECAN STUFFING

I love stuffing, but my family wasn't that fond of it—that is, until I found this recipe. I added a few extras and now they gobble it up. I think the cranberries give it that something special.
—*Robin Lang, Muskegon, MI*

Prep: 30 min. • **Bake:** 40 min.
Makes: 13 servings

- 1 cup orange juice
- ½ cup dried cranberries
- ½ lb. bulk pork sausage
- ¼ cup butter, cubed
- 3 celery ribs, chopped
- 1 large onion, chopped
- 1 tsp. poultry seasoning
- 6 cups seasoned stuffing cubes
- 1 medium tart apple, peeled and finely chopped
- ½ cup chopped pecans
- ¼ tsp. salt
- ⅛ tsp. pepper
- ¾ to 1 cup chicken broth

1. In a small saucepan, bring orange juice and cranberries to a boil. Remove from the heat; let stand for 5 minutes. Meanwhile, in a large skillet, cook the sausage until no longer pink; drain. Transfer to a large bowl.
2. In the same skillet, melt butter. Add the celery and onion; saute until tender. Stir in poultry seasoning.
3. Add to sausage mixture. Stir in the stuffing cubes, orange juice mixture, apple, pecans, salt, pepper and enough broth to reach desired moistness.

4. Transfer to a greased 13x9-in. baking dish. Cover and bake at 325° for 30 minutes. Uncover; bake 10-15 minutes longer or until lightly browned.
Note: This recipe makes enough stuffing to stuff a 14-pound turkey. Bake until a meat thermometer reads 180° for turkey and 165° for stuffing.
¾ cup: 219 cal., 11g fat (4g sat. fat), 16mg chol., 532mg sod., 27g carb. (8g sugars, 2g fiber), 4g pro.

SLOW-COOKER MUSHROOM STUFFING

My grandmother created this recipe after my grandfather left the well-drilling business and invested all their money in a mushroom farm. The farm was a success and saw the family through the Great Depression.
—*Eric Cooper, Durham, NC*

Prep: 30 min. • **Cook:** 3 hours
Makes: 16 servings

- ¼ cup butter, cubed
- 1 lb. baby portobello mushrooms, coarsely chopped
- 4 celery ribs, chopped
- 1 large onion, chopped
- 12 cups unseasoned stuffing cubes
- ¼ cup chopped fresh parsley
- 1½ tsp. rubbed sage
- 1 tsp. salt
- 1 tsp. dried thyme
- 1 tsp. poultry seasoning
- ½ tsp. dried marjoram
- ½ tsp. pepper
- 2 large eggs, lightly beaten
- 3 cups vegetable broth

1. In a 6-qt. stockpot, heat the butter over medium-high heat. Add mushrooms, celery and onion; cook and stir until crisp-tender, 5-7 minutes. Transfer to a bowl. Add stuffing cubes, parsley and seasonings; toss. Whisk together eggs and broth. Pour over stuffing mixture; stir to combine.
2. Transfer to a greased 6-qt. slow cooker. Cook, covered, on low until heated through, 3-4 hours.
¾ cup: 190 cal., 5g fat (2g sat. fat), 31mg chol., 625mg sod., 32g carb. (3g sugars, 3g fiber), 7g pro.

The Best-Kept Secrets for Perfect Homemade Stuffing

Follow these tips and tricks for a homemade stuffing that's so good, your family will ask for it all year long.

YOU DON'T HAVE TO STUFF IT INSIDE THE TURKEY

We won't get into the stuffing versus dressing debate, but technically the dish is only called stuffing if it's stuffed inside a turkey. Otherwise, it's bread dressing. There are some safety issues involved with cooking stuffing inside a turkey, and it also slows down the rate at which the turkey cooks. You'll get plenty of flavor in your dish if you use poultry stock (preferably homemade), so don't feel pressured to stuff it inside the bird.

USE PLENTY OF FRESH HERBS

Dried herbs have their place in lots of recipes, but stuffing isn't one of them. Using a combination of fresh parsley, sage, rosemary and thyme creates the ideal herbaceous backbone to support the savory flavors in the stuffing.

MAKE YOUR OWN BROTH

If you really want that stuffing to shine, use homemade broth. The richer the broth, the better the stuffing, so don't be afraid to go all-out. You may have a container or two of homemade broth in the freezer for occasions like this, but you can also make an incredibly rich broth using the turkey neck.

USE HOMEMADE CROUTONS

Homemade croutons will take your stuffing up a notch. Cut a loaf of bread into 1-inch cubes and toss them into a 300° oven until they're dry and crisp, about 45 minutes. Any loaf of bread will work, but a country loaf, sourdough, brioche or rye yield delicious results.

UNLESS YOU'RE VEGETARIAN, DON'T SKIP THE SAUSAGE

There are some great vegetarian stuffing recipes out there, but there's just something about the combination of sausage and sage that screams Thanksgiving! Plus, the pork fat binds with the bread crumbs, adding an extra layer of delicious flavor. Choose the best sausage to fit your meal: spicy Italian sausage to add a nice kick to the dish, breakfast sausage for its sweet finish or smoky andouille to create extra depth of flavor.

THANKSGIVING KIDS' TABLE

We all love the grand Thanksgiving feast, but sometimes the boisterous festivities and long meal can feel a tad overwhelming to the little guests seated at the table. Make youngsters feel like VIPs by setting up a whimsical kids-only table that will keep them entertained and engaged in between courses. Use these recipes and ideas to cook up tyke-friendly fun the whole family will love!

Gobbler Goodies (p. 93) **Pine Cone Turkeys** (p. 88)

PILGRIM HAT COOKIES

We dreamed up this combination of goodies for a yummy treat to take to school before our Thanksgiving break. Everyone loved them!
—Megan and Mitchell Vogel, Jefferson, WI

- -

Prep: 1 hour • **Makes:** 32 cookies

- 1 cup vanilla frosting
- 7 drops yellow food coloring
- 32 miniature peanut butter cups
- 32 fudge-striped cookies
- 32 pieces orange bubblegum bits

1. In a small shallow bowl, combine frosting and food coloring. Remove paper liners from peanut butter cups.
2. Holding the bottom of a peanut butter cup, dip top of cup in yellow frosting. Position over center hole on the bottom of cookie, forming the hatband and crown. Add a buckle of one orange bubblegum bit. Repeat with remaining cups and cookies.
1 cookie: 130 cal., 7g fat (3g sat. fat), 0 chol., 81mg sod., 16g carb. (11g sugars, 1g fiber), 2g pro.

MINI HOT DOGS & MEATBALLS

I usually double this recipe since it's so popular. Try increasing the heat factor by using a spicier barbecue or spaghetti sauce. It's so easy to make it your own!
—Andrea Chamberlain, Macedon, NY

- -

Prep: 5 min. • **Cook:** 3 hours • **Makes:** 8 cups

- 1 pkg. (12 oz.) frozen fully cooked Italian meatballs
- 1 pkg. (16 oz.) miniature hot dogs or smoked sausages
- 1 pkg. (3½ oz.) sliced pepperoni
- 1 jar (24 oz.) pasta sauce
- 1 bottle (18 oz.) barbecue sauce
- 1 bottle (12 oz.) chili sauce

In a 5-qt. slow cooker, combine all ingredients. Cover and cook on low until heated through, 3-4 hours.
½ cup: 289 cal., 16g fat (6g sat. fat), 34mg chol., 1447mg sod., 28g carb. (21g sugars, 2g fiber), 9g pro.

STUFFING BALLS

This delicious side dish has all the flavors of traditional stuffing that evoke memories of special holiday dinners. The only difference is these are so much faster to fix.
—Mary Beth Jung, Hendersonville, NC

- -

Prep: 15 min. • **Bake:** 20 min.
Makes: 8 servings

- ½ cup chopped celery
- ¼ cup chopped onion
- ⅓ cup butter, cubed
- 5 cups soft bread cubes
- 1 cup chopped walnuts
- ½ cup minced fresh parsley
- 1 tsp. salt
- ½ tsp. poultry seasoning
- ¼ tsp. pepper
- ¼ cup chicken broth
- 1 large egg, well beaten

1. Preheat oven to 375°. In a large skillet, melt butter over medium heat. Add the celery and onion; cook and stir until tender, 3-5 minutes. Remove from the heat. Stir in the remaining ingredients. Shape into 8 balls.
2. Place on a greased baking sheet. Bake until a thermometer reads 160°, about 20 minutes.
1 stuffing ball: 235 cal., 18g fat (6g sat. fat), 47mg chol., 536mg sod., 14g carb. (1g sugars, 2g fiber), 7g pro.

FLUFFY CARAMEL APPLE DIP

This sweet and smooth dip is a crowd-pleaser. Be careful—it's so good that you won't want to stop eating it!
—Taste of Home *Test Kitchen*

- -

Takes: 30 min. • **Makes:** 2 cups

- 1 pkg. (8 oz.) cream cheese, softened
- ½ cup packed brown sugar
- ¼ cup caramel ice cream topping
- 1 tsp. vanilla extract
- 1 cup marshmallow creme
  Apple slices

In a small bowl, beat cream cheese, brown sugar, caramel topping and vanilla until smooth; fold in marshmallow creme. Serve with apple slices.
2 Tbsp.: 110 cal., 5g fat (3g sat. fat), 14mg chol., 69mg sod., 15g carb. (14g sugars, 0 fiber), 1g pro.

CORN & BROCCOLI BAKE

Here's a creamy casserole that resembles corn pudding. I like that this sweet, comforting side dish doesn't require a lot of ingredients.
—Betty Kay Sitzman, Wray, CO

- -

Prep: 10 min. • **Bake:** 45 min.
Makes: 6 servings

- 1 can (16 oz.) cream-style corn
- 3 cups frozen chopped broccoli, thawed
- ½ cup crushed saltines, divided
- 1 large egg, lightly beaten
- 1 Tbsp. dried minced onion
  Dash pepper
- 2 Tbsp. butter, melted

1. Preheat oven to 350°. In a large bowl, combine the corn, broccoli, ¼ cup crushed saltines, egg, onion and pepper. Pour into a greased 1½-qt. baking dish. Combine the butter and remaining ¼ cup crushed saltines; sprinkle over top.
2. Bake, uncovered, until lightly browned and a thermometer reads 160°, 35-40 minutes.
⅔ cup: 136 cal., 6g fat (3g sat. fat), 46mg chol., 341mg sod., 20g carb. (4g sugars, 3g fiber), 4g pro.

FLUFFY
CARAMEL
APPLE DIP

Pine Cone Turkeys

Encourage an atmosphere of gratitude this Thanksgiving with a fun and easy craft that will keep little hands busy.

Supply kids with pieces of multicolored construction paper, a black marker, kid-safe scissors, pairs of googly eyes, liquid glue and pine cones. Assist the children, especially younger ones, as needed.

Have the kids trace their hands onto multicolored construction paper. Cut out the hand shapes, leaves and a small orange triangle for the turkey beak. Ask each child to write something they are thankful for onto leaf and hand cutouts. Use liquid glue to attach 2 googly eyes and a beak to each of the pine cones. Use additional glue to attach the leaves or hand shape to the back of each pine cone for feathers.

CHEESY SAUSAGE PENNE

This lasagna-like entree takes me back to my childhood. I got the recipe from a friend's mother, who fixed it for us when we were kids. I made a few changes to it, but it's still quick and delicious.
—*Dallas McCord, Reno, NV*

- -

Prep: 25 min. • **Bake:** 30 min.
Makes: 12 servings

- 1 lb. bulk Italian sausage
- 1 garlic clove, minced
- 1 jar (26 oz.) spaghetti sauce
- 1 pkg. (16 oz.) uncooked penne pasta
- 1 pkg. (8 oz.) cream cheese, softened
- 1 cup sour cream
- 4 green onions, sliced
- 2 cups shredded cheddar cheese

1. Preheat oven to 350°. In a large skillet, cook sausage over medium heat until the meat is no longer pink. Add garlic; cook 1 minute longer. Drain. Stir in spaghetti sauce; bring to a boil. Reduce heat; cover and simmer 20 minutes.
2. Cook the pasta according to the package directions; drain. Meanwhile, in a small bowl, combine the cream cheese, sour cream and green onions.
3. In a greased shallow 3-qt. baking dish, layer half of the pasta and sausage mixture. Dollop with half the cream cheese mixture; sprinkle with half the cheddar cheese. Repeat layers.
4. Bake casserole, uncovered, until bubbly, 30-35 minutes.
1 cup: 422 cal., 23g fat (13g sat. fat), 71mg chol., 667mg sod., 36g carb. (7g sugars, 2g fiber), 17g pro.

To easily mince garlic, try the smash and chop method. Press the side of your knife down onto a garlic clove until it bursts open. You can press slowly with the heel of your hand, or feel free to give it a good whack—just be careful! Once it's smashed, rock the blade of the knife back and forth through the clove until it's minced into small pieces.

OVEN
CHICKEN
FINGERS

OVEN CHICKEN FINGERS

Kids go crazy for chicken fingers, and they're sure to love these tender, golden strips with two tempting sauces for dipping.
—*Mary Peterson, Charlestown, RI*

Prep: 15 min. • **Bake:** 20 min.
Makes: 6 servings

- 1 cup Italian bread crumbs
- 2 Tbsp. grated Parmesan cheese
- 1 garlic clove, minced
- ¼ cup vegetable oil
- 6 boneless skinless chicken breast halves (5 oz. each)

CRANBERRY ORANGE SAUCE
- ¼ cup sugar
- 2 tsp. cornstarch
- ½ cup fresh or frozen cranberries
- ½ cup orange juice
- ¼ cup water

HONEY MUSTARD SAUCE
- 2 Tbsp. cornstarch
- 1 cup water, divided
- ½ cup honey
- ¼ cup prepared mustard

1. Preheat oven to 375°. In a shallow dish, combine bread crumbs and Parmesan cheese; set aside. In a small bowl, combine garlic and oil. Flatten chicken to ½-in. thickness; cut into 1-in. wide strips. Dip strips in oil; coat with crumb mixture. Place on a greased baking sheet. Bake the chicken strips until golden brown, 20-25 minutes.

2. Meanwhile, combine sugar and cornstarch in a saucepan. Add cranberries, orange juice and water; bring to a boil over medium heat, stirring constantly. Cook and stir 2-3 minutes more, crushing berries while stirring. For the honey mustard sauce, dissolve cornstarch in 1 Tbsp. water in a saucepan. Add the honey, mustard and remaining water; bring to a boil over medium heat. Boil for 1 minute, stirring constantly. Serve with chicken for dipping.

1 serving: 458 cal., 14g fat (2g sat. fat), 80mg chol., 490mg sod., 52g carb. (35g sugars, 1g fiber), 32g pro.

TURKEY
MACARONI
BAKE

BACON CHEESEBURGER BUNS

Try my fun way to serve bacon cheeseburgers to a group without all the fuss of assembling sandwiches. Serve ketchup or barbecue sauce on the side for dipping.
—*Marjorie Miller, Haven, KS*

Prep: 1 hour + rising • **Bake:** 10 min.
Makes: 2 dozen

- 2 **pkg. (¼ oz. each) active dry yeast**
- ⅔ **cup warm water (110° to 115°)**
- ⅔ **cup warm 2% milk (110° to 115°)**
- ¼ **cup sugar**
- ¼ **cup shortening**
- 2 **large eggs, room temperature**
- 2 **tsp. salt**
- 4½ **to 5 cups all-purpose flour**

FILLING

- 1 **lb. sliced bacon, diced**
- 2 **lbs. ground beef**
- 1 **small onion, chopped**
- 1½ **tsp. salt**
- ½ **tsp. pepper**
- 1 **lb. Velveeta, cubed**
- 3 **to 4 Tbsp. butter, melted**
  Optional: Sesame seeds, and ketchup or barbecue sauce

1. In a large bowl, dissolve the yeast in warm water. Add milk, sugar, shortening, eggs, salt and 3½ cups flour; beat until smooth. Stir in enough remaining flour to form a soft dough.
2. Turn onto a floured surface; knead until smooth and elastic, 6-8 minutes. Place in a greased bowl, turning once to grease top. Cover and let rise in a warm place until doubled, about 1 hour.
3. Meanwhile, in a large skillet, cook bacon over medium heat until crisp. Using a slotted spoon, remove to paper towels. In a Dutch oven, cook the beef, onion, salt and pepper over medium heat until meat is no longer pink; drain. Add bacon and cheese; cook and stir until cheese is melted. Remove from the heat.
4. Preheat oven to 400°. Punch dough down. Turn onto a lightly floured surface; divide into fourths. Roll each portion into an 12x8-in. rectangle; cut each into 6 squares. Place ¼ cup meat mixture in the center of each square. Bring corners together in the center and pinch to seal.
5. Place 2 in. apart on greased baking sheets. Bake until lightly browned, 9-11 minutes. Brush with melted butter. If desired, sprinkle with sesame seeds. Serve warm, with ketchup if desired.
1 bun: 310 cal., 17g fat (7g sat. fat), 68mg chol., 720mg sod., 22g carb. (4g sugars, 1g fiber), 16g pro.

TURKEY MACARONI BAKE

A co-worker gave me this recipe when we were discussing quick and easy ways to use leftover turkey. The mild, cheesy casserole is a hit with my family. And it doesn't get much easier than this—you don't even have to cook the macaroni first!
—*Cherry Williams, St. Albert, AB*

Prep: 15 min. • **Bake:** 65 min.
Makes: 6 servings

- 2 **cups cubed cooked turkey**
- 1½ **cups uncooked elbow macaroni**
- 2 **cups shredded cheddar cheese, divided**
- 1 **can (10¾ oz.) condensed cream of chicken soup, undiluted**
- 1 **cup 2% milk**
- 1 **can (8 oz.) mushroom stems and pieces, drained**
- ¼ **tsp. pepper**

1. Preheat the oven to 350°. In a large bowl, combine turkey, macaroni, 1½ cups cheese, soup, milk, mushrooms and pepper. Pour into a greased 2-qt. baking dish.
2. Cover and bake until macaroni is tender, 60-65 minutes. Uncover; sprinkle with the remaining ½ cup cheese. Bake until cheese is melted, 5-10 minutes longer.
1¼ cups: 359 cal., 18g fat (11g sat. fat), 85mg chol., 804mg sod., 21g carb. (3g sugars, 2g fiber), 28g pro.

TEST KITCHEN TIP

Many casseroles use a can of soup, such as cream of chicken or cream of mushroom. Because canned soups are pretty salty on their own, go easy with the salt elsewhere in the recipe or omit it all together. Add any additional flavors with salt-free spice blends or your favorite herbs.

BACON
CHEESEBURGER
BUNS

GOBBLER
GOODIES

GOBBLER GOODIES

The kids and I had a ball making these tasty "turkeys" for Thanksgiving one year. They loved forming the bodies from the gooey cereal mixture and twisting the sandwich cookies apart. Their favorite step was using chocolate frosting to glue on the candy corn. This recipe makes a big batch of treats, so there are plenty for snacking and sharing.
—*Sue Gronholz, Beaver Dam, WI*

Prep: 30 min. • **Cook:** 5 min. + cooling
Makes: 28 servings

- ¼ cup butter, cubed
- 4 cups miniature marshmallows
- 6 cups crisp rice cereal
- 28 Oreo cookies
- 1½ cups chocolate frosting
- 1 pkg. (11 oz.) candy corn
- 28 malted milk balls
  White candy coating, optional

1. In a large saucepan, melt butter. Add the marshmallows; stir over low heat until melted. Stir in the cereal. Cool for 10 minutes. With buttered hands, form cereal mixture into 1½-in. balls. Twist apart the Oreo cookies. If desired, remove filling. Spread chocolate frosting over each cookies half.
2. Place 28 cookie halves under the cereal balls to form the base for each turkey. Place 5 pieces of candy corn in a fan pattern on remaining cookie halves; press each half onto a cereal ball to form the tail. Attach remaining candy corn with frosting to form the turkey wings. For head, attach malted milk ball with frosting; cut white tip off additional candy and attach to head with frosting to form beak. If desired, place melted white candy coating in a piping bag fitted with a #1 round tip; pipe onto head to form eyes. Allow to stand until frosting has set. Store goodies tightly covered at room temperature.
1 piece: 222 cal., 6g fat (2g sat. fat), 0 chol., 125mg sod., 43g carb. (31g sugars, 1g fiber), 1g pro.

CRANBERRY CINNAMON ROLL-UPS

Children of all ages will have a ball assembling these yummy treats that use plain white bread and other fuss-free ingredients. Cranberry sauce adds tons of holiday appeal.
—*Dorothy Pritchett, Wills Point, TX*

Takes: 30 min. • **Makes:** 12 servings

- 12 slices bread, crusts removed
- 7 Tbsp. butter, softened, divided
- ⅔ cup whole-berry cranberry sauce
- ⅓ cup sugar
- 1½ tsp. ground cinnamon

Preheat oven to 400°. Spread bread with 2 Tbsp. butter. Spread each buttered slice with about 1 Tbsp. cranberry sauce. Roll up bread jelly-roll style; secure with a toothpick if desired. Melt remaining 5 Tbsp. butter; add to a shallow bowl. Combine sugar and cinnamon in another shallow bowl. Dip roll-ups in butter, then roll in cinnamon-sugar. Place seam side down on an ungreased baking sheet. Bake roll-ups until browned, 6-8 minutes. Remove toothpicks before serving.
1 piece: 135 cal., 7g fat (4g sat. fat), 18mg chol., 135mg sod., 18g carb. (10g sugars, 1g fiber), 1g pro.

> **TEST KITCHEN TIP**
>
> To make these Cranberry Cinnamon Roll-Ups even more indulgent, drizzle them with an easy vanilla glaze. In a small bowl, combine 1 cup confectioners' sugar, 2 Tbsp. milk and ¼ tsp. vanilla extract. Stir until smooth. Let stand for 5 minutes to thicken if desired. Use a spoon to drizzle over roll-ups.

MAKE-IT-MAPLE DESSERTS

Move over, pumpkin spice! Maple is stepping up as fall's new favorite flavor. These tempting desserts with a splash of maple are sure to hit the sweet spot.

Maple Tree Cake (p. 101)

MAPLE WHOOPIE PIES

3. For filling, in a large bowl, beat the butter, shortening and flavoring until creamy. Beat in confectioners' sugar alternately with cream and syrup until smooth. Spread the filling on bottoms of half of the cookies; cover with remaining cookies. Store whoopie pies in airtight containers.

1 whoopie pie: 306 cal., 15g fat (7g sat. fat), 35mg chol., 183mg sod., 41g carb. (32g sugars, 1g fiber), 2g pro.

MAPLE *&* CREAM APPLE PIE

The cream and maple syrup in this pie make it so rich and delicious. If you are looking for something out of the ordinary, this is it.
—*Glenda Ardoin, Hessmer, LA*

Prep: 40 min. • **Bake:** 40 min. + cooling
Makes: 8 servings

- 1   cup plus ¼ tsp. sugar, divided
- 3   Tbsp. cornstarch
- ½   tsp. salt
- 6   cups thinly sliced peeled Granny Smith apples
- 6   Tbsp. maple syrup
- ¼   cup heavy whipping cream
     Dough for double-crust pie
- ½   tsp. 2% milk

1. Preheat oven to 400°. For filling, in a large bowl, combine 1 cup sugar, cornstarch and salt. Add apples; toss gently to coat. Combine maple syrup and cream; pour over the apple mixture. On a lightly floured surface, roll half of dough to a ⅛-in.-thick circle; transfer to a 9-in. pie plate. Trim crust to ½ in. beyond rim of plate; flute edge. Add filling. Roll remaining dough to ⅛-in. thick. Cut out the crust with a 1½-in. leaf-shaped cookie cutter. With a sharp knife, lightly score cutouts to resemble veins on leaves. Place cutouts over filling. Brush cutouts with milk; sprinkle with remaining ¼ tsp sugar.
2. Cover edge loosely with foil. Bake for 20 minutes. Uncover; bake 20-25 minutes or until crust is golden brown and filling is bubbly. Cool the pie on a wire rack. Refrigerate leftovers.
Note: To make dough for a double-crust pie, combine 2½ cups all-purpose flour and ½ tsp. salt; cut in 1 cup cold butter until crumbly. Gradually add ⅓-⅔ cup ice water, tossing with a fork until dough holds together when pressed. Divide dough in half. Shape each into a disk; wrap and refrigerate 1 hour.

1 piece: 557 cal., 26g fat (16g sat. fat), 69mg chol., 462mg sod., 79g carb. (44g sugars, 2g fiber), 5g pro.

MAPLE WHOOPIE PIES

In New York, we have a huge maple syrup industry. I took a basic whoopie pie and gave it a twist using our beloved maple flavor.
—*Holly Balzer-Harz, Malone, NY*

Prep: 40 min.
Bake: 10 min./batch + cooling
Makes: about 2 dozen

- ⅓   cup butter, softened
- ¾   cup sugar
- 1   large egg, room temperature
- 1   tsp. vanilla extract
- 1   tsp. maple flavoring
- 2¼ cups all-purpose flour
- 1¼ tsp. baking powder
- 1   tsp. salt
- ½   cup heavy whipping cream
- ½   cup maple syrup
- ½   cup finely chopped pecans, divided

FILLING
- ½   cup butter, softened
- ½   cup shortening
- 1   tsp. maple flavoring
- 4   cups confectioners' sugar
- ¼   cup heavy whipping cream
- 2   Tbsp. maple syrup

1. Preheat oven to 375°. In a large bowl, cream butter and sugar until light and fluffy, 5-7 minutes. Beat in egg, vanilla and flavoring. In another bowl, whisk flour, baking powder and salt; add to creamed mixture alternately with cream and syrup, beating well after each addition. Stir in ¼ cup pecans.
2. Drop by rounded tablespoonfuls 2 in. apart onto greased baking sheets; sprinkle with the remaining ¼ cup pecans. Bake until edges are light brown and tops spring back when lightly touched, 8-10 minutes. Remove from pans to wire racks to cool completely.

MAPLE
& CREAM
APPLE PIE

MAPLE PRALINES

This recipe rekindles memories of my grandfather and his love for making maple syrup. When I was in college, my mother would send me a package of her pralines during sugaring season. They were so popular with my friends, I barely managed to tuck away a few for myself.
—*Mary Beth Cool, Canajoharie, NY*

Prep: 10 min. • **Cook:** 10 min. + cooling
Makes: about 1 lb.

- 1 cup sugar
- ⅔ cup heavy whipping cream
- ½ cup maple syrup
- 2 Tbsp. butter
- ¾ cup coarsely chopped pecans, toasted

1. In a heavy 1-qt. saucepan, combine sugar, cream and syrup. Cook and stir over medium heat until mixture boils. Reduce the heat to medium-low. Cook, uncovered, until a candy thermometer reads 234° (soft-ball stage), stirring occasionally.

2. Remove from the heat. Add butter; do not stir. Cool, without stirring, to 160°. Stir in the pecans. Beat vigorously with a wooden spoon until mixture just begins to thicken but is still glossy. Quickly drop by spoonfuls onto waxed paper. Cool. Store in an airtight container.

1 praline: 144 cal., 7g fat (3g sat. fat), 11mg chol., 4mg sod., 20g carb. (19g sugars, 0 fiber), 1g pro.

TEST KITCHEN TIP

When sugar crystallizes, it yields a grainy candy. So when you're cooking the sugar mixture for pralines, don't heat it too fast. Instead, keep the heat at medium and let the mixture come to a boil. Stir only when the recipe specifies to do so. And it's never a good idea to make substitutions or double a candy recipe. Always make one batch at a time for best results.

MAPLE PRALINES

MAPLE PECAN BARS

Baking these bars evokes warm memories of my Grandma Marie, who made a similar recipe. The pecan treats are favorites at our office cookie exchange.
—*Amanda Spearing, Newton, IA*

- -

Prep: 30 min. • **Bake:** 20 min. + cooling
Makes: 5 dozen

- 3 cups all-purpose flour
- ¾ cup confectioners' sugar
- 1½ cups cold butter

TOPPING

- 1½ cups packed brown sugar
- 1 cup butter, cubed
- ½ cup maple syrup
- 2 tsp. ground cinnamon
- ¼ tsp. salt
- 4 cups coarsely chopped pecans
- 2 Tbsp. plus 1 tsp. heavy whipping cream
- ¾ tsp. vanilla extract

1. Preheat oven to 350°. In a large bowl, combine flour and confectioners' sugar. Cut in the butter until crumbly. Press into a greased 15x10x1-in. baking pan. Bake until edges are lightly browned, 12-15 minutes.
2. Meanwhile, in a large heavy saucepan, combine the brown sugar, butter, syrup, cinnamon and salt. Bring to a boil. Cook and stir over low heat until butter is melted. Stir in pecans, cream and vanilla. Remove from heat; spread over crust.
3. Bake until bubbly, 20-25 minutes longer. Cool on a wire rack. Cut into bars.
1 bar: 180 cal., 14g fat (5g sat. fat), 21mg chol., 66mg sod., 15g carb. (9g sugars, 1g fiber), 1g pro.

BEST MAPLE-CRANBERRY CHEESECAKE

While the recipe for this maple cheesecake may look intimidating at first, it's actually easy. If you have to make only one holiday dessert this season, this should be this one!
—*Tonya Burkhard, Davis, IL*

- -

Prep: 30 min. • **Bake:** 1¼ hours + chilling
Makes: 16 servings (2 cups compote)

- 2 cups graham cracker crumbs
- ⅓ cup butter, melted
- 3 Tbsp. sugar
- ½ tsp. ground cinnamon

FILLING

- 1½ cups maple syrup
- 3 pkg. (8 oz. each) cream cheese, softened
- ½ cup packed brown sugar
- ⅔ cup sour cream
- 3 Tbsp. all-purpose flour
- 2 tsp. vanilla extract
- ¼ tsp. salt
- 4 large eggs, room temperature, lightly beaten

COMPOTE

- 2 cups fresh or frozen cranberries, thawed
- ⅔ cup dried cranberries
- 1 cup maple syrup
- ½ cup packed brown sugar

1. Preheat the oven to 375°. Place a greased 9-in. springform pan on a double thickness of heavy-duty foil (about 18 in. square). Securely wrap foil around pan.
2. Combine cracker crumbs, butter, sugar and cinnamon; press onto the bottom and 1½ in. up the sides of prepared pan. Place pan on a baking sheet. Bake until set, 8-10 minutes. Cool on a wire rack. Reduce heat to 325°.
3. Meanwhile, place maple syrup in a small saucepan. Bring to a boil; cook until syrup is reduced to about 1 cup. Cool syrup to room temperature; set aside.
4. In a large bowl, beat cream cheese and brown sugar until smooth. Beat in the sour cream, flour, vanilla, salt and cooled syrup. Add the eggs; beat on low speed just until combined. Pour into crust. Place springform pan in a large baking pan; add 1 in. of hot water to larger pan.
5. Bake until center is just set and top appears dull, 1¼-1½ hours. Remove springform pan from water bath. Cool cheesecake on a wire rack for 10 minutes. Carefully run a knife around edge of pan to loosen; cool 1 hour longer. Refrigerate overnight. Remove sides of pan.
6. In a large saucepan, combine cranberries, syrup and brown sugar. Cook over medium heat until berries pop, about 10 minutes. Serve warm with cheesecake.
1 piece with 2 Tbsp. compote: 483 cal., 23g fat (13g sat. fat), 116mg chol., 284mg sod., 66g carb. (53g sugars, 1g fiber), 6g pro.

MAPLE TREE
CAKE

MAPLE TREE CAKE

Here's a colorful dessert to adorn your fall table. A chocolate-peanut butter tree with pretty leaves tops off the maple-flavored cake.
—*Lorraine Tishmack, Casselton, ND*

Prep: 25 min. • **Bake:** 30 min. + cooling
Makes: 16 servings

- 4 large eggs, room temperature
- 2 cups sugar
- 2 cups sour cream
- 2 tsp. maple flavoring
- 2½ cups all-purpose flour
- 2 tsp. baking soda
  Dash salt
- ½ cup chopped pecans
FROSTING
- 6 Tbsp. butter, softened
- 4½ cups confectioners' sugar
- ¾ cup plus 2 Tbsp. maple syrup
- ¼ cup semisweet chocolate chips
- ¼ cup peanut butter chips
- ½ tsp. red paste food coloring
- ¼ tsp. yellow paste food coloring

1. Preheat oven to 350°. In a large bowl, beat eggs and sugar. Add sour cream and maple flavoring. Combine flour, baking soda and salt; add to sour cream mixture and mix well. Fold in pecans.
2. Pour into 2 greased and floured 9-in. round baking pans. Bake for 30 minutes or until a toothpick inserted in the center comes out clean. Cool 10 minutes before removing from pans to wire racks to cool completely.
3. For frosting, in a bowl, cream butter and confectioners' sugar. Add syrup; mix well. Set aside ⅔ cup frosting for decoration. Spread remaining frosting between layers and over top and sides of cake.
4. In a microwave-safe bowl, melt chocolate and peanut butter chips; stir until smooth. Transfer to a pastry bag or heavy-duty resealable plastic bag; cut a small hole in the corner of bag. Pipe a tree trunk and branches on top of cake.
5. For decorative leaves, divide the reserved frosting between 2 small bowls. Add the red food coloring to 1 bowl; stir to combine. Add yellow food coloring to other bowl; stir to combine. Cut a small hole in the tip of a pastry bag; insert #21 star tip. Spoon the frostings alternately into the bag. Pipe frosting on top of cake to resemble leaves of tree.
1 piece: 475 cal., 11g fat (5g sat. fat), 54mg chol., 205mg sod., 90g carb. (72g sugars, 1g fiber), 6g pro.

MAPLE-RAISIN BREAD PUDDING

We love this bread pudding on cold Sunday mornings. It also makes a satisfying dessert when served with a dollop of whipped cream or a dusting of powdered sugar.
—*Trisha Kruse, Eagle, ID*

Takes: 30 min. • **Makes:** 8 servings

- 16 slices raisin bread, cubed
- ½ cup packed brown sugar
- ½ cup raisins
- ½ tsp. ground cinnamon
- 5 large eggs
- 2 cups 2% milk
- ½ cup maple syrup
- ¼ cup butter, melted

1. Place the bread cubes in a greased 2-qt. microwave-safe dish. Sprinkle with brown sugar, raisins and cinnamon.
2. In a large bowl, whisk eggs, milk, syrup and butter until smooth. Pour over bread; gently press bread cubes into egg mixture.
3. Cover and microwave at 50% power until center is soft-set and a knife inserted near the center comes out clean, 10-12 minutes. Let stand 5 minutes. If desired, serve with additional syrup.
1 piece: 398 cal., 11g fat (5g sat. fat), 136mg chol., 266mg sod., 67g carb. (40g sugars, 4g fiber), 12g pro.

MAPLE WALNUT FONDUE

Sized right for a pair, this warm, praline-flavored fondue is great with cake cubes, berries, apple wedges and other tasty dippers.
—*Angela Pohl, Marquette, MI*

Takes: 15 min. • **Makes:** 2 servings (½ cup)

- 1½ tsp. cornstarch
- ⅓ cup evaporated milk
- ¼ cup maple syrup
- 3 Tbsp. corn syrup
- 2 Tbsp. finely chopped walnuts
- 1 Tbsp. butter
- ¼ tsp. vanilla extract
  Pound cake cubes and assorted fresh fruit

1. In a small saucepan, combine cornstarch and milk until smooth. Stir in maple syrup and corn syrup. Bring to a boil over medium heat; cook and stir for 2 minutes or until thickened. Remove from the heat.
2. Stir in walnuts, butter and vanilla. Transfer to a small fondue pot and keep warm. Serve with cake cubes and fruit.
¼ cup: 353 cal., 13g fat (7g sat. fat), 28mg chol., 124mg sod., 57g carb. (0 sugars, 1g fiber), 4g pro.

MAPLE MOCHA POPS

My husband can't stop at just one of these creamy pops. They're a breeze to make and a fun way to enjoy a frozen treat in fall. For a pretty presentation, freeze them in serving cups and add a dollop of whipped cream.
—*Caroline Sperry, Allentown, MI*

Prep: 15 min. + freezing • **Makes:** 10 servings

- 2 cups heavy whipping cream
- ½ cup half-and-half cream
- ¼ cup maple syrup
- ¼ cup chocolate syrup
- 1 Tbsp. instant coffee granules
- 12 freezer pop molds or 12 paper cups (3 oz. each) and wooden pop sticks

1. In a large bowl, whisk whipping cream, half-and-half, maple syrup, chocolate syrup and coffee granules until coffee is dissolved.
2. Fill molds or cups with ¼ cup cream mixture. Top molds with holders. If using cups, top with foil and insert sticks through foil. Freeze until firm.
1 pop: 221 cal., 19g fat (12g sat. fat), 60mg chol., 23mg sod., 12g carb. (11g sugars, 0 fiber), 2g pro.

Try this easy trick to remove a popsicle from the mold. After pulling your frozen treats from the freezer, give them a quick dip in hot water. They'll fall right out of the mold.

GLAZED MAPLE SHORTBREAD COOKIES

When I visit friends in the United States, I make sure to purchase maple syrup and maple sugar because it's the best I've ever had. These cookies can be decorated with sprinkles, but they're also delicious as is.
—*Lorraine Caland, Shuniah, ON*

Prep: 25 min. + chilling
Bake: 20 min./batch + cooling
Makes: 1½ dozen

- 1 cup butter, softened
- ¼ cup sugar
- 3 Tbsp. cornstarch
- 1 tsp. maple flavoring
- 1¾ cups all-purpose flour

GLAZE
- ¾ cup plus 1 Tbsp. confectioners' sugar
- ⅓ cup maple syrup

1. In a large bowl, beat butter, sugar and cornstarch until blended. Beat in flavoring. Gradually beat in flour.
2. Shape dough into a disk; cover. Refrigerate until firm enough to roll, about 45 minutes.
3. Preheat oven to 325°. On a lightly floured surface, roll dough to ¼-in. thickness. Cut with a floured 2¾-in. leaf-shaped cookie cutter. Place 1 in. apart on parchment-lined baking sheets.
4. Bake 20-25 minutes or until the edges are light brown. Remove from pans to wire racks to cool completely.
5. In a small bowl, mix confectioners' sugar and maple syrup until smooth. Spread over cookies. Let stand until set.
1 cookie: 188 cal., 10g fat (7g sat. fat), 27mg chol., 82mg sod., 23g carb. (12g sugars, 0 fiber), 1g pro.

GINGERED MAPLE CUPCAKES

Tickle your taste buds with a creamy maple frosting. A woman from church brought these yummy cupcakes to a winter potluck. Now my husband and three children enjoy them often.
—*Elesha Freeman, Mount Pleasant, MI*

Prep: 20 min. + chilling
Bake: 20 min. + cooling
Makes: 1½ dozen

- ½ cup butter, softened
- ½ cup packed brown sugar
- 2 large eggs, room temperature
- 1¼ cups maple syrup
- 2 tsp. vanilla extract
- 2½ cups all-purpose flour
- 2 tsp. baking powder
- ¾ tsp. ground ginger
- ½ tsp. salt
- ¼ tsp. baking soda
- ½ cup 2% milk
- ½ cup finely chopped pecans

FROSTING
- 1 cup butter, softened
- 3 oz. cream cheese, softened
- ⅔ cup packed brown sugar
- ¼ tsp. salt
- ½ cup maple syrup
- ¾ tsp. vanilla extract
- 1½ cups confectioners' sugar
- 18 pecan halves

1. Preheat the oven to 350°. In a large bowl, cream butter and brown sugar until light and fluffy, 5-7 minutes. Beat in eggs. Beat in syrup and vanilla. Combine flour, baking powder, ginger, salt and baking soda; add to creamed mixture alternately with milk, beating well after each addition. Stir in pecans.
2. Fill paper-lined muffin cups two-thirds full. Bake until a toothpick inserted in the center comes out clean, 20-25 minutes. Cool for 10 minutes before removing from pans to wire racks to cool completely.
3. Meanwhile, in a small bowl, cream butter, cream cheese, brown sugar and salt until light and fluffy, 5-7 minutes. Beat in maple syrup and vanilla. Gradually beat in confectioners' sugar until smooth. Refrigerate for 1 hour.
4. Frost cupcakes; top each with a pecan half. Store in the refrigerator.
1 cupcake: 425 cal., 20g fat (11g sat. fat), 71mg chol., 348mg sod., 59g carb. (44g sugars, 1g fiber), 4g pro.

MAPLE MOUSSE

MAPLE MOUSSE

I make this with maple syrup produced in our area. Try it if you're looking for a change from heavier cakes and pies. It's a luscious ending to a holiday meal.
—*Jane Fuller, Ivoryton, CT*

Prep: 30 min. + chilling • **Makes:** 6 servings

- ¾ cup plus 6 tsp. maple syrup, divided
- 3 large egg yolks, lightly beaten
- 2 cups heavy whipping cream
- 2 Tbsp. chopped hazelnuts, toasted
  Additional heavy whipping cream, whipped, optional

1. In a small saucepan over medium heat, heat ¾ cup syrup just until it simmers. Reduce heat to low. Whisk a small amount of hot syrup into egg yolks; return all to the pan, whisking constantly. Cook and stir until mixture is thickened and reaches 160°. Transfer to a large bowl; set bowl in ice water and stir for 2 minutes. Cool to room temperature.
2. In a large bowl, beat cream until stiff peaks form. Gently fold into syrup mixture. Spoon into dessert dishes. Chill for at least 2 hours. If desired, top with additional whipped cream. Just before serving, drizzle with the remaining syrup and sprinkle with hazelnuts.
¾ cup: 441 cal., 33g fat (19g sat. fat), 215mg chol., 38mg sod., 34g carb. (32g sugars, 0 fiber), 3g pro.

TEST KITCHEN TIP

A perfect mousse is thick, creamy and luxurious—too thin and it's just pudding. To achieve the perfect texture, make sure the whipped cream is fully aerated with nice peaks before folding it into the syrup mixture. And make sure the syrup has cooled to room temperature when it's folded in, or it will deflate the whipped cream. Mousse will firm up even more in the refrigerator. Store in the refrigerator, covered, for 2 days or frozen for 2 months.

COMFORTING SOUPS & BREADS

Soup is serious comfort food. It's even better when it's soaked up with a slice of warm, toothsome bread. Look here for a lineup of recipes brimming with delicious homemade soups and fresh-baked dunkable breads that will let you savor every last drop. Autumn's chill doesn't stand a chance.

Homemade Broccoli Beer Cheese Soup (p. 111) **Caraway Cheese Bread** (p. 109)

POPPY SEED CHEESE BREAD

This easy bread goes well with a salad lunch or a casserole dinner. But I especially like to serve it with spaghetti and pasta dishes.
—*Elaine Mundt, Detroit, MI*

Prep: 20 min. + rising • **Bake:** 15 min.
Makes: 15 servings

- 1 pkg. (¼ oz.) active dry yeast
- 2 tsp. sugar
- ¼ cup warm water (110° to 115°)
- ¾ cup warm whole milk (110° to 115°)
- 2 Tbsp. shortening
- 1 tsp. salt
- 2¼ to 2½ cups all-purpose flour

TOPPING
- 2 cups shredded cheddar cheese
- 1 large egg
- ⅓ cup whole milk
- 1 tsp. finely chopped onion
  Poppy seeds

1. Dissolve yeast and sugar in water. Combine the milk, shortening and salt; stir into yeast mixture. Add enough flour to form a soft dough. Turn onto a floured surface; knead until smooth and elastic, about 3 minutes. Place in a greased bowl, turning once to grease top. Cover and let rise in a warm place until doubled, about 1½ hours.
2. Punch down dough; press into a greased 13x9-in. baking pan. Cover and let rise in a warm place until doubled, about 45 minutes.
3. Preheat oven to 425°. Combine cheese, egg, milk and onion; spread over dough. Sprinkle dough with poppy seeds. Bake for 15-20 minutes. Cut the bread into squares; serve warm.
1 piece: 163 cal., 8g fat (4g sat. fat), 30mg chol., 267mg sod., 16g carb. (2g sugars, 1g fiber), 7g pro.

GRANDMA'S CHICKEN & DUMPLING SOUP

I've enjoyed making this rich soup for over 40 years. Every time I serve it, I remember my grandma, who was very special to me and a great cook.
—*Paulette Balda, Prophetstown, IL*

Prep: 20 min. + cooling • **Cook:** 2¾ hours
Makes: 12 servings (3 qt.)

- 1 broiler/fryer chicken (3½ to 4 lbs.), cut up
- 2¼ qt. cold water
- 5 chicken bouillon cubes
- 6 whole peppercorns
- 3 whole cloves
- 1 can (10¾ oz.) condensed cream of chicken soup, undiluted
- 1 can (10¾ oz.) condensed cream of mushroom soup, undiluted
- 1½ cups chopped carrots
- 1 cup fresh or frozen peas
- 1 cup chopped celery
- 1 cup chopped peeled potatoes
- ¼ cup chopped onion
- 1½ tsp. seasoned salt
- ¼ tsp. pepper
- 1 bay leaf

DUMPLINGS
- 2 cups all-purpose flour
- 4 tsp. baking powder
- 1 tsp. salt
- ¼ tsp. pepper
- 1 large egg, beaten
- 2 Tbsp. butter, melted
- ¾ to 1 cup 2% milk
  Snipped fresh parsley, optional

1. Place the chicken, water, bouillon cubes, peppercorns and cloves in a stockpot. Cover and bring to a boil; skim foam. Reduce heat; cover and simmer 45-60 minutes or until the chicken is tender. Strain broth; return to stockpot.
2. Remove chicken and set aside until cool enough to handle. Remove meat from bones; discard bones and skin and cut chicken into chunks. Cool broth and skim off fat.
3. Return chicken to stockpot with soups, vegetables and seasonings; bring to a boil. Reduce heat; cover and simmer for 1 hour. Uncover; increase heat to a gentle boil. Discard bay leaf.
4. For dumplings, combine the dry ingredients in a medium bowl. Stir in the egg, butter and enough milk to make a moist stiff batter. Drop by teaspoonfuls into soup. Cover and cook without lifting the lid for 18-20 minutes. Sprinkle with parsley if desired.
1 cup: 333 cal., 14g fat (5g sat. fat), 79mg chol., 1447mg sod., 28g carb. (4g sugars, 3g fiber), 22g pro.

CREAMY CARROT & TOMATO SOUP

I often double this recipe and freeze half so we can enjoy a taste of summer during the cold winter months. If I do freeze it, I omit the yogurt and stir it in after the soup's reheated.
—*Sue Gronholz, Beaver Dam, WI*

Prep: 15 min. • **Cook:** 25 min.
Makes: 4 servings

- 1 Tbsp. olive oil
- 1 medium onion, chopped
- 3 garlic cloves, minced
- 3 cups peeled and shredded carrots (4 to 5 medium carrots)
- 2 cups reduced-sodium chicken broth
- ⅓ cup minced fresh basil
- 3 Tbsp. minced fresh parsley
- 3 cups reduced-sodium tomato juice
- 2 Tbsp. butter
- 2 Tbsp. all-purpose flour
- ¼ tsp. salt
- ¼ tsp. pepper
- ½ cup plain Greek yogurt
  Additional plain Greek yogurt, optional
  Additional torn fresh basil, optional

1. In a large saucepan, heat oil over medium heat. Add onion; cook and stir until tender. Add garlic; cook 1 minute longer. Stir in the carrots, chicken broth, basil and parsley. Bring to a boil. Reduce heat; simmer, covered, until carrots are tender, 10-12 minutes. Stir in the tomato juice. Pulse the mixture in a blender until smooth.
2. In another large saucepan, melt butter over medium heat. Stir in flour until smooth; gradually whisk in the tomato mixture, salt and pepper.
3. Bring to a boil, stirring constantly; cook and stir until slightly thickened, 5-7 minutes. Remove from heat; stir in the yogurt until blended. If desired, top with additional yogurt and basil.
Freeze option: Before stirring in yogurt, cool soup; freeze in freezer containers. To use, partially thaw in refrigerator overnight. Heat through in a large saucepan over medium-low heat, stirring occasionally; add broth or water if necessary. Stir in ½ cup Greek yogurt and, if desired, add toppings before serving.
1¼ cups: 225 cal., 12g fat (6g sat. fat), 23mg chol., 683mg sod., 25g carb. (14g sugars, 5g fiber), 5g pro.

CREAMY CARROT
& TOMATO SOUP

Soup-Freezing Tips

Keep this expert advice in mind so your soup tastes just as good as it did the day you made it.

1. Avoid freezing soups with pasta, rice or pieces of potato. These starches soak up liquid and get soggy when reheated. Pureed potatoes, though, hold up well. If you need to freeze one of these soups, hold the pasta, rice or potato pieces. Add them after you've thawed the soup.

2. Omit the dairy, too. A freezer does odd things to milk's texture, and the soup will be grainy when it thaws. It's best to add milk and other dairy products when you're reheating the thawed soup.

3. Never freeze hot soup. If you do, it will develop large ice crystals and freeze unevenly, translating to mushy soup when you thaw it. For best freezing results, cool your soup to at least room temperature (but, preferably, below 40° in the refrigerator) to help it freeze faster and better.

4. Consider portion size. Freezing your soup in one- or two-person portions makes for easy meal planning, and it also helps the soup freeze faster.

5. Opt for freezer-safe containers and leave about 1½ inches of headspace. Soup will expand as it freezes, and you don't want your container to crack or break. When you're ready to eat, run cold water over the outside of the container to loosen the frozen soup. It will pop right out into your pot.

BACON-PIMIENTO CHEESE CORN MUFFINS

Cornbread is essential at family dinners, and with the addition of bacon and pimiento cheese, you'll have requests for more long after the get-together!
—*Holly Jones, Kennesaw, GA*

Takes: 25 min. • **Makes:** 10 muffins

- 1 jar (5 oz.) pimiento cheese spread
- ¼ cup butter, melted
- ¼ cup sour cream
- 1 large egg, room temperature
- 1 pkg. (8½ oz.) cornbread/muffin mix
- 4 bacon strips, cooked and crumbled

1. Preheat oven to 400°. Whisk together cheese spread, butter, sour cream and egg until blended. Add muffin mix; stir just until moistened. Fold in bacon.
2. Fill 10 greased or paper-lined muffin cups three-fourths full. Bake 10-12 minutes or until a toothpick inserted in the center comes out clean. Cool 5 minutes before removing from pan to a wire rack. Serve warm.

1 muffin: 212 cal., 13g fat (7g sat. fat), 47mg chol., 376mg sod., 18g carb. (6g sugars, 2g fiber), 5g pro.

CHICKEN TORTILLA SOUP

This colorful soup is as good as (if not better than) any I've had in a restaurant. It also freezes well; just save the chips and cheese until ready to serve.
—*Laura Black Johnson, Largo, FL*

Takes: 30 min. • **Makes:** 8 servings (2½ qt.)

- 2 Tbsp. olive oil
- 1 large onion, chopped
- 1 can (4 oz.) chopped green chiles
- 2 garlic cloves, minced
- 1 jalapeno pepper, seeded and chopped
- 1 tsp. ground cumin
- 1 can (15 oz.) tomato sauce
- 1 can (14½ oz.) diced tomatoes with garlic and onion, undrained
- 5 cups reduced-sodium chicken broth
- 1 rotisserie chicken, shredded, skin removed
- ¼ cup minced fresh cilantro
- 2 tsp. lime juice
- ¼ tsp. salt
- ¼ tsp. pepper
  Crushed tortilla chips
  Shredded Monterey Jack or cheddar cheese

1. In a Dutch oven, heat oil over medium heat; saute onion until tender, about 5 minutes. Add chiles, garlic, jalapeno and cumin; cook 1 minute. Stir in the tomato sauce, tomatoes and broth. Bring to a boil; reduce heat. Stir in the chicken.
2. Simmer, uncovered, 10 minutes. Add the cilantro, lime juice, salt and pepper. Top servings with chips and cheese.
Freeze option: Before adding the chips and cheese, cool soup; freeze in freezer containers. To use, partially thaw the soup in refrigerator overnight. Heat through in a large saucepan over medium-low heat, stirring occasionally; add broth or water if necessary. Add chips and cheese before serving.

1¼ cups: 200 cal., 8g fat (2g sat. fat), 55mg chol., 941mg sod., 9g carb. (4g sugars, 2g fiber), 22g pro.

CARAWAY CHEESE BREAD
(PICTURED ON PAGE 105)

We enjoy cheese in so many different ways. In this bread, cheddar blends with just the right amount of caraway.
—*Homer Wooten, Ridgetown, ON*

Prep: 10 min. • **Bake:** 30 min. + cooling
Makes: 1 loaf (16 pieces)

- 2½ cups all-purpose flour
- 2 cups shredded cheddar cheese
- 1½ to 2 tsp. caraway seeds
- ¾ tsp. salt
- ½ tsp. baking powder
- ½ tsp. baking soda
- 2 large eggs, room temperature
- 1 cup plain yogurt
- ½ cup butter, melted
- 1 Tbsp. Dijon mustard

1. Preheat oven to 375°. In a large bowl, combine the first 6 ingredients. In another bowl, combine remaining ingredients. Stir into dry ingredients just until moistened.
2. Pour into a greased 9x5-in. loaf pan. Bake 30-35 minutes or until a toothpick comes out clean. Cool 10 minutes before removing from pan to a wire rack. Serve the bread warm. Refrigerate leftovers.

1 piece: 199 cal., 12g fat (7g sat. fat), 55mg chol., 338mg sod., 16g carb. (1g sugars, 1g fiber), 7g pro.

CHICKEN TORTILLA SOUP

BACON-PIMIENTO CHEESE CORN MUFFINS

STEAK &
VEGETABLE
SOUP

1. Preheat oven to 400°. In a small skillet over medium heat, melt 1 Tbsp. butter. Add leeks; cook until tender, 6-7 minutes. Cool.

2. Whisk together flour, baking powder, salt and baking soda. Cut in remaining butter until the mixture resembles coarse crumbs. Stir in the leeks, sour cream and water just until moistened. Turn dough onto a lightly floured surface; knead 8-10 times.

3. Pat or roll out to ½-in. thickness; cut with a floured 2½-in. biscuit cutter. Place in a cast-iron or other ovenproof skillet. Bake until golden brown, 12-16 minutes. Serve warm.

1 biscuit: 166 cal., 7g fat (4g sat. fat), 20mg chol., 241mg sod., 20g carb. (2g sugars, 3g fiber), 4g pro. **Diabetic exchanges:** 1½ fat, 1 starch.

SOUTHWESTERN PORK & SQUASH SOUP

One day I adapted a pork and squash stew recipe using tomatoes and southwestern-style seasonings. My husband and sons loved it, and the leftovers were even better the next day! Try it with fresh corn muffins.
—*Molly Newman, Portland, Oregon*

Prep: 20 min. **Cook:** 4 hours
Makes: 6 servings (2¼ qt.)

- 1 lb. pork tenderloin, cut into 1-in. cubes
- 1 medium onion, chopped
- 1 Tbsp. canola oil
- 3 cups reduced-sodium chicken broth
- 1 medium butternut squash, peeled and cubed
- 2 medium carrots, sliced
- 1 can (14½ oz.) diced tomatoes with mild green chiles, undrained
- 1 Tbsp. chili powder
- 1 tsp. ground cumin
- 1 tsp. dried oregano
- ½ tsp. pepper
- ¼ tsp. salt

In a large skillet, brown pork and onion in oil; drain. Transfer to a 4- or 5-qt. slow cooker. Stir in the remaining ingredients. Cover and cook on low for 4-5 hours or until the meat is tender.

1½ cups: 220 cal., 5g fat (1g sat. fat), 42mg chol., 708mg sod., 26g carb. (10g sugars, 7g fiber), 19g pro. **Diabetic exchanges:** 4 vegetable, 2 lean meat, ½ fat.

STEAK & VEGETABLE SOUP

This weeknight steak soup packs rich flavor into a light broth. My family loves the blend of southwestern flavors.
—*Rebecca Ridpath, Cedar Park, TX*

Prep: 10 min. • **Cook:** 30 min.
Makes: 8 servings (2½ qt.)

- 1 Tbsp. canola oil
- 1 beef top sirloin steak (about 1 lb.), cut into 1-in. pieces
- 1 tsp. dried basil
- ½ tsp. salt
- ¼ tsp. pepper
- 2 garlic cloves, minced
- 1 pkg. (16 oz.) frozen vegetables for stew, thawed
- 1 jar (16 oz.) picante sauce
- 2 cans (14½ oz. each) beef broth
- 1 can (15½ oz.) great northern beans, rinsed and drained
- 1 cup fresh baby spinach

1. In a Dutch oven, heat oil over medium-high heat. Add steak, basil, salt and pepper. Stir-fry until the meat is no longer pink, 4-5 minutes; drain. Add the garlic; cook 1 minute more.

2. Stir in vegetables and picante sauce. Add broth; bring to a boil. Reduce heat; simmer, uncovered, 15-20 minutes or until vegetables are tender. Stir in the beans; cook until heated through, 4-5 minutes. Add spinach; cook until just starting to wilt, 1-2 minutes.

1¼ cups: 191 cal., 5g fat (1g sat. fat), 23mg chol., 1144mg sod., 19g carb. (3g sugars, 3g fiber), 17g pro.

SOUR CREAM-LEEK BISCUITS

These biscuits are a wonderful pairing for soups. I've made them with all-purpose white flour as well as whole wheat, and both work equally well.
—*Bonnie Appleton, Canterbury, CT*

Takes: 30 min. • **Makes:** about 1 dozen

- ⅓ cup cold unsalted butter, divided
- 1½ cups finely chopped leeks (white portion only)
- 2 cups white whole wheat flour
- 2½ tsp. baking powder
- ½ tsp. salt
- ¼ tsp. baking soda
- ¾ cup reduced-fat sour cream
- ¼ cup water

HOMEMADE BROCCOLI BEER CHEESE SOUP

If you don't like beer, this recipe tastes just as wonderful without it. I always make extra and pop individual servings in the freezer.
—Lori Lee, Brooksville, FL

Prep: 20 min. • **Cook:** 30 min.
Makes: 10 servings (2½ qt.)

- 3 Tbsp. butter
- 5 celery ribs, finely chopped
- 3 medium carrots, finely chopped
- 1 small onion, finely chopped
- 4 cups fresh broccoli florets, chopped
- ¼ cup chopped sweet red pepper
- 4 cans (14½ oz. each) chicken broth
- ½ tsp. pepper
- ½ cup all-purpose flour
- ½ cup water
- 3 cups shredded cheddar cheese
- 1 pkg. (8 oz.) cream cheese, cubed
- 1 bottle (12 oz.) beer or nonalcoholic beer
  Optional toppings: Additional shredded cheddar cheese, cooked and crumbled bacon strips, chopped green onions, sour cream and salad croutons

1. In a Dutch oven, melt butter over medium-high heat. Add the celery, carrots and onion; saute until crisp-tender. Add broccoli and red pepper; stir in broth and pepper. Combine flour and water until smooth; gradually stir into pan. Bring to a boil. Reduce the heat; simmer, uncovered, until soup is thickened and vegetables are tender, 25-30 minutes.
2. Stir in cheeses and beer until cheeses are melted (do not boil). Top with additional shredded cheese, bacon, green onions, sour cream and croutons as desired.

Freeze option: Before adding toppings, cool soup; transfer to freezer containers. Freeze for up to 3 months. To use, partially thaw in the refrigerator overnight; heat through in a large saucepan over medium-low heat, stirring occasionally (do not boil). Add the optional toppings as desired.
1 cup: 316 cal., 23g fat (13g sat. fat), 69mg chol., 1068mg sod., 13g carb. (5g sugars, 2g fiber), 12g pro.

QUICK & EASY BREAD BOWLS

Impress your friends by serving cream soups in bread bowls. It's one of the most popular recipes on my blog, *yammiesnoshery.com.*
—Rachel Preus, Marshall, MI

Prep: 35 min. + rising • **Bake:** 20 min+ cooling
Makes: 6 servings

- 2 Tbsp. active dry yeast
- 3 cups warm water (110° to 115°)
- 2 Tbsp. sugar
- 2 tsp. salt
- 6½ to 7½ cups bread flour
  Optional: Cornmeal and sesame seeds

1. In a small bowl, dissolve yeast in warm water. In a large bowl, combine sugar, salt, yeast mixture and 3 cups flour; beat on medium speed 3 minutes. Stir in enough remaining flour to form a soft dough (the dough will be sticky).
2. Turn onto a floured surface; knead until smooth and elastic, 6-8 minutes. Place in a greased bowl, turning once to grease the top. Cover with a kitchen towel and let rise in a warm place until doubled, about 30 minutes.
3. Preheat oven to 500°. Punch dough down. Divide and shape into 6 balls. Place 3 in. apart on 2 baking sheets that have been generously sprinkled with cornmeal or greased. Cover with a kitchen towel; let rise in a warm place until doubled, about 15 minutes. Spray loaves with water; if desired, generously sprinkle with sesame seeds. Using a sharp knife, score surface with shallow cuts in an "X" pattern. Bake 2 minutes. Reduce oven setting to 425°. Bake until golden brown and the internal temperature reaches 190°-200°. Remove from pans to wire racks to cool completely.
4. Cut a thin slice off the top of the bread. Hollow out bottom portion of loaf, leaving a ½-in.-thick shell. Discard removed bread or save for another use, such as croutons.
1 bread bowl: 283 cal., 1g fat (0 sat. fat), 0 chol., 396mg sod., 57g carb. (2g sugars, 2g fiber), 10g pro.

How to Cut and Shape a Bread Bowl

Crispy on the outside and soft and tender on the inside, bread bowls are everyone's favorite soup vessel. Follow these easy steps before filling.

1. Cut a thin slice off the top of the round bread loaf.

2. Hollow out bottom of loaf, leaving a ¼-in.-thick shell. Add soup, stew or chili when ready to serve.

EASTER GATHERINGS

Like the warm air rendered by winter's thaw, spring's arrival fosters a lighter mood, a slower pace and the opportunity to savor foods at the height of their season. The sun-kissed weather awakens our senses to nature's garden-fresh goodness and lets us break free from huddling indoors, so we can finally take the party outside. Enjoy the dawn of a new season with these knock-out, no-sweat ideas for chic and cheerful spring gatherings.

EASY EASTER DINNER

With plenty of spring cheer in the air, Easter is a glorious time to come together with loved ones. Brighten up your dinner menu with a host of breezy, carefree foods that will make this year's celebration the best ever. These fuss-free recipes—from roasted lamb and asparagus to lemon risotto and other side dishes and desserts—let you savor the fresh flavors of the season while spending less time in the kitchen and more time with guests.

Roast Leg of Lamb (p. 120) **Chilled Asparagus with Basil Cream** (p. 119)
Lemon Risotto with Broccoli (p. 119)

Easter Day Countdown

This year, make Easter an event to remember. But don't stress over all the details. Refer to this handy cooking and prep timeline to help you create a fuss-free, yet elegant gathering that pulls out all the stops.

A FEW WEEKS BEFORE

☐ Prepare two grocery lists—one for nonperishable items to buy now and one for perishable items to buy a few days before Easter.

TWO DAYS BEFORE

☐ Buy remaining grocery items.

☐ Bake the Dill Bread and Sour Cream Biscotti. Cover baked goods and store in airtight containers.

☐ Wash china, stemware and table linens.

THE DAY BEFORE

☐ Prepare the Ham Spread. Cover and store in the refrigerator.

☐ Prepare and bake the Fudge Truffle Cheesecake. Cover and place in the refrigerator to chill overnight.

☐ Prepare the Refreshing Berry Wine. Cover and place in the refrigerator to chill overnight.

☐ Set the table.

EASTER DAY

☐ About 3 hours before dinner, prepare and bake the Roast Leg of Lamb. Let stand 15 minutes before slicing.

☐ About 2 hours before dinner, prepare the Chilled Asparagus with Basil Cream. Store in the refrigerator or, if desired, arrange the asparagus around the cooked leg of lamb on a serving platter.

☐ About 1-2 hours before dinner, prep the raspberries for the Rose & Raspberry Fool. Place sugared berries in the refrigerate and chill for 1-2 hours.

☐ About an hour before dinner, prepare and bake the Ricotta-Stuffed Chicken Breasts. Keep warm until ready to serve.

☐ About an hour before dinner, prepare the Lemon Risotto with Broccoli. Keep warm until ready to serve.

☐ About 35 minutes before dinner, prepare the Spring Pea Crostini with Lemon Creme.

☐ About 20 minutes before dinner, prepare the Warm Wilted Lettuce Salad.

JUST BEFORE DINNER

☐ Just before your guests arrive, remove the Ham Spread from the refrigerator. Set Ham Spread and Spring Pea Crostini with Lemon Creme on the buffet table.

☐ As guests arrive, remove the Refreshing Berry Wine from the refrigerator. Add ice and garnish individual servings with mint.

☐ Following dinner, remove the sugared raspberries from the refrigerator. Whip cream with rose water; add berries and scoop into individual dessert dishes. Remove the cheesecake from the refrigerator. Add whipped cream and chocolate chips to individual slices if desired. Serve desserts with biscotti. If desired, serve the biscotti with hot coffee or tea for dunking.

DILL BREAD

This golden-brown loaf is moist and flavorful. Dill weed gives each wedge an herbed zest, making it a nice complement to most any meal. As an added bonus, this easy yeast bread requires no kneading!
—*Corky Huffsmith, Salem, OR*

- -

Prep: 10 min. + rising
Bake: 35 min. + cooling
Makes: 12 servings

1 pkg. (¼ oz.) active dry yeast
¼ cup warm water (110° to 115°)
1 cup 2% cottage cheese
¼ cup snipped fresh dill or 4 tsp. dill weed
1 Tbsp. butter, melted
1½ tsp. salt
1 tsp. sugar
1 tsp. dill seed
1 large egg, room temperature, lightly beaten
2¼ to 2¾ cups all-purpose flour

1. In a large bowl, dissolve yeast in warm water. In a small saucepan, heat cottage cheese to 110°-115°; add to yeast mixture. Add fresh dill, butter, salt, sugar, dill seed, egg and 1 cup flour; beat until smooth. Stir in enough remaining flour to form a soft dough. Do not knead. Cover and let rise in a warm place until doubled, about 1 hour.
2. Punch dough down. Turn onto a lightly floured surface; shape into a 6-in. circle. Transfer to a greased 9-in. round baking pan. Cover and let rise in a warm place until doubled, about 45 minutes. Preheat oven to 350°.
3. Bake until golden brown and bread sounds hollow when tapped, 35-40 minutes. Remove from pan to a wire rack to cool completely. Cut into wedges.
1 piece: 118 cal., 2g fat (1g sat. fat), 22mg chol., 385mg sod., 19g carb., 1g fiber), 6g pro.
Diabetic exchanges: 1 starch, ½ fat.

HAM SPREAD

SPRING PEA CROSTINI WITH LEMON CREME

Peas and lemon are classic springtime flavors and they work really well together for this crostini appetizer. The best part for me, though, is the combination of the creamy spread and crunchy toasts.
—*Elizabeth Godecke, Chicago, IL*

Prep: 25 min. • **Bake:** 10 min.
Makes: 3 dozen

- 1   **French bread baguette, cut into 36 slices**
- 1   **Tbsp. olive oil**
- 3   **cups fresh peas, shelled**
- ¼   **cup fresh mint leaves**
- 2   **Tbsp. brown sugar**
- 2   **Tbsp. white vinegar**
- 2   **garlic cloves, minced**
- 1   **tsp. grated lemon peel**
- ¼   **tsp. salt**
- ¼   **tsp. pepper**
- ¼   **cup creme fraiche or sour cream**
- 1   **tsp. lemon juice**

1. Brush baguette slices with oil. Place on ungreased baking sheets. Bake at 400° for 6-8 minutes or until toasted.
2. Place peas in a large saucepan and cover with water. Bring to a boil. Reduce heat; cover and simmer for 5-8 minutes or until tender. Drain, reserving 3 Tbsp. cooking liquid.
3. Transfer peas to a food processor; add sugar, mint, vinegar, garlic, lemon peel, salt, pepper and reserved cooking liquid. Cover and process until pureed.
4. In a small bowl, combine creme fraiche and lemon juice. Spread 2 tsp. pea puree over each baguette slice; top with ¼ tsp. lemon creme.
1 piece: 44 cal., 1g fat (0 sat. fat), 1mg chol., 71mg sod., 7g carb. (2g sugars, 1g fiber), 1g pro. **Diabetic exchanges:** ½ starch.

↑

Creme fraiche is a French soured cream that is thicker and less sour than American sour cream. Creme fraiche is prized for cooking because it does not separate with heat like sour cream. It can also be used to top desserts and fresh fruit. Look for it in specialty food stores in the dairy case. If you're not able to find it, you can use regular sour cream with good results.

HAM SPREAD

My husband Keith and I enjoy simple recipes when entertaining. We share the cooking responsibilities and make this ham spread when our kids and grandkids are home for different holidays.
—*Marilyn Strahm, Lincoln, NE*

Prep: 15 min. + chilling • **Makes:** 2½ cups

- 1   **pkg. (8 oz.) cream cheese, softened**
- ¼   **cup mayonnaise**
- ¼   **cup ranch salad dressing**
- 2   **Tbsp. minced fresh parsley**
- 1   **tsp. finely chopped onion**
- ½   **tsp. ground mustard**
- ½   **tsp. hot pepper sauce, optional**
- 2   **cups finely chopped fully cooked ham**
- ⅓   **cup chopped pecans**
      Assorted crackers

1. In a small mixing bowl, combine cream cheese, mayonnaise, salad dressing, parsley, onion, mustard and, if desired, pepper sauce until smooth. Stir in ham. (Mixture will be soft.) Line a 3-cup bowl with plastic wrap. Spoon ham mixture into bowl; cover and refrigerate at least 8 hours or overnight.
2. Invert ham mixture onto a serving plate; discard plastic wrap. Press pecans onto surface of ham mixture. Serve with crackers.
2 Tbsp.: 100 cal., 9g fat (3g sat. fat), 20mg chol., 248mg sod., 1g carb. (1g sugars, 0 fiber), 4g pro.

CHILLED ASPARAGUS
WITH BASIL CREAM

CHILLED ASPARAGUS WITH BASIL CREAM

This recipe is an all-time family favorite that has been served at many of our holiday meals. I like it because it's simple and can be prepared ahead of time.

—*Melissa Puccetti, Rohnert Park, CA*

Takes: 20 min. • **Makes:** 8 servings

- 2 lbs. fresh asparagus, trimmed
- 1 cup mayonnaise
- ¼ cup heavy whipping cream
- 4 Tbsp. minced fresh basil, divided
- 2 garlic cloves, peeled and halved
- ½ tsp. salt
- ¼ tsp. pepper
- 2 Tbsp. pine nuts, toasted
- 1 Tbsp. grated lemon peel

1. In a large saucepan, bring 8 cups water to a boil. Add half the asparagus; cook, uncovered, just until crisp-tender, 2-4 minutes. Remove and immediately drop into ice water. Drain and pat dry. Repeat with remaining asparagus. Arrange on a serving platter.

2. Place mayonnaise, cream, 3 Tbsp. basil, garlic, salt and pepper in a food processor; cover and process until blended. Spoon over asparagus. Garnish with pine nuts, lemon peel and remaining 1 Tbsp. basil.

1 serving: 235 cal., 24g fat (5g sat. fat), 10mg chol., 296mg sod., 3g carb. (1g sugars, 1g fiber), 2g pro.

TEST KITCHEN TIP

Always buy the freshest asparagus you can find and be sure to store it properly when you get home. Asparagus bunches tend to come tightly belted by a rubber band. As soon as you get home, snip off this constrictive belt! It can easily bruise your vegetable and can cause an unpleasant rubbery texture. Keep the loose asparagus in a produce bag in the fridge until you use it.

LEMON RISOTTO WITH BROCCOLI

LEMON RISOTTO WITH BROCCOLI

This rich and creamy risotto is a nice change of pace from standard mashed potatoes. You won't be disappointed!

—*Judy Grebetz, Racine, WI*

Prep: 25 min. • **Cook:** 30 min.
Makes: 8 servings

- 3 cans (14½ oz. each) reduced-sodium chicken broth
- 1 small onion, finely chopped
- 1 Tbsp. olive oil
- 1½ cups uncooked arborio rice
- 2 tsp. grated lemon zest
- ½ cup dry white wine or additional reduced-sodium chicken broth
- 3 cups chopped fresh broccoli
- ⅓ cup grated Parmesan cheese
- 1 Tbsp. lemon juice
- 2 tsp. minced fresh thyme

1. In a large saucepan, bring the broth to a simmer; keep hot. In another large saucepan heat oil over medium heat. Add onion; cook and stir until tender, 3-5 minutes. Add rice and lemon zest; cook and stir until rice is coated, 1-2 minutes.

2. Stir in wine. Reduce heat to maintain a simmer; cook and stir until wine is absorbed. Add hot broth, ½ cup at a time, cooking and stirring until broth has been absorbed after each addition, adding broccoli after half the broth has been added. Cook until rice is tender but firm to the bite, and risotto is creamy. Remove from heat; stir in cheese and lemon juice. Sprinkle with fresh thyme. Serve immediately.

⅔ cup: 201 cal., 3g fat (1g sat. fat), 3mg chol., 460mg sod., 35g carb. (2g sugars, 2g fiber), 7g pro. **Diabetic exchanges:** 2 starch, ½ fat.

WARM WILTED LETTUCE SALAD

Fresh, colorful and lightly coated with a delectable dressing, this salad is perfect for a special meal or Sunday dinner. Mom made it look so tempting with the crisp radishes and crumbled bacon.
—Vera Reid, Laramie, WY

Takes: 15 min. • **Makes:** 8 servings

- 1 bunch leaf lettuce, torn
- 6 to 8 radishes, thinly sliced
- 4 to 6 green onions with tops, thinly sliced

DRESSING
- 4 to 5 bacon strips
- 2 Tbsp. red wine vinegar
- 1 Tbsp. lemon juice
- 1 tsp. sugar
- ½ tsp. pepper

Toss lettuce, radishes and onions in a large salad bowl; set aside. In a skillet, cook bacon until crisp. Remove to paper towels to drain. To the hot drippings, add vinegar, lemon juice, sugar and pepper; stir well. Immediately pour dressing over salad; toss gently. Crumble the bacon and sprinkle on top.

1 cup: 76 cal., 7g fat (2g sat. fat), 8mg chol., 94mg sod., 3g carb. (1g sugars, 1g fiber), 2g pro. **Diabetic exchanges:** 1½ fat, 1 vegetable.

RICOTTA-STUFFED CHICKEN BREASTS

This chicken dish is great for entertaining. It's easy to put together, but elegant, too. Served with pasta or rice and a salad, it makes a lovely dinner for guests.
—Subrina Blubaugh, Loris, SC

Prep: 15 min. • **Bake:** 35 min.
Makes: 8 servings

- 1 cup whole-milk ricotta cheese
- 1 cup shredded Italian cheese blend
- ⅔ cup grated Parmesan and Romano cheese blend
- 2 garlic cloves, minced
- ½ tsp. dried basil
- ¼ tsp. dried oregano
- ¼ tsp. lemon-pepper seasoning
- 8 bone-in chicken breast halves (14 oz. each)
- 4 tsp. olive oil

1. In a small bowl, combine first 7 ingredients. Gently loosen skin from chicken breasts; stuff cheese mixture under skin.
2. Place on a greased 15x10x1-in. baking pan; brush with oil. Bake at 375° for 35-45 minutes or until a thermometer reads 170°.

1 stuffed chicken breast half: 605 cal., 29g fat (11g sat. fat), 226mg chol., 486mg sod., 2g carb. (2g sugars, 0 fiber), 79g pro.

ROAST LEG OF LAMB

Lamb can seem intimidating at first, but this simple recipe is perfect for veteran cooks and beginners alike. A blend of garlic and dried herbs amp up the flavor.
—Sharon Cusson, Augusta, ME

Prep: 5 min. • **Bake:** 2 hours + standing
Makes: 10 servings

- 1 bone-in leg of lamb (6 to 8 lbs.), trimmed
- 2 garlic cloves, minced
- ½ tsp. dried thyme
- ½ tsp. dried marjoram
- ½ tsp. dried oregano
- ¼ tsp. salt
- ⅛ tsp. pepper
- 1 tsp. canola oil

1. Preheat oven to 325°. Place the lamb on a rack in a shallow roasting pan, fat side up. Cut 12-14 slits ½-in. deep in roast. Combine garlic, thyme, marjoram, oregano, salt and pepper; spoon 2 tsp. into the slits. Brush roast with oil; rub with remaining herb mixture.
2. Bake, uncovered, until meat reaches desired doneness (for medium-rare, a thermometer should read 135°; medium, 140°; medium-well, 145°), 2-2½ hours. Let meat stand 15 minutes before slicing.

5 oz. cooked lamb: 227 cal., 9g fat (4g sat. fat), 122mg chol., 114mg sod., 0 carb. (0 sugars, 0 fiber), 34g pro. **Diabetic exchanges:** 5 lean meat.

ROAST LEG OF LAMB

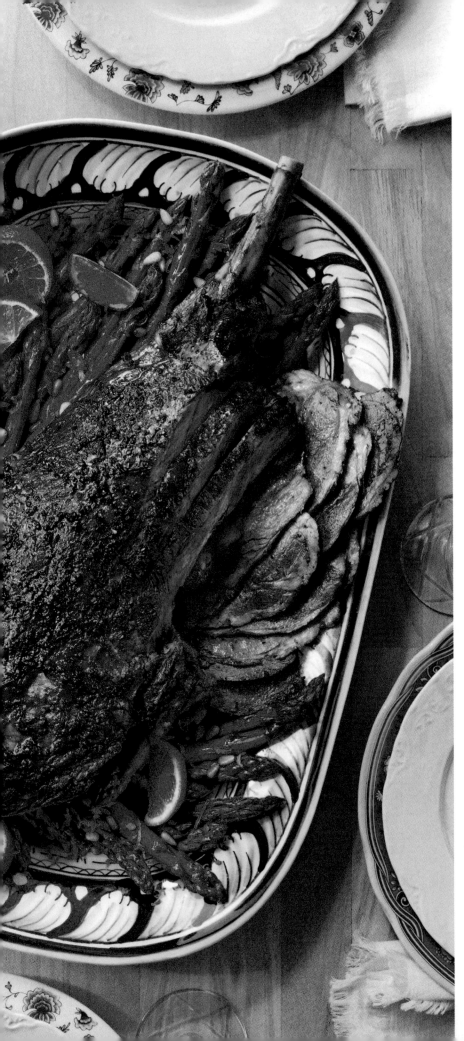

SOUR CREAM BISCOTTI

I received this recipe from my uncle's mother. These crisp traditional cookies are perfect for dunking in milk, coffee or hot chocolate.
—*Anna Ciraco, Hawthorne, NY*

Prep: 20 min. • **Bake:** 45 min. + cooling
Makes: 2½ dozen

- 1 cup butter, softened
- 1 cup sugar
- 2 large egg, room temperature
- ½ cup sour cream
- 1½ tsp. almond or vanilla extract
- 3½ cups all-purpose flour
- 1½ tsp. baking powder
- 1 tsp. baking soda

1. Preheat oven to 350°. In a bowl, cream the butter and sugar. Add the eggs, 1 at a time, beating well after each addition. Stir in sour cream and extract. Combine dry ingredients; gradually add to creamed mixture.
2. Line 2 baking pans with foil; grease the foil. Divide dough into thirds. On a floured surface, shape dough into three 8x2½x¾-in. loaves; place on foil. Bake until golden, 20-25 minutes. Remove from the oven. Lift loaves with foil onto a wire rack; cool for 15 minutes.
3. Place on a cutting board; using a serrated knife, slice diagonally ¾-in. thick. Place slices, cut side down, on ungreased baking sheets. Bake until golden, 8-10 minutes. Turn cookies over; bake 10 minutes longer. Cool on wire racks. Store in an airtight container.
1 cookie: 147 cal., 7g fat (4g sat. fat), 30mg chol., 121mg sod., 18g carb. (7g sugars, 0 fiber), 2g pro.

TEST KITCHEN TIP

Dress up your biscotti by dipping one end in melted chocolate. Start by melting about 10 oz. of milk chocolate candy coating. Then dip each cookie halfway into the melted candy coating, allowing excess to drip off. Place each piece of biscotti on waxed paper until set. Store in an airtight container.

REFRESHING BERRY WINE
(PICTURED ON COVER)
Here's an easy way to dress up wine for a party. Other fruit, such as watermelon balls or sliced peaches, can be used in place of the strawberry slices.
—*Laura Wilhelm, West Hollywood, CA*

Prep: 35 min. + chilling • **Makes:** 8 servings

- 1¼ cups frozen unsweetened raspberries
- 1 cup white grape juice
- 1 bottle (750 milliliters) dry rose wine
- 2 cups sliced fresh strawberries
  Ice cubes
  Fresh mint or rosemary sprigs

In a small saucepan, combine raspberries and juice. Bring to a boil; reduce heat. Cook and stir over medium heat until liquid is almost evaporated, about 30 minutes. Remove from the heat. Press through a fine-mesh strainer into a bowl; discard seeds. Transfer puree to a pitcher. Stir in the wine and strawberries. Refrigerate, covered, until chilled. Serve with ice; garnish with mint.

¾ cup: 122 cal., 0 fat (0 sat. fat), 0 chol., 3mg sod., 14g carb. (7g sugars, 1g fiber), 0 pro.

⬆

Increase sweetness by choosing a sweeter type of wine. Add white or club soda to make this a wine spritzer.

FUDGE TRUFFLE CHEESECAKE
This cheesecake is perfect for a holiday gathering. It serves a lot of people, and everyone seems to savor the rich chocolaty flavor. Best of all, because you need to make it a day ahead of time, dessert will be ready when you are!
—*S.E. Sanborn, Perry, MI*

Prep: 15 min. + chilling
Bake: 65 min. + cooling
Makes: 16 servings

CRUST
- 1½ cups vanilla wafer crumbs (about 45 wafers)
- ½ cup confectioners' sugar
- ⅓ cup baking cocoa
- ⅓ cup butter, melted

FILLING
- 3 pkg. (8 oz. each) cream cheese, softened
- 1 can (14 oz.) sweetened condensed milk
- 2 tsp. vanilla extract
- 4 large eggs, room temperature, lightly beaten
- 2 cups semisweet chocolate chips, melted and cooled
  Optional: Whipped cream and additional chocolate chips

1. Preheat oven to 350°. Combine all crust ingredients and press onto bottom and 2 in. up sides of a 9-in. springform pan; refrigerate until ready to fill.
2. For filling, in a large bowl, beat cream cheese, milk and vanilla until smooth. Add eggs; beat on low speed just until combined. Stir in melted chips. Pour into crust. Place pan on a baking sheet.
3. Bake until the center is almost set, 60-65 minutes. Cool on a wire rack for 10 minutes. Carefully run a knife around edge of the pan to loosen; cool 1 hour longer. Refrigerate overnight, covering when completely cooled.
4. Remove rim from pan. If desired, garnish with whipped cream and chocolate chips.

1 piece: 451 cal., 30g fat (17g sat. fat), 110mg chol., 256mg sod., 42g carb. (34g sugars, 2g fiber), 8g pro.

ROSE & RASPBERRY FOOL
I came up with this recipe when I was going through a floral phase. I put rose or lavender in everything. This dessert is easy to make, but it's also elegant and simple to serve when company comes.
—*Carolyn Eskew, Dayton, OH*

Prep: 15 min. + chilling • **Makes:** 8 servings

- 2 cups fresh or frozen raspberries
- 6 Tbsp. sugar, divided
- 1½ cups heavy whipping cream
- 1 tsp. rose water
  Fresh mint leaves

1. In a small bowl, lightly crush raspberries and 2 Tbsp. sugar. Cover and refrigerate for 1-2 hours.
2. In a large bowl, beat cream until it begins to thicken. Add remaining 4 Tbsp. sugar and rose water; beat until soft peaks form. Gently fold in raspberry mixture. Spoon into dessert dishes. Garnish with fresh mint leaves and, if desired, additional berries. Serve immediately.

½ cup: 206 cal., 16g fat (10g sat. fat), 51mg chol., 13mg sod., 14g carb. (12g sugars, 2g fiber), 2g pro.

Bunny Napkin Fold
Easter bunny-shaped napkins with an Easter egg nestled inside make adorable accents to your place settings. Look online for easy tutorials for folding. Make sure to use starched cloth square napkins and hard-boiled eggs. Plastic eggs work, too. Tie the napkin with pretty ribbon or twine.

ROSE &
RASPBERRY
FOOL

LIGHT &
LIVELY CREPES

Bring a touch of France to your table with a plate stacked high with delicate, buttery crepes. Crepes can be simple or extravagant, hot or cold, sweet or savory, and filled and shaped to suit any meal or occasion. Look here for fresh ideas on how to dress up the humble crepe with endless fillings, toppings and garnishes.

Crepe Board with Buckwheat Brunch Crepes (p. 131)

ASPARAGUS CREPES

ASPARAGUS CREPES

I love serving these tender crepes with their light lemony sauce in spring. But my husband likes them any time of year. In fact, it's the only way he'll eat asparagus!
—*Carol Hemker, Phenix City, AL*

Prep: 25 min. + chilling • **Bake:** 10 min.
Makes: 2 servings

- ½ cup 2% milk
- 1 large egg
- ⅓ cup plus 2 tsp. all-purpose flour
- 24 asparagus spears,
  cooked and drained

SAUCE
- 2 large egg yolks
- ¼ cup water
- 1 Tbsp. butter, melted
- 1 Tbsp. lemon juice
- ⅛ tsp. salt
  Dash cayenne pepper
  Paprika

1. For batter, combine the milk and egg in a blender; cover and process until blended. Add flour; cover and process until blended. Refrigerate, covered, 1 hour.
2. Preheat oven to 350°. Heat a lightly greased 8-in. skillet over medium heat. Stir the batter. Pour ¼ cup batter into center of pan. Quickly lift and tilt pan to coat bottom evenly. Cook until top appears dry; turn crepe over and cook until bottom is cooked, 15-20 seconds longer. Remove to a wire rack. Repeat with remaining batter, greasing pan as needed.
3. Place 6 asparagus spears on 1 side of each crepe; roll up. Place seam side down in a greased 11x7-in. baking dish. Bake, uncovered, until heated through, 10-15 minutes.
4. In a saucepan, whisk egg yolks and water. Cook over low heat, stirring constantly, until mixture is thickened and coats the back of a metal spoon and a thermometer reads at least 160°. Whisk in the butter, lemon juice, salt and cayenne. Pour over warm crepes; sprinkle with paprika. Serve immediately.
2 crepes: 299 cal., 15g fat (7g sat. fat), 298mg chol., 291mg sod., 30g carb. (6g sugars, 4g fiber), 15g pro.

CREAMY
BANANA CREPES

CREAMY BANANA CREPES

My husband and I enjoy taking turns fixing breakfast on the weekend. These crepes are frequently on our menus. The sweet-and-sour banana filling is delicious. You'll want to serve them for lunch, dinner and dessert!
—*Parrish Smith, Lincoln, NE*

Prep: 10 min. + chilling • **Cook:** 10 min.
Makes: 6 servings

- 2 large eggs
- ¾ cup water
- ¾ cup 2% milk
- 2 Tbsp. butter, melted
- ½ tsp. vanilla extract
- 1 cup all-purpose flour
- 1 Tbsp. sugar
- ½ tsp. salt

BANANA FILLING
- 3 Tbsp. butter
- 3 Tbsp. brown sugar
- 3 medium firm bananas,
  cut into ¼-in. slices

SOUR CREAM FILLING
- 1 cup sour cream
- 2 Tbsp. confectioners' sugar
- ½ cup slivered almonds, toasted

1. In a small bowl, whisk eggs, water, milk, butter and vanilla. In another bowl, mix flour, sugar and salt; add to egg mixture and mix well. Refrigerate, covered, 1 hour.
2. Heat a lightly greased 8-in. nonstick skillet over medium heat. Stir batter. Fill a ¼-cup measure three-fourths full with batter; pour into center of pan. Quickly lift and tilt pan to coat bottom evenly. Cook until top appears dry; turn crepe over and cook until bottom is cooked, 15-20 seconds longer. Remove to a wire rack. Repeat with remaining batter, greasing pan as needed. When cool, stack crepes between pieces of waxed paper or paper towels.
3. In a small skillet, heat butter and brown sugar over medium heat until the sugar is dissolved. Add the bananas; toss to coat. Remove from heat; keep warm.
4. In a small bowl, combine sour cream and confectioners' sugar. Spread over half of each crepe. Top with banana filling and almonds; fold crepes over filling. If desired, sprinkle with additional confectioners' sugar and almonds.
2 crepes: 429 cal., 25g fat (12g sat. fat), 99mg chol., 327mg sod., 46g carb. (22g sugars, 3g fiber), 9g pro.

SUNSHINE CREPES

CHOCOLATE-ALMOND DESSERT CREPES

What's better than a tender crepe filled with rich chocolate and topped with chocolate sauce, whipped cream and a sprinkling of almonds? These make a sweet ending to a special-occasion meal.
—*Taste of Home Test Kitchen*

- -

Prep: 25 min. + chilling • **Cook:** 15 min.
Makes: 12 servings

- 3 large eggs
- 1¼ cups 2% milk
- 2 Tbsp. butter, melted
- ¾ cup all-purpose flour
- 1 Tbsp. sugar
- ¼ tsp. salt
- 1 envelope unflavored gelatin
- 2 Tbsp. cold water
- ¼ cup boiling water
- 1 cup sugar
- ½ cup baking cocoa
- 2 cups cold heavy whipping cream
- 2 tsp. vanilla extract
  Optional: Hot fudge ice cream topping, whipped cream and toasted sliced almonds

1. In a large bowl, whisk eggs, milk and butter. In another bowl, mix the flour, sugar and salt; add to egg mixture and mix well. Refrigerate, covered, 1 hour.
2. Meanwhile, in a small bowl, sprinkle gelatin over cold water; let stand 2 minutes to soften. Add the boiling water; stir until the gelatin is completely dissolved and the mixture is clear. Cool slightly.
3. In a large bowl, mix sugar and cocoa; add cream and vanilla. Beat on medium speed until well blended. Gradually beat in gelatin mixture. Refrigerate, covered, at for least 30 minutes.
4. Heat a lightly greased 8-in. nonstick skillet over medium heat. Stir batter. Pour ¼ cup batter into center of pan. Quickly lift and tilt pan to coat bottom evenly. Cook until top appears dry; turn crepe over and cook until bottom is cooked,15-20 seconds longer. Remove to a wire rack. Repeat with remaining batter, greasing pan as needed. When cool, stack crepes between pieces of waxed paper or paper towels.
5. Spoon filling down center of each crepe; roll up. If desired, garnish with fudge topping, whipped cream and almonds.
1 crepe: 320 cal., 21g fat (11g sat. fat), 115mg chol., 107mg sod., 29g carb. (19g sugars, 1g fiber), 6g pro.

SUNSHINE CREPES

My family wanted something light to go with coffee for a special breakfast, so I whipped up these sweet and fruity crepes. They were a big hit! Fill them with whatever canned or fresh fruit you have available.
—*Mary Hobbs, Campbell, MO*

- -

Prep: 15 min. + chilling • **Cook:** 15 min.
Makes: 6 servings

- 2 large eggs
- ⅔ cup 2% milk
- 1 Tbsp. canola oil
- ½ cup all-purpose flour
- 1 tsp. sugar
- ¼ tsp. salt
  FILLING
- 1 can (20 oz.) crushed pineapple, drained
- 1 can (11 oz.) mandarin oranges, drained
- 1 tsp. vanilla extract
- 1 carton (8 oz.) frozen whipped topping, thawed
  Confectioners' sugar

1. In a large bowl, whisk eggs, milk and oil. In another bowl, mix flour, sugar and salt; add to the egg mixture and mix well. Refrigerate, covered, 1 hour.
2. Heat a lightly greased 8-in. nonstick skillet over medium heat. Stir batter. Fill a ¼-cup measure halfway with batter; pour into center of pan. Quickly lift and tilt pan to coat bottom evenly. Cook until top appears dry; turn the crepe over and cook until bottom is cooked, 15-20 seconds longer. Remove to a wire rack. Repeat with remaining batter, greasing pan as needed. When cool, stack crepes between pieces of waxed paper or paper towels.
3. For the filling, in a large bowl, combine pineapple, oranges and vanilla; fold in the whipped topping. Spread ⅓ cup over each crepe; fold into quarters. Dust with crepes confectioners' sugar.
2 crepes: 299 cal., 11g fat (7g sat. fat), 64mg chol., 139mg sod., 43g carb. (31g sugars, 1g fiber), 5g pro.

CREAMY STRAWBERRY CREPES

Wrap summer-ripe strawberries and creamy filling into these delicate crepes for an elegant brunch entree.
—*Kathy Kochiss, Huntington, CT*

Prep: 15 min. + chilling • **Cook:** 25 min.
Makes: 7 servings

- 4 large eggs
- 1 cup 2% milk
- 1 cup water
- 2 Tbsp. butter, melted
- 2 cups all-purpose flour
- ¼ tsp. salt

FILLING
- 1 pkg. (8 oz.) cream cheese, softened
- 1¼ cups confectioners' sugar
- 1 Tbsp. lemon juice
- 1 tsp. grated lemon zest
- ½ tsp. vanilla extract
- 4 cups fresh strawberries, sliced, divided
- 1 cup heavy whipping cream, whipped

1. In a large bowl, whisk eggs, milk, water and butter. In another bowl, mix flour and salt; add to the egg mixture and mix well. Refrigerate, covered, 1 hour.
2. Heat a lightly greased 8-in. nonstick skillet over medium heat. Stir batter. Fill a ¼-cup measure halfway with batter; pour into center of pan. Quickly lift and tilt pan to coat bottom evenly. Cook until top appears dry; turn crepe over and cook until the bottom is cooed, 15-20 seconds longer. Remove to a wire rack.

Repeat with remaining batter, greasing pan as needed. When cool, stack crepes between pieces of waxed paper or paper towels.
3. For filling, in a small bowl, beat the cream cheese, confectioners' sugar, lemon juice and zest, and vanilla until smooth. Fold in 2 cups berries and the whipped cream. Spoon about ⅓ cup filling down the center of each crepe; roll up. Garnish with remaining berries and, if desired, additional confectioner's sugar. Cover and refrigerate or freeze remaining crepes in an airtight container, unfilled, for another use.

2 crepes: 415 cal., 26g fat (16g sat. fat), 115mg chol., 163mg sod., 40g carb. (28g sugars, 2g fiber), 7g pro.

Voila, Crepes!

Mastering this French morning treat is no big deal. Pour, swirl, flip, fill and serve.

For the batter: In a bowl, beat the eggs, milk, water and butter. Add flour and salt; beat until smooth. Cover and refrigerate for 1 hour.

1. Pour and swirl. In an 8-in. nonstick skillet, melt 1 tsp. butter; pour 2 Tbsp. batter into center of skillet. Lift and tilt pan, swirling to evenly coat the bottom.

2. Cook crepes. Cook until top appears dry; turn and cook 15-20 seconds longer. Remove to wire rack. Repeat, adding butter as needed. Stack cooled crepes between waxed paper or paper towels.

3. Make filling. In a bowl, beat the cream cheese, confectioners' sugar, lemon juice and zest, and vanilla until smooth. Fold in 2 cups berries and whipped cream.

4. Assemble. Spoon about ⅓ cup filling down the center of each of 14 crepes; roll up. Garnish with remaining berries. Freeze remaining crepes for another use.

BROCCOLI CHEESE CREPES

Here's a perfect recipe for a special brunch or light dinner for two. I tuck a cheesy broccoli mixture into tender homemade crepes with delicious results.

—*Jane Shapton, Irvine, CA*

Prep: 25 min. + chilling • **Bake:** 5 min.
Makes: 2 servings

- 2 large eggs
- ¼ cup water
- 6 Tbsp. all-purpose flour
- ½ tsp. salt

FILLING
- 1 Tbsp. butter
- 2 Tbsp. chopped onion
- 1 Tbsp. all-purpose flour
- 1 cup whole milk
- 1 cup shredded cheddar cheese, divided
- 1 to 1½ tsp. Dijon mustard
- 1 tsp. Worcestershire sauce
- ¼ tsp. pepper
- ⅛ tsp. salt
- 2 cups frozen chopped broccoli, thawed

1. For batter, combine eggs, water, flour and salt in a blender. Cover and process until blended. Refrigerate, covered, 30 minutes.

2. Meanwhile, in a small saucepan, melt butter over medium heat; add onion. Cook and stir until tender, 1-2 minutes. Stir in flour until blended. Gradually whisk in milk. Bring to a boil, stirring constantly; cook and stir until slightly thickened, about 2 minutes. Reduce heat to low. Stir in ½ cup cheese, mustard, Worcestershire sauce, pepper and salt until cheese is melted. Stir in the broccoli. Cover; keep warm.

3. Preheat oven to 350°. Heat a lightly greased 8-in. nonstick skillet over medium heat. Stir the batter. Fill a ¼-cup measure halfway with batter; pour into the center of pan. Quickly lift and tilt pan to coat bottom evenly. Cook until the top appears dry; turn crepe over and cook until bottom is cooked, 15-20 seconds longer. Remove to a wire rack. Repeat with remaining batter, greasing pan as needed.

4. Spoon about ½ cup filling down the center of each crepe; roll up. Place seam side down in an ungreased 11x7-in. baking dish. Sprinkle the crepes with remaining ½ cup cheese. Bake, uncovered, 5-7 minutes or until cheese is melted.

3 crepes: 586 cal., 34g fat (18g sat. fat), 269mg chol., 1412mg sod., 40g carb. (10g sugars, 7g fiber), 32g pro.

BROCCOLI CHEESE CREPES

BUCKWHEAT
BRUNCH CREPES

BUCKWHEAT BRUNCH CREPES

My husband and I enjoy these delicious crepes with sweet berry sauce and cream on Saturday mornings or even at supper time with sausage and eggs. They're considered a delicacy here, especially with a drizzle of maple syrup.
—*Sharon Dyck, Roxton Falls, QC*

- -

Prep: 20 min. + standing • **Cook:** 15 min.
Makes: 3 servings

- 5 Tbsp. heavy whipping cream
- ½ cup sour cream
- 2 large eggs
- ½ cup 2% milk
- ⅓ cup all-purpose flour
- 3 Tbsp. buckwheat flour or whole wheat flour
- ½ tsp. salt

BERRY SAUCE

- ½ cup sugar
- 1 Tbsp. cornstarch
  Dash salt
- ½ cup water
- ⅓ cup fresh blueberries
- ⅓ cup fresh raspberries
- 4½ tsp. butter, divided
- 1 tsp. lemon juice

1. In a small bowl, beat whipping cream until stiff peaks form; fold into sour cream. Cover and refrigerate. In a large bowl, whisk eggs and milk. In another bowl, mix flours and salt; add to egg mixture and mix well. Refrigerate, covered, 1 hour.

2. Meanwhile, in a small saucepan, combine sugar, cornstarch and salt; whisk in water until smooth. Bring to a boil; cook and stir until thickened, 1-2 minutes. Add berries; cook over medium-low heat until berries pop. Stir in 1½ tsp. butter and lemon juice until butter is melted. Set aside and keep warm.

3. Heat 1 tsp. remaining butter in an 8-in. nonstick skillet over medium heat. Stir batter. Fill a ¼-cup measure halfway with batter; pour into center of pan. Quickly lift and tilt pan to coat bottom evenly. Cook until top appears dry; turn crepe over and cook until bottom is cooked, 15-20 seconds longer. Remove to a wire rack. Repeat with remaining batter, adding butter to skillet as needed. When cool, stack crepes between pieces of waxed paper or paper towels. Serve crepes with berry sauce and cream mixture.

2 crepes: 516 cal., 27g fat (16g sat. fat), 180mg chol., 577mg sod., 60g carb. (40g sugars, 2g fiber), 10g pro.

BASIC CREPES

Enjoy this basic crepe the way the French do—with melted butter and sprinkle of sugar. Or enhance it with sweet or savory ingredients that suit your fancy (see some suggested toppings on opposite page). It's best to make the batter at least 30 minutes ahead so it can be chilled to allow the flour to absorb all the moisture before you start cooking the crepes.
—Taste of Home *Test Kitchen*

Prep: 10 min. + chilling • **Cook:** 20 min.
Makes: 20 crepes

- 4 large eggs
- 1½ cups 2% milk
- 1 cup all-purpose flour
- 1½ tsp. sugar
- ⅛ tsp. salt
- 8 tsp. butter

1. In a small bowl, whisk the eggs and milk. In another bowl, mix the flour, sugar and salt; add to egg mixture and mix well. Refrigerate, covered, 1 hour.

2. Melt 1 tsp. butter in an 8-in. nonstick skillet over medium heat. Stir the batter. Fill a ¼-cup measure halfway with batter; pour into center of pan. Quickly lift and tilt pan to coat bottom evenly. Cook until top appears dry; turn crepe over and cook until the bottom is cooked, 15-20 seconds longer. Remove to a wire rack. Repeat with remaining batter, adding butter to skillet as needed. When cool, stack the crepes between pieces of waxed paper or paper towels.

1 crepe: 61 cal., 3g fat (2g sat. fat), 43mg chol., 50mg sod., 6g carb. (1g sugars, 0 fiber), 3g pro.

SALMON & GOAT CHEESE CREPES

Homemade crepes filled with a creamy goat cheese mixture and topped with smoked salmon add a real wow factor to a brunch table. The flavors will impress your guests.
—Amy Burton, Fuquay-Varina, NC

Prep: 20 min. + chilling • **Cook:** 10 min.
Makes: 5 servings

- 3 large eggs
- 1¼ cups 2% milk
- ½ cup water
- 1 cup whole wheat pastry flour
- 1 cup all-purpose flour
- ¾ tsp. salt
FILLING
- 12 oz. fresh goat cheese
- ¾ cup roasted sweet red peppers
- 1 Tbsp. plus 1½ tsp. lemon juice
- 1½ tsp. smoked paprika
- 1 garlic clove, peeled and halved
- 1 lb. smoked salmon fillets
- 2 cups fresh baby spinach
- 3 Tbsp. capers, drained
- 1 Tbsp. snipped fresh dill

1. In a large bowl, whisk eggs, milk and water. In another bowl, mix flours and salt; add to the egg mixture and mix well. Refrigerate, covered, 1 hour.

2. Meanwhile, in a food processor, combine the goat cheese, red peppers, lemon juice, paprika and garlic; cover and process until blended, 2-3 minutes. Refrigerate until ready to use.

3. Heat a lightly greased 8-in. nonstick skillet over medium heat. Stir batter. Pour ¼ cup batter into center of pan. Quickly lift and tilt pan to coat bottom evenly. Cook until top appears dry; turn crepe over and cook until the bottom is cooked, 15-20 seconds longer. Remove to a wire rack. Repeat with remaining batter, greasing pan as needed. When cool, stack crepes between pieces of waxed paper or paper towels.

4. Spread 2 Tbsp. cheese mixture down the center of each crepe. Top with the salmon, spinach, capers and dill; roll up. If desired, garnish with additional cheese, capers and dill.

2 crepes: 235 cal., 8g fat (4g sat. fat), 91mg chol., 837mg sod., 21g carb. (2g sugars, 2g fiber), 17g pro. **Diabetic exchanges:** 2 medium-fat meat, 1½ starch.

HAM & APRICOT CREPES

A sweet apricot sauce nicely complements these savory ham crepes.
—Candy Evavold, Samammish, WA

Prep: 35 min. + chilling • **Bake:** 10 min.
Makes: 10 servings

- 2 large eggs
- 1½ cups 2% milk
- 1 Tbsp. butter, melted
- 1 cup all-purpose flour
- 20 thin slices deli ham
SAUCE
- 1 can (15¼ oz.) apricot halves
- ⅔ cup sugar
- 2 Tbsp. cornstarch
- ⅛ tsp. salt
- 2 cans (5½ oz. each) apricot nectar
- 2 Tbsp. butter
- 2 tsp. lemon juice

1. In a large bowl, whisk eggs, milk and butter. Add flour and mix well. Refrigerate, covered, 1 hour.

2. Preheat oven to 350°. Heat a lightly greased 8-in. nonstick skillet over medium heat. Stir batter. Fill a ¼-cup measure halfway with batter; pour into center of pan. Quickly lift and tilt pan to coat bottom evenly. Cook until top appears dry; turn crepe over and cook until bottom is cooked, 15-20 seconds longer. Remove to a wire rack. Repeat with remaining batter, greasing pan as needed. When cool, stack crepes between pieces of waxed paper or paper towels.

3. Place a slice of ham on each crepe; roll up. Arrange crepes in 2 greased 13x9-in. baking dishes. Bake, uncovered, until heated through, 8-10 minutes.

4. Meanwhile, drain apricots, reserving syrup. Cut apricots into ¼-in. slices; set aside. In a large saucepan, combine sugar, cornstarch and salt. Whisk in apricot nectar and reserved syrup until smooth. Bring to a boil over medium heat; cook and stir until thickened, 1-2 minutes. Remove from the heat; stir in butter, lemon juice and apricot slices. Serve with crepes.

2 crepes: 235 cal., 6g fat (3g sat. fat), 56mg chol., 224mg sod., 40g carb. (28g sugars, 1g fiber), 7g pro.

Crepe Toppers

Sweet ideas: Fresh fruit, berries, jam, honey, marmalade, maple syrup, lemon curd, nut butters, chocolate chips, whipped cream, pie filling, hot fudge, caramel sauce, chopped nuts, ice cream, shaved chocolate.

Savory ideas: Shredded cheese, mushrooms, grape tomatoes, mixed greens, ham, salami, prosciutto, pesto, bacon, avocado.

READY FOR RHUBARB!

The arrival of rhubarb is a surefire sign that spring has sprung. This ruby-red plant is responsible for some of our favorite warm-weather recipes, both sweet and savory. Whether you grow your own in the garden or pick some up at the farmers market, you'll love all the creative ways you can use this sweet-tart treat.

Rhubarb Strawberry Pie (p. 140)

RHUBARB BEEF

My daughter made a trip around the world and brought home this recipe from Iran. I've served it often to many of my friends, and they always seem to savor its unique zingy taste.
—*Bertha Davis, Springfield, MO*

- -

Prep: 10 min. • **Cook:** 2¼ hours
Makes: 6 servings

- 2 to 2½ lbs. beef stew meat, cut into 1-in. cubes
- 2 Tbsp. butter
- 2 large onions, chopped
- 1 tsp. saffron
- 1 can (10½ oz.) beef broth
- 1 cup water
- ¼ cup lemon juice
- ¼ cup chopped fresh parsley
- 1½ tsp. dried mint
- 2 tsp. salt
- ¼ tsp. pepper
- 2 to 3 cups sliced fresh or frozen rhubarb
    Hot cooked rice
    Fresh mint leaves, torn

In a Dutch oven, brown the beef in butter. Remove meat from pan; drain all but 2 Tbsp. drippings. Saute onions until lightly browned. Return meat to pan. Add the saffron, broth, water, lemon juice, parsley, mint, salt and pepper; cover and simmer until meat is tender, about 2 hours. Add more water as needed. Add the rhubarb during the last 15 minutes of cooking. Serve over rice; top with fresh mint.
1 cup: 287 cal., 15g fat (6g sat. fat), 104mg chol., 1072mg sod., 8g carb. (5g sugars, 2g fiber), 30g pro.

RHUBARB KETCHUP

I received this recipe from a friend many years ago. It's a nice surprise for ketchup lovers, and it's so easy to prepare. The spicy flavor makes it one of the tastiest condiments I've ever had!
—*Faith McLillian, Rawdon, QC*

- -

Prep: 5 min. • **Cook:** 1 hour + chilling
Makes: 6 cups

- 4 cups diced fresh or frozen rhubarb
- 3 medium onions, chopped
- 1 can (28 oz.) diced tomatoes, undrained
- 1 cup sugar
- 1 cup packed brown sugar
- 1 cup white vinegar
- 2 tsp. salt
- 1 tsp. ground cinnamon
- 1 Tbsp. pickling spice

1. In a large saucepan, combine the first 8 ingredients. Place the pickling spice on a double thickness of cheesecloth. Gather corners of cloth to enclose seasoning; tie securely with string. Add to saucepan. Cook 1 hour or until thickened.
2. Discard spice bag. Cool ketchup. Store in airtight containers in the refrigerator.
2 Tbsp.: 43 cal., 0 fat (0 sat. fat), 0 chol., 122mg sod., 11g carb. (10g sugars, 1g fiber), 0 pro.

PINK RHUBARB PUNCH

Toast the arrival of guests and springtime with this blush-colored rhubarb punch. It has a crisp, refreshing taste everyone will love.
—*Rebecca Mininger, Jeromesville, OH*

- -

Prep: 30 min. + chilling
Makes: 20 servings (about 5 qt.)

- 8 cups chopped fresh or frozen rhubarb
- 8 cups water
- 2½ cups sugar
- 2 Tbsp. strawberry gelatin powder
- 2 cups boiling water
- 2 cups pineapple juice
- ¼ cup lemon juice
- 6 cups ginger ale, chilled
    Optional: Fresh pineapple wedges, sliced strawberries and sliced lemons

1. In a Dutch oven, bring rhubarb and water to a boil. Reduce heat; simmer, uncovered, for 10 minutes. Drain, reserving liquid (save rhubarb for another use).
2. In a large bowl, dissolve sugar and gelatin powder in boiling water. Stir in pineapple and lemon juices. Stir in rhubarb liquid; refrigerate until chilled.
3. Just before serving, pour into a punch bowl and stir in ginger ale. If desired, garnish with fresh fruit.
1 cup: 152 cal., 0 fat (0 sat. fat), 0 chol., 11mg sod., 38g carb. (37g sugars, 1g fiber), 1g pro.

RHUBARB CHUTNEY

This tangy-sweet chutney is one of our favorite garnishes. We love it with pork or chicken, but it brightens up almost anything. Spread it on toasted baguette slices with cream cheese for a yummy snack.
—*Jan Paterson, Anchorage, AK*

- -

Takes: 20 min. • **Makes:** about 3 cups

- ¾ cup sugar
- ⅓ cup cider vinegar
- 1 Tbsp. minced garlic
- ¾ tsp. ground ginger
- ½ tsp. ground cumin
- ½ tsp. ground cinnamon
- ¼ tsp. crushed red pepper flakes
- ⅛ to ¼ tsp. ground cloves
- 4 cups coarsely chopped fresh or frozen rhubarb, thawed
- ½ cup chopped red onion
- ⅓ cup golden raisins
- 1 tsp. red food coloring, optional

1. In a large saucepan, combine the sugar, vinegar, garlic, ginger, cumin, cinnamon, red pepper flakes and cloves. Bring to a boil. Reduce heat; simmer, uncovered, until sugar is dissolved, about 2 minutes.
2. Add the rhubarb, onion and raisins. Cook and stir over medium heat 5-10 minutes or until rhubarb is tender and mixture is slightly thickened. Stir in food coloring if desired. Cool completely. Store in the refrigerator.
¼ cup: 75 cal., 0 fat (0 sat. fat), 0 chol., 3mg sod., 19g carb. (17g sugars, 1g fiber), 1g pro.

During the simmering process, the vinegar aroma will be very pungent. So do it in a well-ventilated area.

RHUBARB
CHUTNEY

HONEY-RHUBARB
CHICKEN

RHUBARB DUMPLINGS

I love trying new recipes. I received lots of compliments when I served these delectable dumplings at a family gathering.
—*Elsie Shell, Topeka, IN*

- -

Prep: 25 min. • **Bake:** 35 min.
Makes: 12 servings

SAUCE
- 1½ cups sugar
- 1 Tbsp. all-purpose flour
- ½ tsp. ground cinnamon
- ¼ tsp. salt
- 1½ cups water
- ⅓ cup butter
- 1 tsp. vanilla extract
  Red food coloring, optional

DOUGH
- 2 cups all-purpose flour
- 2 Tbsp. sugar
- 2 tsp. baking powder
- ¼ tsp. salt
- 2½ Tbsp. cold butter
- ¾ cup 2% milk

FILLING
- 2 Tbsp. butter, softened
- 2 cups finely chopped fresh or frozen rhubarb
- ½ cup sugar
- ½ tsp. ground cinnamon

1. In a saucepan, combine the sugar, flour, cinnamon and salt. Stir in water; add the butter. Bring to a boil; cook and stir 1 minute. Remove from heat. Add vanilla and, if desired, enough food coloring to tint sauce a deep pink. Set sauce aside.
2. For dough, in a medium bowl, combine flour, sugar, baking powder and salt. Cut in butter until the mixture resembles coarse crumbs. Add milk and mix quickly. (Do not overmix.) Gather dough into a ball and roll out on a floured surface into a 12x9-in. rectangle. Spread with softened butter; arrange rhubarb on top.
3. Combine sugar and cinnamon; sprinkle over rhubarb. Roll up from a long side and place on a cutting board, seam side down. Cut roll into 12 slices. Arrange slices cut side up in a greased 13x9-in. baking dish. Pour sauce over. Bake at 350° for 35-40 minutes or until golden brown.
1 piece: 312 cal., 10g fat (6g sat. fat), 27mg chol., 269mg sod., 54g carb. (36g sugars, 1g fiber), 3g pro.

HONEY-RHUBARB
CHICKEN

The sauce on this honey chicken is like a sweet-tart spin on teriyaki. Everyone who has tried it raves about it—even my husband, who's not usually a rhubarb lover.
—*Rachel Beach, Whitley City, KY*

- -

Prep: 30 min. • **Bake:** 35 min.
Makes: 6 servings

- 1¼ cups all-purpose flour
- 1 Tbsp. poultry seasoning
- 1 large egg
- 1 cup 2% milk
- 1 broiler/fryer chicken (3 to 4 lbs.), cut up
- ¼ cup canola oil

HONEY-RHUBARB SAUCE
- ¼ cup cornstarch
- 1¾ cups cold water, divided
- ½ cup packed brown sugar
- ½ cup honey
- 3 Tbsp. soy sauce
- 1½ cups chopped fresh or frozen rhubarb
- 2 Tbsp. chopped onion
- 2 garlic cloves, peeled

1. Preheat oven to 400°. Combine flour and poultry seasoning. In another bowl, whisk egg and milk. Dip chicken, 1 piece at a time, into flour mixture, then into egg mixture; coat again with flour mixture.
2. In a large skillet, heat oil over medium-high heat. Brown chicken on both sides. Place in a greased 13x9-in. baking dish.
3. For sauce, combine the cornstarch and 1½ cups cold water in a large saucepan until smooth; stir in brown sugar, honey and soy sauce. Pulse the rhubarb, onion, garlic and remaining water in a food processor until blended. Stir into cornstarch mixture. Bring to a boil over medium heat; cook and stir until thickened, 2-3 minutes. Pour over chicken.
4. Bake, uncovered, 35-40 minutes or until a thermometer inserted into a thigh reads 170°.
1 serving: 639 cal., 25g fat (5g sat. fat), 114mg chol., 565mg sod., 70g carb. (43g sugars, 2g fiber), 34g pro.

PORK CHOPS WITH RHUBARB

A surprising rhubarb sauce makes these tender chops extra special. I like it on the tangy side, but you can always add more honey to sweeten up the fruity sauce if it's too puckery for your family's tastes.
—Bonnie Bufford, Nicholson, PA

Takes: 25 min. • Makes: 2 servings

- 1 Tbsp. all-purpose flour
  Salt and pepper to taste
- 2 bone-in pork loin chops (½ to ¾ in. thick)
- 2 Tbsp. butter
- ½ lb. fresh or frozen rhubarb, chopped
- 1 Tbsp. honey
- ⅛ tsp. ground cinnamon
- 1½ tsp. minced fresh parsley

In a shallow dish, combine the flour, salt and pepper; add pork chops and turn to coat. In a skillet, melt butter over medium heat. Add pork chops; cook until a thermometer reads 145°, 4-5 minutes on each side. Remove and keep warm. Add the rhubarb, honey and cinnamon to the skillet; cook until rhubarb is tender, about 5 minutes. Serve sauce over pork chops. Sprinkle with parsley.

1 pork chop: 390 cal., 19g fat (7g sat. fat), 111mg chol., 82mg sod., 17g carb. (10g sugars, 2g fiber), 38g pro.

RHUBARBECUE

This simmered sauce is a roller-coaster ride for your tongue. It's a wonderful blend of complex flavors that goes with any meat.
—Rd Stendel-Freels, Albuquerque, NM

Prep: 45 min. • Bake: 2½ hours
Makes: 8 servings

- 1½ tsp. salt
- 1½ tsp. paprika
- 1 tsp. coarsely ground pepper
- 3 to 4 lbs. boneless country-style pork ribs
SAUCE
- 3 cups sliced fresh or frozen rhubarb (about 7 stalks)
- 2 cups fresh strawberries, halved
- 2 to 3 Tbsp. olive oil
- 1 medium onion, chopped
- 1 cup packed brown sugar
- ¾ cup ketchup
- ½ cup red wine vinegar
- ½ cup bourbon
- ¼ cup reduced-sodium soy sauce
- ¼ cup honey
- 2 Tbsp. Worcestershire sauce
- 2 tsp. garlic powder
- 1 tsp. crushed red pepper flakes
- 1 tsp. coarsely ground pepper

1. Preheat oven to 325°. Mix the salt, paprika and pepper; sprinkle over ribs. Refrigerate, covered, while preparing sauce.
2. In a large saucepan, combine rhubarb and strawberries; add water to cover. Bring to a boil. Cook, uncovered, until rhubarb is tender, 8-10 minutes. Drain; return to pan. Mash the rhubarb and strawberries until blended.
3. In a Dutch oven, heat 1 Tbsp. oil over medium heat. Brown ribs in batches, adding more oil as needed. Remove from pan.
4. Add the onion to same pan; cook and stir until tender, 4-6 minutes. Add the remaining ingredients; stir in rhubarb mixture. Return ribs to pan, turning to coat. Bring to a boil. Cover and bake until ribs are tender, about 2 hours. Bake, uncovered, until the sauce is slightly thickened, 30-35 minutes.

⅓ cup sauce: 533 cal., 19g fat (6g sat. fat), 98mg chol., 1158mg sod., 52g carb. (45g sugars, 2g fiber), 31g pro.

Rhubarb 101

What exactly is rhubarb? Here are some fun facts on the sweet-tart treat.

WHAT IS RHUBARB?

Rhubarb is a perennial plant that grows well in cool climates. The stalks are edible, but it's sometimes planted as an ornamental plant because of its beautiful, vibrant red stalks and wide green leaves. Consumed raw, rhubarb has an intensely tart flavor. But toss it with sugar and rhubarb's bitterness fades and becomes quite enjoyable.

IS RHUBARB POISONOUS?

Rhubarb stalks are safe to eat, but the leaves contain a compound called oxalic acid, which is toxic to both humans and animals. But don't worry; you'd have to eat several pounds of rhubarb leaves to reach a toxic level.

WHEN IS RHUBARB IN SEASON?

Rhubarb grows best in cool weather below 75°, so it's widely available in spring. You'll find it in most areas beginning in April or May, although some regions tolerate rhubarb growth throughout the summer.

HOW TO PICK OR CHOOSE RHUBARB

If you're harvesting rhubarb from the plant, choose stalks that are firm and upright. Frost can cause the toxic oxalic acid from the leaves to migrate into the stalks, so avoid anything that's flimsy or soft. Dark red rhubarb is sweeter and more flavorful, but the green stalks are edible, too. At the store or farmers market, look for firm, shiny stalks without any blemishes. If the rhubarb has the leaves attached, look for leaves that look fresh and haven't wilted.

RHUBARB STRAWBERRY PIE

(PICTURED ON PAGE 135)

This strawberry rhubarb pie has become a favorite in our house. My husband never liked rhubarb until he tasted this pie. Now he asks me to make it often.

—Sandy Brown, Lake Worth, FL

- -

Prep: 15 min. + standing
Bake: 40 min. + cooling
Makes: 8 servings

- ¾ cup sugar
- ¼ cup quick-cooking tapioca
- 3 cups sliced fresh or frozen rhubarb (¼-in. pieces)
- 3 cups sliced fresh or frozen strawberries, thawed
- ⅓ cup orange juice
- 4½ tsp. orange marmalade, optional
- ¼ tsp. grated orange zest
  Dough for double-crust pie

1. Preheat oven to 400°. In a large bowl, combine sugar and tapioca. Add fruit; toss to coat. Gently stir in the juice, marmalade if desired, and orange zest. Let stand for 15 minutes.
2. On a lightly floured surface, roll half of dough to a ⅛-in.-thick circle; transfer to 9-in. deep-dish pie plate. Trim to ½ in beyond rim of plate. Add filling.
3. Roll remaining dough to a ⅛-in.-thick circle; cut into ¼-in.-wide strips. Arrange over filling in a lattice pattern. Trim and seal the strips to edge of bottom crust; flute edge. Cover edge loosely with foil.
4. Bake until filling is bubbly and rhubarb is tender, 40-50 minutes. Remove foil. Cool on a wire rack. Store in the refrigerator.
1 piece: 470 cal., 23g fat (14g sat. fat), 60mg chol., 312mg sod., 62g carb. (24g sugars, 3g fiber), 5g pro.
Dough for double-crust pie: Combine 2½ cups all-purpose flour and ½ tsp. salt; cut in 1 cup cold butter until crumbly. Gradually add ⅓ to ⅔ cup ice water, tossing with a fork until dough holds together when pressed. Divide dough in half. Shape each into a disk; wrap and refrigerate 1 hour.

⬆

If using frozen rhubarb, measure rhubarb while still frozen, then thaw completely. Drain in a colander, but do not press liquid out.

RHUBARB CRUMBLE

To tell you the truth, I'm not sure how well my crumble keeps in the fridge—we usually eat it all in a day! You can make this with all rhubarb, but the apples and strawberries make the dessert extra good.

—Linda Enslen, Schuler, AB

- -

Prep: 20 min. • **Bake:** 40 min.
Makes: 8 servings

- 3 cups sliced fresh or frozen rhubarb (½-in. pieces)
- 1 cup diced peeled apples
- ½ to 1 cup sliced strawberries
- ⅓ cup sugar
- ½ tsp. ground cinnamon
- ½ cup all-purpose flour
- 1 tsp. baking powder
- ¼ tsp. salt
- 4 Tbsp. cold butter
- ⅔ cup packed brown sugar
- ⅔ cup quick-cooking oats
  Vanilla ice cream, optional

1. Preheat oven to 350°. Combine rhubarb, apples and strawberries; spoon into a greased 8-in. square baking dish. Combine the sugar and cinnamon; sprinkle over rhubarb mixture. Set aside.
2. In a bowl, combine flour, baking powder and salt. Cut in butter until mixture resembles coarse crumbs. Stir in brown sugar and oats. Sprinkle over rhubarb mixture.
3. Bake at 350° for 40-50 minutes or until lightly browned. Serve warm or cold, with a scoop of ice cream if desired.
1 serving: 227 cal., 6g fat (4g sat. fat), 15mg chol., 191mg sod., 41g carb. (29g sugars, 2g fiber), 2g pro.

STRAWBERRY-RHUBARB UPSIDE-DOWN CAKE

STRAWBERRY-RHUBARB UPSIDE-DOWN CAKE

I prepare this colorful dessert often in the spring and summer when fresh rhubarb is abundant. It may have simple ingredients, but the result is stunning! When I take it to church potlucks, people always line up.
—*Bonnie Krogman, Thompson Falls, MT*

Prep: 15 min. • **Bake:** 40 min. + cooling
Makes: 12 servings

- 5 cups sliced fresh or frozen rhubarb, thawed and drained
- 1 pkg. (6 oz.) strawberry gelatin
- ½ cup sugar
- 2 cups miniature marshmallows
- 1 pkg. white or yellow cake mix (regular size)
  Whipped topping, optional

1. Place the rhubarb in a greased 13x9-in. baking pan. Sprinkle with gelatin, sugar and marshmallows. Prepare cake mix according to the package directions; pour batter over the marshmallows.

2. Bake at 350° until a toothpick inserted in the center comes out clean, 40-45 minutes. Cool for 10 minutes; invert the cake onto a serving plate. Serve the cake with whipped topping if desired.

1 piece: 353 cal., 9g fat (2g sat. fat), 47mg chol., 359mg sod., 65g carb. (44g sugars, 2g fiber), 5g pro.

DID YOU KNOW?

Curious minds want to know—is rhubarb a fruit or a vegetable? We already know the line between fruits and vegetables is blurry from the tomato debate. But rhubarb is a bit of an interesting case. Botanically, a fruit contains seeds and vegetables consist of leaves, stalks and roots. That definitely makes rhubarb a vegetable, but the U.S. Customs Court legally classified rhubarb as a fruit in 1947. Since it is most often used to make sweet desserts (like other fruits), they deemed that importers shouldn't have to pay the higher vegetable tax on the stalks.

SPECIAL CELEBRATIONS

Your table is not only the place where you gather for meals—it's also a canvas for your creativity. Whether you're an avid entertainer or just looking for some fresh ideas for new celebrations or traditions to incorporate into your seasonal calendar, this section offers so many exciting and ingenious ways to amp up the fun factor. Let's get this party started!

LET'S PAWTY!

It's time to pawty! This fun chapter shows you how to throw the ulti-mutt pet birthday party or any type of four-legged get-together with food for people and pets. Prepare to be pawstruck at all the fetching ideas.

Puppy Dog Cake (p. 148) **Beefy Dog Treats** (p. 153)

Dog Paw Balm

WHAT YOU'LL NEED
- ☐ 2 Tbsp. beeswax
- ☐ 2 Tbsp. shea butter
- ☐ 2 Tbsp. coconut oil
- ☐ 2 Tbsp. olive oil
- ☐ 20 drops lavender essential oil
- ☐ Toothpick
- ☐ 4 oz. Mason jar with lid
- ☐ Small glass bowl

DIRECTIONS
1. Microwave beeswax, shea butter, and coconut and olive oils in glass bowl for about 1 minute or until there is just a small amount of unmelted wax. Use toothpick to stir until the mixture is completely melted.
2. Add lavender oil and stir with the toothpick.
3. Pour mixture into Mason jar. Allow to cool and solidify. Screw lid onto jar.

HARVEST EMPANADAS

Here's an easy recipe that can be served as appetizers, or pair it with a salad for a main course. Bonus: It's easy to freeze extras for when surprise guests show up.
—*Megan Smith, Chandler, AZ*

Prep: 30 min. • **Bake:** 15 min./batch
Makes: 4 dozen

- 1 large Granny Smith apple, peeled and cut into ½-in. cubes
- 1½ cups cubed peeled sweet potatoes (½-in. cubes)
- 1½ tsp. olive oil
- ¼ tsp. salt
- ¼ tsp. pepper
- ⅛ tsp. ground cinnamon
- ½ lb. bulk pork sausage
- 1 oz. crumbled goat cheese
- 2 sheets refrigerated pie crust
- 1 large egg
- ¼ tsp. water

1. Preheat oven to 400°. Place apples and sweet potato on a foil-lined rimmed baking sheet. Drizzle with oil; sprinkle with salt, pepper and cinnamon. Toss to coat. Roast until tender, about 20 minutes.
2. Meanwhile, in a large skillet, cook sausage over medium heat 4-6 minutes or until no longer pink, breaking into crumbles; drain. Add the apple mixture and goat cheese; stir to combine.
3. On a lightly floured surface, roll crust to ¼-in. thickness. Cut with a floured 3-in. round biscuit cutter. Place the circles 2 in. apart on parchment-lined baking sheets. Place 1 heaping teaspoon filling on 1 side of each circle. Beat egg and water. Brush edges of pastry with egg wash; fold circles in half. With a fork, press edges to seal. Brush with egg wash. Bake until golden brown, 12-15 minutes per batch.

Freeze option: Bake and cool empanadas. Freeze the cooled empanadas in freezer containers. To use, reheat empanadas on a baking sheet in a preheated 400° oven until heated through, 12-15 minutes.

1 empanada: 61 cal., 4g fat (1g sat. fat), 7mg chol., 80mg sod., 6g carb. (1g sugars, 0 fiber), 1g pro.

BEST HUSH PUPPIES

Some years ago, I was a cook on a large cattle ranch. One day, I recalled the hush puppies I tried as a child on a southern trip, and I ended up creating my own homemade version of them. They make a fun snack or side dish at parties. I enjoy them as part of a fried chicken dinner with mashed potatoes, biscuits, corn on the cob and watermelon pickles!
—*Karyl Goodhart, Geraldine, MT*

Prep: 15 min. • **Cook:** 20 min.
Makes: 3 dozen

- 2 cups yellow cornmeal
- ½ cup all-purpose flour
- 2 Tbsp. sugar
- 2 tsp. baking powder
- 1 tsp. salt
- ½ tsp. baking soda
- 1 large egg, room temperature, lightly beaten
- ¾ cup 2% milk
- ¾ cup cream-style corn
  Oil for deep-fat frying

1. In a large bowl, whisk cornmeal, flour, sugar, baking powder, salt and baking soda. Add the egg, milk and cream-style corn; stir just until combined.
2. In a deep-fat fryer, heat oil to 375°. Drop tablespoons of batter, a few at a time, into hot oil. Fry until golden brown on both sides. Drain on paper towels. Serve warm.

1 hush puppy: 66 cal., 2g fat (0 sat. fat), 6mg chol., 129mg sod., 10g carb. (1g sugars, 0 fiber), 1g pro.

TEST KITCHEN TIP

Hush puppies are said to have originated in New Orleans in 1727. They are a traditional accompaniment to fried catfish. It is said that hush puppies got their name from hunters and fishermen who would deep-fry a basic cornmeal mixture (possibly the same mixture they would use to coat their own fried fish or meat) into small balls. They would feed the fried balls to their dogs to "hush the puppies" during mealtime.

BEST HUSH PUPPIES

PUPPY DOG CAKE

PUPPY DOG CAKE

Transform a coconut cake into an adorable pooch. This recipe contains chocolate, which is toxic to dogs, so only serve to human pals.
—*Nancy Reichert, Thomasville, GA*

- -

Prep: 1 hour + standing
Bake: 35 min. + cooling
Makes: 16 servings

- 5 oz. semisweet chocolate, chopped
- 2 Tbsp. plus 1½ tsp. corn syrup
- 4 large eggs

CAKE
- 4 oz. white baking chocolate, chopped
- ½ cup water
- 1 cup butter, softened
- 2 cups sugar
- 3 tsp. vanilla extract
- 2½ cups all-purpose flour
- 1 tsp. baking soda
- 1 cup buttermilk
- 1 cup sweetened shredded coconut
- 1 cup chopped pecans

FROSTING/DECORATING
- 2 pkg. (8 oz. each) cream cheese, softened
- 1 cup butter, softened
- 7½ cups confectioners' sugar
- 2 Tbsp. 2% milk
- 2 tsp. vanilla extract
- 1 red fruit Roll-up
  Brown food coloring

1. In a microwave-safe bowl, melt semisweet chocolate; stir until smooth. Stir in corn syrup just until the mixture is well blended, forms a ball and is no longer shiny. Turn onto an 8-in. square of waxed paper. Press the chocolate mixture into a 7-in. square. Let mixture stand at room temperature until dry to the touch, about 2 hours.

2. Separate eggs. Place yolks and whites in separate small bowls. Let eggs stand at room temperature for 30 minutes. In a microwave-safe bowl, microwave white chocolate with water at 30% power until chocolate is melted; cool to room temperature.

3. In a large bowl, cream butter and sugar until light and fluffy, 5-7 minutes. Beat in the egg yolks, vanilla and white chocolate mixture. Combine the flour and baking soda; add to creamed mixture alternately with buttermilk. In a small bowl, beat egg whites on high speed until stiff peaks form. Fold into the white chocolate mixture with coconut and pecans.

4. Fill 4 greased muffin cups half full with cake batter. Spoon remaining batter into 2 greased 9-in. round baking pans. Bake the cupcakes at 350° for 15 minutes and cakes for 35 minutes or until a toothpick comes out clean. Cool for 10 minutes before removing from pans to wire racks to cool completely.

5. In a large bowl, beat cream cheese and butter. Add confectioners' sugar, milk and vanilla. Color 1 cup of frosting brown. Fill separate piping bags with white and brown frostings, set aside.

6. Roll out chocolate mixture on waxed paper to ⅛-in. thickness. Using a sharp knife, cut out two 4x3-in. ears; round 1 end of each. Cut out two 1¼-in. circles for eyes, two ½-in.-long strips for mouth and one 1-in. triangle for the nose; set aside.

7. To assemble, place 1 cake on a large platter or covered board (about 14x11 in.). Cut off the cupcake tops; cut a ¼-in. piece from a rounded edge from each cupcake and discard. Place cut side of 2 cupcakes against side of cake with edges touching; frost top of cake and cupcakes. Top with remaining cake and cupcakes; lightly frost top and sides. Place ears on top of the cupcakes.

8. Using a grass piping tip, pipe 1 ear with white frosting on 1 ear with brown. Then, using a small star tip, pipe frosting on the top of the cake in white and brown. Place eyes, nose and mouth. With scissors, cut the fruit roll-up into a 2-in. strip and round 1 end; place straight end under nose for tongue.

1 piece: 894 cal., 47g fat (27g sat. fat), 137mg chol., 422mg sod., 112g carb. (95g sugars, 2g fiber), 8g pro.

PINEAPPLE GELATIN SALAD

My family enjoys this lovely layered salad with grilled hamburgers. Although I just started using this recipe, it's quickly become a favorite. A good friend shared it with me, and every time I make it, I think of her.
—Susan Kirby, Tipton, IN

- -

Prep: 25 min. + chilling • **Makes:** 20 servings

- 1 can (20 oz.) crushed pineapple
- 1 pkg. (6 oz.) lemon gelatin
- 3 cups boiling water
- 1 pkg. (8 oz.) cream cheese, softened
- 1 carton (16 oz.) frozen whipped topping, thawed
- ¾ cup sugar
- 3 Tbsp. lemon juice
- 3 Tbsp. water
- 2 Tbsp. all-purpose flour
- 2 large egg yolks, lightly beaten

1. Drain pineapple, reserving juice. Dissolve gelatin in water; add pineapple. Pour into a 13x9-in. dish coated with cooking spray; chill until almost set, about 45 minutes.

2. In a bowl, beat cream cheese and whipped topping until smooth. Carefully spread over gelatin; chill for 30 minutes. Meanwhile, in a saucepan over medium heat, combine the sugar, lemon juice, water, flour, egg yolks and reserved pineapple juice; bring to a boil, stirring constantly. Cook until thickened, about 1 minute. Cool. Carefully spread over cream cheese layer. Chill for at least 1 hour.

1 piece: 189 cal., 8g fat (6g sat. fat), 30mg chol., 56mg sod., 26g carb. (25g sugars, 0 fiber), 2g pro.

HOT DOG SLIDERS

Turn classic all-American hot dogs into a tasty international treat at your next party. Guests will go hog wild for one (or all!) of these three special treatments: Chicago-style, Bavarian and South of the Border. We bet you can't eat just one!
—Taste of Home Test Kitchen

- -

Prep: 50 min. + rising • **Bake:** 15 min.
Makes: 3½ dozen

- 21 frozen bread dough dinner rolls, thawed
- 1 large egg
- 1 Tbsp. water
- ¾ tsp. poppy seeds
- ¾ tsp. caraway seeds
- 3 Tbsp. shredded Mexican cheese blend
- 1 pkg. (16 oz.) miniature smoked sausages

HOT DOG SLIDERS

CHICAGO DOGS
- ⅓ cup prepared mustard
- ⅓ cup sweet pickle relish
- ⅓ cup chopped sweet onion
- ⅓ cup chopped tomato
- 2 whole dill pickles, julienned

BAVARIAN DOGS
- 1 can (14 oz.) Bavarian sauerkraut, rinsed, drained and chopped
- 1 small apple, diced
- ⅓ cup chopped sweet onion
- ¼ cup chopped celery

CHIHUAHUA DOGS
- 1 cup salsa verde
- 1 can (8 oz.) unsweetened crushed pineapple, drained
- ¼ cup minced fresh cilantro
- 2 tsp. chopped seeded jalapeno pepper
- 1 tsp. grated lime zest

1. Cut each roll in half; roll each into an oblong shape. Arrange in 2 greased 13x9-in. baking pans. Cover and let rise in a warm place until doubled, about 30 minutes.

2. In a small bowl, whisk egg and water; brush over rolls. Sprinkle a third of the buns with poppy seeds, another third with caraway seeds and the remaining buns with cheese. Bake at 350° for 14-16 minutes or until golden brown. Remove to wire racks to cool.

3. Meanwhile, place sausages in a 15x10x1-in. baking pan. Bake at 350° for 12-14 minutes or until heated through.

1 slider: 86 cal., 4g fat (1g sat. fat), 12mg chol., 214mg sod., 9g carb. (1g sugars, 1g fiber), 3g pro.

For Chicago Dogs: Place a sausage in a poppy seed bun. Top sausage with a teaspoon each of mustard, relish, onion and tomato. Repeat. Top each with pickles.

For Bavarian Dogs: In a bowl, combine the sauerkraut, apple, onion and celery. Place a sausage in each caraway seed bun; top with sauerkraut mixture.

For Chihuahua Dogs: In a bowl, combine the salsa, pineapple, cilantro, jalapeno and lime zest. Place a sausage in each cheese bun; top with salsa mixture.

CHICKEN & GNOCCHI SOUP

My family loves filling, hearty soups like this one. It's great to include on the buffet table at parties, too. I serve it with thick slices of Italian bread and butter. Use leftover or rotisserie chicken to speed up prep time.
—*Meredith Sayre, Burlington, KY*

Prep: 30 min. • **Cook:** 15 min.
Makes: 10 servings (3¾ qt.)

- ⅓ cup butter, cubed
- 2 Tbsp. olive oil
- 2 medium onions, chopped
- 4 celery ribs, chopped
- 6 garlic cloves, minced
- ¾ cup all-purpose flour
- 6 cups half-and-half cream
- 4 cups cubed rotisserie chicken
- 3 large carrots, shredded
- 1 Tbsp. chicken base
- 1½ tsp. dried thyme
- 1 tsp. dried parsley flakes
- ¾ tsp. salt
- ½ tsp. poultry seasoning
- 3 cans (14½ oz. each) chicken broth
- 1 pkg. (16 oz.) potato gnocchi
- 1 cup fresh baby spinach, thinly sliced

1. In a stockpot, heat the butter and oil over medium heat. Add onions and celery. Cook and stir until tender, 7-9 minutes. Add garlic; cook 1 minute longer.
2. Stir in flour until blended; gradually add the cream. Bring to a boil. Cook and stir 2 minutes or until thickened. Stir in the chicken, carrots, chicken base, thyme, parsley, salt and poultry seasoning; heat through.
3. Meanwhile, in a Dutch oven, bring broth to a boil. Add gnocchi and cook until they float (do not drain). Carefully add gnocchi and broth to the soup. Stir in spinach. Cook and stir until spinach is wilted.
1½ cups: 544 cal., 29g fat (15g sat. fat), 148mg chol., 1338mg sod., 38g carb. (8g sugars, 3g fiber), 27g pro.

SOUTHWEST VEGETARIAN CHILI

My daughter is a vegetarian, and she inspired me to create this veggie-filled meatless chili. I use vine-ripened tomatoes, cilantro and peppers from my garden plus fresh local corn from the farmers market. No one ever misses the meat.
—*Cindy Beberman, Orland Park, IL*

Prep: 20 min. • **Cook:** 15 min.
Makes: 6 servings

- 1 Tbsp. olive oil
- 1 medium sweet onion, chopped
- 1 jalapeno pepper, seeded and finely chopped
- 3 garlic cloves, minced
- 1½ tsp. ground cumin
- 1 tsp. chili powder
- 2 cups diced fresh tomatoes (about 3 medium)
- 1½ cups fresh or frozen corn (about 8 oz.)
- 1 can (15 oz.) black beans, rinsed and drained
- 1 can (15 oz.) garbanzo beans or chickpeas, rinsed and drained
- 2 cups reduced-sodium vegetable broth
- ½ tsp. salt
- ⅓ cup chopped fresh cilantro
 Optional: Sour cream, diced avocado and lime wedges

1. In a Dutch oven, heat oil over medium heat. Add onion and jalapeno; cook and stir until tender, 4-5 minutes. Add garlic, cumin and chili powder; cook 1 minute longer.
2. Stir in the tomatoes, corn, beans, broth and salt; bring to a boil. Reduce heat; cover and simmer until heated through, about 5 minutes. Stir in cilantro. If desired, serve with optional toppings.
1 cup: 214 cal., 4g fat (0 sat. fat), 0 chol., 496mg sod., 37g carb. (10g sugars, 8g fiber), 9g pro. **Diabetic exchanges:** 2½ starch, 1 lean meat, ½ fat.

PUPP-ERONI PIZZA CRACKERS

Kids love making (and eating!) these simple treats. I use pizza sauce from a squeeze bottle to make it easier for them. Just make sure an adult is present to put the crackers in the oven.
—*Tonya Sanders, Geneva, IA*

Takes: 20 min. • **Makes:** 2 dozen

- 24 Ritz crackers
- 24 slices pepperoni
- ¼ cup pizza sauce
- 2 Tbsp. finely shredded Colby-Monterey Jack cheese
- 1 Tbsp. minced fresh oregano or 1 tsp. dried oregano

Preheat oven to 400°. Place crackers on a baking sheet. Top with pepperoni, pizza sauce, cheese and oregano. Bake until cheese is melted, 5-7 minutes.
1 cracker: 29 cal., 2g fat (1g sat. fat), 2mg chol., 78mg sod., 2g carb. (0 sugars, 0 fiber), 1g pro.

PUPP-ERONI PIZZA CRACKERS

Treat, Play, Love

Humans can't have all the fun. Try these thoughtful ways to show your furriest friend how much you care.

TOSS 'EM A NEW TOY
Show Fido some love by adding a new toy to his or her collection. Many dogs love playing tug of war with long, squeaky toy animals or chasing moving objects, like balls.

SCHEDULE A PLAY DATE
For your outgoing doggy, there is nothing more exhilarating than puppy playtime. Have your human honey over for dinner and invite Scout along, too, for the best kind of double date.

LAY OUT A LUXE BED
Comfort your dog with a cuddly new bed. Choose one that's soft and the appropriate size (the bed should be 6 to 12 inches longer than the pet). This will give your snuggler plenty of space to sprawl and rest.

TAKE A HIKE
Treat yourself and your active pup to an afternoon of exercise. Pick an activity appropriate for the age and energy level of your dog. Hikes, swims, long walks and camping are great ways to spend quality time together.

BAKE UP SOME PUPPY BITES
Make some dog-friendly treats to show your special buddy how much you love him or her. Try the Cheddar Dog Treats or Beefy Dog Treats on page 153.

151

PUPPY CHOW

Here's a fun chocolate-peanut butter twist on traditional puppy chow. Despite its name, it's not safe for four-legged friends. But bring it to a party or potluck, and watch how quickly human comrades devour it.
—*Mary Obeilin, Selinsgrove, PA*

Takes: 15 min. • **Makes:** about 6 cups

- 1 cup semisweet chocolate chips
- ¼ cup creamy peanut butter
- 6 cups Corn or Rice Chex
- 1 cup confectioners' sugar

1. In a large microwave-safe bowl, melt the chocolate chips on high for 30 seconds. Stir; microwave 30 seconds longer or until the chips are melted. Stir in peanut butter. Gently stir in cereal until well coated; set aside.
2. Place confectioners' sugar in a large airtight container. Add cereal mixture and shake until well coated. Store in an airtight container in the refrigerator.
½ cup: 194 cal., 7g fat (3g sat. fat), 0 chol., 170mg sod., 33g carb. (19g sugars, 1g fiber), 3g pro.

CHEDDAR DOG TREATS

Any pampered pup will be lucky to fetch these goodies. The yummy strips are made with real cheese, which most dogs can't resist.
—*Lydia Driscoll, Milwaukee, WI*

Prep: 15 min. • **Bake:** 15 min. + standing
Makes: 3 dozen

- 1 cup all-purpose flour
- 1 cup shredded cheddar cheese
- 1 Tbsp. butter, softened
- ⅓ cup whole milk

1. In a small bowl, combine flour and cheese. Stir in butter until combined. Gradually add milk just until moistened. Turn onto a lightly floured surface; knead 8-10 times.
2. Roll dough into a 12x9-in. rectangle; cut into 3x1-in. strips. Place on ungreased baking sheets. Bake at 350° for 15 minutes or until golden brown. Let stand in the oven with the door slightly open until cooled completely. Store in an airtight container.
1 treat: 30 cal., 1g fat (1g sat. fat), 4mg chol., 24mg sod., 3g carb. (0 sugars, 0 fiber), 1g pro.

BEEFY DOG TREATS

Your canine companions will go crazy for these healthy meat-flavored biscuits.
—*Lori Kimble, Mascoutah, IL*

Prep: 20 min. • **Bake:** 20 min. + standing
Makes: 3 dozen

- 1 pkg. (¼ oz.) active dry yeast
- ¼ cup warm water (110° to 115°)
- 1 tsp. beef bouillon granules
- 2 Tbsp. boiling water
- 2½ cups all-purpose flour
- 1 cup nonfat dry milk powder
- 1 cup whole wheat flour
- 1 cup cooked long grain rice
- 1 envelope unflavored gelatin
- 1 jar (4 oz.) vegetable beef dinner baby food
- 1 large egg
- 2 Tbsp. vegetable oil

1. Preheat the oven to 325°. In a small bowl, dissolve yeast in warm water. In another small bowl, dissolve bouillon in boiling water. In a large bowl, combine all-purpose flour, milk powder, wheat flour, rice and gelatin. Stir in baby food, egg, oil, yeast mixture and bouillon mixture until combined.
2. On a lightly floured surface, knead dough 8-10 times until the mixture forms a ball. Roll to ¼-in. thickness. Cut dough with a floured 2-in. bone-shaped cookie cutter. Place 1 in. apart on ungreased baking sheets.
3. Bake until set, 18-25 minutes. Remove to wire racks to cool. Let stand 24 hours or until hardened. Store treats in an airtight container in the refrigerator.
1 treat: 66 cal., 1g fat (0 sat. fat), 6mg chol., 39mg sod., 11g carb. (2g sugars, 1g fiber), 3g pro.

GAME-NIGHT GATHERING

We're not bluffing when we say a game night is the best way to spend quality time with those you love most. Gather your crew for a evening of card shufflin', dice rollin' and snack dunkin'. The rules? Must come hungry and eager to play. Now get your game face on!

Mini Corn Dogs (p. 157) **Lake Charles Dip** (p. 157) **Cran & Cherry Punch** (p. 160)

LAKE CHARLES DIP

LAKE CHARLES DIP

Italian salad dressing mix gives this dip its delicious flavor. Serve it with fresh veggies or crackers for an easy appetizer.
—*Shannon Copley, Upper Arlington, OH*

Prep: 15 min. + chilling • **Makes:** 1½ cups

- 1 cup sour cream
- 2 Tbsp. reduced-fat mayonnaise
- 1 Tbsp. Italian salad dressing mix
- ⅓ cup finely chopped avocado
- 1 tsp. lemon juice
- ½ cup finely chopped seeded tomato
  Optional: Assorted crackers, cucumber slices, julienned sweet red pepper and carrot sticks

In a small bowl, combine the sour cream, mayonnaise and dressing mix. Toss avocado with lemon juice; stir into sour cream mixture. Stir in tomato. Cover and refrigerate for at least 1 hour. Serve with crackers and assorted vegetables as desired.

¼ cup: 111 cal., 9g fat (5g sat. fat), 27mg chol., 216mg sod., 3g carb. (2g sugars, 1g fiber), 2g pro.

HOT PIZZA DIP

You can assemble this effortless appetizer in a jiffy. The pizza-flavored dip goes very fast, so you may want to make two batches.
—*Stacie Morse, South Otselic, NY*

Takes: 10 min.
Makes: 24 servings (about 3 cups)

- 1 pkg. (8 oz.) cream cheese, softened
- 1 tsp. Italian seasoning
- 1 cup shredded part-skim mozzarella cheese
- ¾ cup grated Parmesan cheese
- 1 can (8 oz.) pizza sauce
- 2 Tbsp. chopped green pepper
- 2 Tbsp. thinly sliced green onion
  Breadsticks or tortilla chips

1. In a bowl, beat cream cheese and Italian seasoning. Spread in an ungreased 9-in. microwave-safe pie plate.
2. Combine the mozzarella and Parmesan cheeses; sprinkle half over the cream cheese. Top with the pizza sauce, remaining cheese mixture, green pepper and onion.
3. Microwave, uncovered, on high until the cheese is almost melted, 2-3 minutes, rotating a half-turn several times. Let the dip stand for 1-2 minutes. Serve dip with breadsticks or tortilla chips.

2 Tbsp.: 62 cal., 5g fat (3g sat. fat), 16mg chol., 131mg sod., 1g carb. (1g sugars, 0 fiber), 3g pro.

MINI CORN DOGS

MINI CORN DOGS

Bring a county fair favorite into your home with these bite-sized corn dogs. It's easy to make your own by wrapping cornmeal dough around mini hot dogs. Kids and the young at heart love them.
—*Geralyn Harrington, Floral Park, NY*

Takes: 30 min. • **Makes:** 2 dozen

- 1⅔ cups all-purpose flour
- ⅓ cup cornmeal
- 3 tsp. baking powder
- 1 tsp. salt
- 3 Tbsp. cold butter
- 1 Tbsp. shortening
- 1 large egg, room temperature
- ¾ cup 2% milk
- 24 miniature hot dogs

HONEY MUSTARD SAUCE
- ⅓ cup honey
- ⅓ cup prepared mustard
- 1 Tbsp. molasses

1. In a large bowl, combine first 4 ingredients. Cut in butter and shortening until mixture resembles coarse crumbs. Beat egg and milk; stir into dry ingredients until a soft dough forms; dough will be sticky.
2. Turn onto a generously floured surface; knead 6-8 times or until smooth, adding additional flour as needed. Roll out to ¼-in. thickness. Cut with a 2¼-in. biscuit cutter. Fold each dough circle over a hot dog and press the edges to seal. Place on greased baking sheets.
3. Bake at 450° 10-12 minutes or until golden brown. In an small bowl, combine the sauce ingredients. Serve with corn dogs.

1 mini corn dog: 109 cal., 5g fat (2g sat. fat), 18mg chol., 306mg sod., 14g carb. (5g sugars, 0 fiber), 3g pro.

MOZZARELLA STICKS

I'm particularly fond of these mozzarella sticks because they are baked instead of deep-fried. Cheese is one of my family's favorite foods. Being of Italian descent, I cook often with ricotta and mozzarella cheeses.
—*Mary Merchant, Barre, VT*

Prep: 15 min. + freezing • **Bake:** 10 min.
Makes: 6 servings

- 3 Tbsp. all-purpose flour
- 2 large eggs
- 1 Tbsp. water
- 1 cup dry bread crumbs
- 2½ tsp. Italian seasoning
- ½ tsp. garlic powder
- ⅛ tsp. pepper
- 12 sticks string cheese
- 1 Tbsp. butter, melted
- 1 cup marinara or spaghetti sauce, heated

1. Place flour in a shallow bowl. In another shallow bowl, beat eggs and water. In a third shallow bowl, combine the bread crumbs, Italian seasoning, garlic powder and pepper. Coat cheese sticks with flour, then dip in egg mixture and coat with bread crumb mixture. Repeat egg and bread crumb coatings. Cover and freeze for at least 2 hours or overnight.
2. Place on a parchment-lined baking sheet; spray with cooking spray. Bake, uncovered, at 400° for 6-8 minutes or until heated through. Allow to stand for 3-5 minutes before serving. Serve with warm marinara or spaghetti sauce for dipping.

2 sticks: 312 cal., 17g fat (10g sat. fat), 116mg chol., 749mg sod., 22g carb. (4g sugars, 1g fiber), 20g pro.

BARBECUE CHICKEN SLIDERS

Thanks to store-bought rotisserie chicken, these cheesy, smoky sliders are a snap to make on a busy night. The special barbecue sauce takes it up a notch.
—*Nancy Heishman, Las Vegas, NV*

Takes: 25 min. • **Makes:** 4 servings

- ¾ cup beer or reduced-sodium chicken broth
- ½ cup barbecue sauce
- 1 Tbsp. bourbon
- 1 tsp. hot pepper sauce
- ¼ tsp. seasoned salt
- ¼ tsp. ground mustard
- 2 cups shredded rotisserie chicken
- 8 slider buns, split
- 1½ cups shredded smoked cheddar cheese

1. Preheat broiler. In a large saucepan, mix first 6 ingredients; bring to a boil. Reduce heat; simmer, uncovered, until mixture is slightly thickened, 8-10 minutes, stirring occasionally. Stir in chicken; heat through.
2. Place buns on a baking sheet, cut side up. Broil 3-4 in. from heat until lightly toasted, 30-60 seconds.
3. Remove tops of buns from baking sheet. Top bottoms with chicken mixture; sprinkle with cheese. Broil 3-4 in. from heat until cheese is melted, 1-2 minutes. Add bun tops.
Freeze option: Freeze cooled chicken mixture in freezer containers. To use, partially thaw in the refrigerator overnight. Heat through in a saucepan, stirring occasionally; add water if necessary.

2 sliders: 529 cal., 23g fat (10g sat. fat), 106mg chol., 1023mg sod., 42g carb. (15g sugars, 1g fiber), 36g pro.

POPCORN NUT MIX

Traditional popcorn nut mix gets a makeover with orange and cinnamon flavors.
—*Sandi Pichon, Memphis, TN*

Prep: 10 min. • **Bake:** 15 min. + cooling
Makes: 18 servings (9 cups)

- 10 cups popped popcorn
- 1 cup mixed nuts
- ¼ cup honey
- 2 Tbsp. grated orange zest
- 2 Tbsp. orange juice
- ¼ tsp. ground cinnamon

Place popcorn and nuts in a large bowl; set aside. In a small saucepan, combine the honey, orange zest, orange juice and cinnamon. Bring to a boil. Pour over popcorn mixture; toss to coat. Transfer to an ungreased 13x9-in. baking pan. Bake at 350° for 15 minutes, stirring twice. Cool completely on waxed paper. Store in an airtight container.

½ cup: 97 cal., 7g fat (1g sat. fat), 0 chol., 68mg sod., 9g carb. (4g sugars, 1g fiber), 2g pro.

→

A half cup of unpopped kernels equals about 4 cups popped popcorn. So you'll need 1¼ cups unpopped kernels for this recipe.

POPCORN NUT MIX

How to Host a Family Game Night

With these ideas, your family game night will be fun- and food-filled with a little friendly competition, of course.

PICK WHAT TO PLAY

After you and your crew decide on a night that works for everyone, here comes the hard part: agreeing on a game. Be sure to gear your selection toward your group. If you have little ones, opt for a classic like Candy Land. School-age kids love Sequence. And teens and adults can't seem to get enough of Catan.

Editor's Tip: Short on games? Buy some from a local thrift store (just check to make sure all of the pieces are in place) or check the library—some lend board games in addition to books.

SELECT YOUR SNACKS

You'll want your menu full of small, mess-free munchies that can be grabbed, dunked and devoured in between rounds.

SET THE TABLE

First, place the game and its pieces on the table to ensure there's enough space. You can even divvy up tokens, deal cards and set up scorecards in advance. Next, set out your snacks in the remaining space.

Editor's Tip: Serve the small bites on a lazy Susan. That way everyone can reach, even as they're strategizing.

PLAY CLEAN

And no, we don't mean playing by the rules! That's important, too, but so is keeping the table and game pieces tidy. Place slices of lemon and a shallow dish of warm water at each place setting (see photo and description on page 160). When fingers get greasy from snacking, simply splash 'em in the water and rub with the fruit to freshen up quickly. A spritz of hand sanitizer will help, too.

GAME ON!

You're finally ready to call in the crew and get gaming. For optimal family bonding, make game night a tech-free zone. Place phones in a separate room and turn off the TV. Now, it's time to snack—then attack!

159

CRAN & CHERRY PUNCH

This crimson-colored beverage makes a great thirst quencher for any celebration. The ice cubes give it an extra pretty touch.
—*Lori Daniels, Beverly, WV*

Prep: 15 min. + freezing • **Makes:** 3½ qt.

- ⅓ cup fresh or frozen cranberries
- 2 lemon slices, cut into 6 wedges
- 1 pkg. (3 oz.) cherry gelatin
- 1 cup boiling water
- 3 cups cold water
- 6 cups cranberry juice, chilled
- ¾ cup thawed lemonade concentrate
- 1 liter ginger ale, chilled

1. Place several cranberries and a piece of lemon in each compartment of an ice cube tray; fill with water and freeze.
2. In a punch bowl or large container, dissolve gelatin in boiling water. Stir in the cold water, cranberry juice and lemonade concentrate. Just before serving, stir in ginger ale. Serve over cranberry-lemon ice cubes.
¾ cup: 99 cal., 0 fat (0 sat. fat), 0 chol., 17mg sod., 25g carb. (24g sugars, 0 fiber), 1g pro.
Diabetic exchanges: 1 starch, ½ fruit.

CHAI TEA

Warm up a chilly evening—or any day at all—with this inviting tea. The spices make it divine, and it's even more delicious when stirred with a cinnamon stick.
—*Kelly Pacowta, Danbury, CT*

Takes: 20 min. • **Makes:** 4 servings

- 4 whole cloves
- 2 whole peppercorns
- 4 tea bags
- 4 tsp. sugar
- ¼ tsp. ground ginger
- 1 cinnamon stick (3 in.)
- 2½ cups boiling water
- 2 cups 2% milk

1. Place cloves and peppercorns in a large bowl; with the end of a wooden spoon handle, crush spices until aromas are released.
2. Add the tea bags, sugar, ginger, cinnamon stick and boiling water. Cover and steep for 6 minutes. Meanwhile, in a small saucepan, heat the milk.
3. Strain tea, discarding spices and tea bags. Stir in hot milk. Pour into mugs.
1 cup: 92 cal., 4g fat (2g sat. fat), 12mg chol., 49mg sod., 10g carb. (10g sugars, 0 fiber), 4g pro.

ONE-POT MAC & CHEESE

Who likes cleaning up after making mac and cheese? Not this girl. This one-pot mac and cheese is a family favorite, and my youngster is thrilled to see it coming to the dinner table. We love to add sliced smoked sausage to this creamy mac recipe!
—*Ashley Lecker, Green Bay, WI*

Prep: 5 min. • **Cook:** 30 min.
Makes: 10 servings

- 3½ cups whole milk
- 3 cups water
- 1 pkg. (16 oz.) elbow macaroni
- 4 oz. Velveeta, cubed
- 2 cups shredded sharp cheddar cheese
- ½ tsp. salt
- ½ tsp. coarsely ground pepper

In a Dutch oven, combine milk, water and macaroni; bring to a boil over medium heat. Reduce heat and simmer until macaroni is tender and almost all the cooking liquid has been absorbed, 12-15 minutes, stirring frequently. Reduce heat to low; stir in cheeses until melted. Season with salt and pepper.
1 cup: 344 cal., 14g fat (8g sat. fat), 42mg chol., 450mg sod., 39g carb. (6g sugars, 2g fiber), 16g pro.

EASY BACON CHEESE FONDUE

Here's my go-to recipe when I'm looking for a rich appetizer with mass appeal but want a change from the usual cheese spread.
—*Bernice Morris, Marshfield, MO*

Takes: 30 min. • **Makes:** 3¾ cups

- 4 to 5 bacon strips, diced
- ¼ cup chopped onion
- 2 Tbsp. all-purpose flour
- 1 lb. Velveeta, cubed
- 2 cups sour cream
- 1 jalapeno pepper, seeded and chopped, optional
- 1 loaf (1 lb.) French bread, cubed
  Optional: Soft pretzel bites and halved miniature sweet peppers

1. In a large skillet, cook bacon over medium heat until crisp. Using a slotted spoon, remove to paper towels. In the drippings, saute onion until tender. Stir in flour until blended; cook and stir until thickened.
2. Reduce heat to low. Add cheese cubes; cook and stir until melted. Stir in sour cream, jalapeno if desired, and bacon; cook and stir just until heated through. Transfer to a fondue pot and keep warm. Serve with bread cubes.
4 Tbsp.: 305 cal., 18g fat (11g sat. fat), 48mg chol., 647mg sod., 21g carb. (4g sugars, 1g fiber), 11g pro.

Hand 'Em Lemons

Place slices of the puckery fruit and a shallow dish of warm water at each place setting. When fingers get greasy from snacking (no shame!), simply splash 'em in the water and rub with the lemon to freshen up quickly and keep your game pieces clean. We call that a win-win.

EASY BACON
CHEESE FONDUE

CHOCOLATE CARAMEL COOKIES

This is my favorite recipe for bazaars, bake sales and casual get-togethers. Each sweet chocolate cookie has a fun caramel surprise in the middle, thanks to a Rolo candy.
—*Melissa Vannoy, Childress, TX*

- -

Prep: 25 min. • **Bake:** 10 min. + cooling
Makes: 5 dozen

- 1 cup butter, softened
- 1 cup plus 1 Tbsp. sugar, divided
- 1 cup packed brown sugar
- 2 large eggs, room temperature
- 2 tsp. vanilla extract
- 2½ cups all-purpose flour
- ¾ cup baking cocoa
- 1 tsp. baking soda
- 1 cup chopped pecans, divided
- 1 pkg. (13 oz.) Rolo candies

1. In a large bowl, cream butter, 1 cup sugar and brown sugar. Beat in eggs and vanilla. Combine flour, cocoa and baking soda; gradually add to creamed mixture just until combined. Stir in ½ cup pecans.

2. Shape dough by tablespoonfuls around each candy. In a small bowl, combine the remaining pecans and sugar; dip each cookie halfway.

3. Place with nut side up on ungreased baking sheets. Bake at 375° until the top is slightly cracked, 7-10 minutes. Cool for 3 minutes; remove to wire racks to cool completely.

1 cookie: 121 cal., 6g fat (3g sat. fat), 15mg chol., 60mg sod., 16g carb. (11g sugars, 1g fiber), 1g pro.

CHOCOLATE
CARAMEL COOKIES

CHUNKY MONKEY CUPCAKES

Peanut butter is a favorite of ours, and it brings a fun element to these cupcakes. They're good with or without garnishes.
—*Holly Jones, Kennesaw, GA*

Prep: 30 min. • **Bake:** 20 min. + cooling
Makes: 2 dozen

- 2 cups mashed ripe bananas (about 5 medium)
- 1½ cups sugar
- 3 large eggs, room temperature
- ½ cup unsweetened applesauce
- ¼ cup canola oil
- 3 cups all-purpose flour
- 1 tsp. baking soda
- ½ tsp. baking powder
- ½ tsp. salt
- 1 cup semisweet chocolate chunks

FROSTING
- 4 oz. reduced-fat cream cheese
- ¼ cup creamy peanut butter
- 3 Tbsp. butter, softened
- 1 to 1¼ cups confectioners' sugar
  Chopped salted peanuts, optional

1. Preheat oven to 350°. Line 24 muffin cups with paper liners.
2. Beat first 5 ingredients until well blended. In another bowl, whisk together flour, baking soda, baking powder and salt; gradually beat into banana mixture. Fold in the semisweet chocolate chunks.
3. Fill prepared cups three-fourths full. Bake until a toothpick inserted in center comes out clean, 20-25 minutes. Cool cupcakes in pans 10 minutes before removing to wire racks to cool completely.
4. For frosting, beat cream cheese, peanut butter and butter until smooth. Gradually beat in enough confectioners' sugar to reach desired consistency. Spread over cupcakes. If desired, sprinkle with peanuts. Refrigerate leftover cupcakes.
1 cupcake: 250 cal., 9g fat (4g sat. fat), 30mg chol., 165mg sod., 40g carb. (25g sugars, 2g fiber), 4g pro.

RASPBERRY WHITE CHOCOLATE BARS

A co-worker's mother gave me this gem of a recipe a few years back. I can never decide what's more appealing—the attractive look of the bars or their incredible aroma while they're baking!
—*Mimi Priesman, Pace, FL*

Prep: 20 min. • **Bake:** 45 min.
Makes: 2 dozen

- ½ cup butter, cubed
- 1 pkg. (10 to 12 oz.) white baking chips, divided
- 2 large eggs
- ½ cup sugar
- 1 tsp. almond extract
- 1 cup all-purpose flour
- ½ tsp. salt
- ½ cup seedless raspberry jam
- ¼ cup sliced almonds

1. In a small saucepan, melt butter. Remove from the heat; add 1 cup chips (do not stir). In a small bowl, beat eggs until foamy; gradually add sugar. Stir in the chip mixture and almond extract. Combine flour and salt; gradually add to egg mixture just until combined.
2. Spread half of the batter into a greased 9-in. square baking pan. Bake at 325° for 15-20 minutes or until golden brown.
3. In a small saucepan, melt jam over low heat; spread over warm crust. Stir remaining chips into the remaining batter; drop by spoonfuls over the jam layer. Sprinkle with almonds.
4. Bake 30-35 minutes longer or until a toothpick inserted in the center comes out clean. Cool on a wire rack. Cut into bars.
1 serving: 162 cal., 9g fat (5g sat. fat), 30mg chol., 104mg sod., 20g carb. (8g sugars, 0 fiber), 2g pro.

MARCH MADNESS

Turn the man cave into the most delicious spot in your house by serving up these b-ball greats. You'll make everyone's hoop dreams come true when you turn on the games as they settle in with savory favorites. In fact, these full-flavored dishes are so satisfying, you'll crave them all year long! Turn here any time you want to surprise the gang with a few finger-lickin' bites.

Maple-Barbecue Pork Sandwiches (p. 170)
Chili-Chocolate Caramel Corn (p. 166) **Sticky Honey Chicken Wings** (p. 166)

CHILI-CHOCOLATE
CARAMEL CORN

1. Preheat oven to 350°. In a large saucepan, melt butter over medium heat. Add garlic; cook and stir until tender, 1-2 minutes. Add tomatoes, pasta sauce, basil, salt and pepper; heat through. Transfer to an ungreased 1½ qt. shallow baking dish. Spoon cheese into center of sauce; dollop pesto over cheese. Bake, uncovered, until bubbly, 25-30 minutes.

2. Meanwhile, brush baguette slices with oil. Arrange on ungreased baking sheets. Bake until toasted, 2-4 minutes on each side. Serve with dip.

2 Tbsp.: 83 cal., 5g fat (3g sat. fat), 12mg chol., 208mg sod., 8g carb. (1g sugars, 1g fiber), 2g pro.

STICKY HONEY CHICKEN WINGS

This recipe was given to me by a special lady who was like a grandmother to me. The wings make the perfect game-day food.
—*Marisa Raponi, Vaughan, ON*

Prep: 15 min. + marinating
Bake: 30 min. • **Makes:** 3 dozen

- ½ cup orange blossom honey
- ⅓ cup white vinegar
- 2 Tbsp. paprika
- 2 tsp. salt
- 1 tsp. pepper
- 4 lbs. chicken wings

1. Combine honey, vinegar, paprika, salt and pepper in a small bowl.

2. Cut through the 2 wing joints with a sharp knife, discarding wing tips. Add remaining wing pieces and honey mixture to a large bowl; stir to coat. Cover and refrigerate for 4 hours or overnight.

3. Preheat oven to 375°. Remove wings; reserve honey mixture. Place the wings on greased 15x10x1-in. baking pans. Bake until juices run clear, about 30 minutes, turning halfway through.

4. Meanwhile, place reserved honey mixture in a small saucepan. Bring to a boil; cook for 1 minute.

5. Remove wings from oven; preheat broiler. Place wings on a greased rack in a broiler pan; brush with honey mixture. Broil 4-5 in. from heat until crispy, 3-5 minutes. Serve with the remaining honey mixture.

1 piece: 71 cal., 4g fat (1g sat. fat), 16mg chol., 147mg sod., 4g carb. (4g sugars, 0 fiber), 5g pro.

CHILI-CHOCOLATE CARAMEL CORN

Warning: It's not easy to walk away from this sweet, salty, spicy, crunchy snack. If you are taking it to a party, consider making a double batch because you won't come home with any leftovers. It's truly that good!
—Taste of Home *Test Kitchen*

Takes: 10 min. • **Makes:** 14 servings (3½ qt.)

- 2⅓ cups chocolate chips
- 2 Tbsp. shortening
  Dash ground ancho chili pepper
  Dash ground cinnamon
- 3½ qt. caramel popcorn with peanuts
- 1 cup dried cranberries, optional

In a microwave, melt chocolate chips and shortening; stir until smooth. Stir in chili pepper and cinnamon. Drizzle over caramel popcorn with peanuts; toss to coat. Arrange popcorn on a waxed paper-lined baking sheet. Refrigerate until set; break into pieces. If desired, add dried cranberries. Store in an airtight container.

1 cup: 336 cal., 13g fat (6g sat. fat), 6mg chol., 97mg sod., 51g carb. (34g sugars, 3g fiber), 5g pro.

TOMATO-BASIL PARTY DIP

If you're short on time, look for prepared seasoned crostini, which are available in many grocery stores. Heat the small bread baguettes briefly in the oven or for a few seconds in the microwave before serving.
—*Bee Engelhart, Bloomfield Township, MI*

Prep: 25 min. • **Bake:** 25 min.
Makes: 28 servings (3½ cups)

- ¼ cup butter, cubed
- 2 garlic cloves, minced
- 1 can (14½ oz.) diced tomatoes, drained
- 1 cup tomato basil pasta sauce
- 1 Tbsp. minced fresh basil
- ¼ tsp. salt
- ¼ tsp. pepper
- 1 pkg. (6½ oz.) garlic-herb spreadable cheese
- 1 Tbsp. prepared pesto
- 1 French bread baguette (10½ oz.), cut into ¼-in. slices
- 1 Tbsp. olive oil

STICKY HONEY
CHICKEN WINGS

REUBEN PUFF PASTRY STROMBOLI

I love this layered Reuben stromboli. I used another sandwich recipe as a guide but made it with Reuben fixings. You can easily change it to a Rachel by using sliced turkey and coleslaw instead of corned beef and sauerkraut.
—*Joan Hallford, North Richland Hills, TX*

Prep: 25 min. • **Bake:** 40 min. + standing
Makes: 6 servings

- 1 sheet frozen puff pastry, thawed
- ⅔ cup Thousand Island salad dressing, divided
- 3 Tbsp. dill pickle relish
- ½ lb. thinly sliced deli corned beef
- ½ lb. thinly sliced deli pastrami
- 4 Tbsp. spicy brown mustard
- 8 slices Swiss or fontina cheese
- 1½ cups sauerkraut, rinsed and well drained
- 1 large egg white, lightly beaten
- 2 tsp. caraway seeds or sesame seeds

1. Preheat oven to 400°. On a lightly floured surface, unfold the puff pastry. Roll into a 14x11-in. rectangle. Spread ⅓ cup dressing to within ½ in. of edges. Sprinkle with relish. Layer with corned beef, pastrami, mustard, cheese and sauerkraut. Roll up jelly-roll style, starting with a long side. Place stromboli on a parchment-lined baking sheet, seam side down; tuck ends under and press to seal.
2. Brush with egg white and sprinkle with caraway seeds; cut small slits in top. Bake until golden brown and pastry is cooked through, 40-45 minutes. Let stand 10 minutes before slicing. Serve with remaining dressing.
1 piece: 491 cal., 32g fat (10g sat. fat), 50mg chol., 1566mg sod., 32g carb. (4g sugars, 4g fiber), 18g pro.

REUBEN
PUFF PASTRY
STROMBOLI

ZESTY CITRUS SNACK MIX

This mix combines two of my favorite snacks—pita chips and roasted garbanzo beans—with nuts, pretzels and a flavorful citrus blend. It's perfect for parties and for taking on the go. You can substitute premade pita chips for the pita bread with good results.
—*Elisabeth Larsen, Pleasant Grove, UT*

Prep: 30 min. • **Bake:** 40 min. + cooling
Makes: 14 servings (10 cups)

- 1 can (15 oz.) garbanzo beans or chickpeas, drained and patted dry
- 1 Tbsp. olive oil
- ⅛ tsp. salt
- ¼ cup butter, melted
- 1 tsp. brown sugar
- ½ tsp. grated orange zest
- ½ tsp. grated lime zest
- ½ tsp. soy sauce
- ¼ tsp. ground ginger
- ¼ tsp. onion powder
- ⅛ tsp. garlic powder
- 4 pita pocket halves, cut into 1-in. squares
- 2 cups miniature pretzels
- ¾ cup unsalted cashews
- ¾ cup unblanched almonds

1. Preheat oven to 400°. Remove skins from garbanzo beans; discard. Toss beans with oil and salt; spread in a single layer in a foil-lined 15x10x1-in. pan. Bake until very crunchy, 30-35 minutes, stirring every 15 minutes. Remove from oven; cool completely.
2. Whisk melted butter, brown sugar, orange and lime zest, soy sauce and seasonings. Add pita squares, pretzels, cashews and almonds; toss to coat. Spread evenly into 2 foil-lined 15x10x1-in. baking pans. Bake until dry and crisp, 10-15 minutes, stirring occasionally. Add garbanzo beans to pita mixture. Cool completely. Store in an airtight container.
¾ cup: 235 cal., 15g fat (4g sat. fat), 10mg chol., 281mg sod., 21g carb. (2g sugars, 3g fiber), 6g pro.

ROASTED RED PEPPER, SPINACH & ARTICHOKE SPREAD

I found a simple spinach and artichoke spread in a cookbook and added my own touches—roasted red peppers, pesto, lemon zest and wine. You'll be surprised at how much your guests enjoy it.
—*Be Jones, Brunswick, MO*

Prep: 20 min. • **Bake:** 30 min.
Makes: 20 servings (5 cups)

- ½ cup white wine or chicken broth
- 2 shallots, minced
- 1 garlic clove, minced
- 1 can (10¾ oz.) reduced-fat reduced-sodium condensed cream of mushroom soup, undiluted
- 1 cup reduced-fat sour cream
- ½ cup prepared pesto
- 2 Tbsp. all-purpose flour
- 1 Tbsp. reduced-sodium soy sauce
- 1 tsp. grated lemon zest
- ½ tsp. hot pepper sauce
- 2 pkg. (10 oz. each) frozen chopped spinach, thawed and squeezed dry
- 1 can (14 oz.) water-packed artichoke hearts, rinsed, drained and chopped
- ¾ cup roasted sweet red peppers, drained and chopped
- 2 cups shredded part-skim mozzarella cheese, divided
  Assorted crackers and/or breads

1. In a large skillet, combine the wine, shallots and garlic. Bring to a boil; cook until liquid is reduced to about 2 Tbsp. Stir in the soup, sour cream, pesto, flour, soy sauce, lemon zest and pepper sauce. Fold in the spinach, artichokes, red peppers and half the cheese.
2. Transfer to a greased 11x7-in. baking dish; sprinkle with remaining cheese. Bake at 400° until set, 30-35 minutes. Serve with crackers and/or breads.
¼ cup: 104 cal., 6g fat (2g sat. fat), 9mg chol., 341mg sod., 8g carb. (2g sugars, 1g fiber), 6g pro.

BEER & SMOKED SAUSAGE STEW

This slow-cooker stew is perfect for keeping warm on even the coldest nights, and the meal is ready when you are. Feel free to add corn, peas, green beans or other veggies.
—*Jesi Allen, Gastonia, NC*

Prep: 10 min. • **Cook:** 8 hours
Makes: 12 servings (3 qt.)

- 4 large potatoes, cubed
- 2 lbs. smoked sausage, cut into ¾-in. pieces
- 2 bottles (12 oz. each) beer
- 2 cups reduced-sodium chicken broth
- 2 ribs celery, sliced
- 1 medium onion, chopped
- 2 garlic cloves, minced
- 2 bay leaves
- ½ tsp. minced fresh thyme
- ¼ tsp. minced fresh rosemary
- 2 Tbsp. butter, cubed

In a 6-qt. slow cooker, combine the first 10 ingredients. Dot with cubed butter. Cook, covered, on low until vegetables are tender, 8-10 hours. Discard bay leaves before serving.

1 cup: 357 cal., 22g fat (10g sat. fat), 56mg chol., 979mg sod., 25g carb. (4g sugars, 3g fiber), 14g pro.

HOISIN CHICKEN PIZZA

Use leftover or rotisserie chicken if you have it on hand. During the summer, it's worth taking the time to grill fresh chicken to add a smokier flavor to the pizza.
—*Jessie Apfel, Berkeley, CA*

Takes: 30 min.
Makes: 2 pizzas (6 servings each)

- ¾ cup hoisin sauce, divided
- 1 Tbsp. rice vinegar
- 1 Tbsp. sesame oil
- 1½ tsp. minced fresh gingerroot
- 1 garlic cloves, minced
- 2 pkg. (6 oz. each) ready-to-use grilled chicken breast strips
- 16 large fresh mushrooms, thinly sliced
- 2 prebaked 12-in. pizza crusts
- 4 green onions, chopped
- 1 can (8 oz.) sliced water chestnuts, drained
- 4 cups shredded part-skim mozzarella cheese

1. Preheat oven to 350°. In a small bowl, combine ½ cup hoisin, vinegar, oil, gingerroot and garlic. In a large bowl, combine chicken strips, mushrooms and remaining hoisin; toss to coat.

2. Place crusts on 2 ungreased 12-in. pizza pans. Spread hoisin mixture over crusts. Top with chicken mixture, onions, water chestnuts and cheese.

3. Bake until heated through and cheese is melted, 10-15 minutes.

1 piece: 380 cal., 13g fat (5g sat. fat), 41mg chol., 877mg sod., 44g carb. (8g sugars, 2g fiber), 23g pro.

MAPLE-BARBECUE PORK SANDWICHES

If you're serving this pork at a party, keep it warm in a slow cooker. Stir in water, a little at a time, if the mixture gets too thick.
—*Sharlene Heatwole, McDowell, VA*

Prep: 30 min. • **Bake:** 2½ hours
Makes: 10 servings

- 1 boneless pork shoulder butt roast (3 to 4 lbs.)
- 1 Tbsp. cider vinegar
- 1 cup ketchup
- 1 cup barbecue sauce
- ½ cup maple syrup
- 2 Tbsp. Dijon mustard
- 1 tsp. liquid smoke, optional
- ½ tsp. pepper
- ¼ tsp. salt
- 10 hamburger buns, split

1. Preheat oven to 350°. Place pork in a large roasting pan; brush with vinegar. Add ½ in. water to pan. Cover and bake until tender, 2½-3 hours. Remove the roast; when cool enough to handle, shred meat with 2 forks.

2. In a large saucepan, combine ketchup, barbecue sauce, syrup, mustard, liquid smoke if desired, pepper and salt. Bring to a boil over medium heat. Reduce the heat; simmer, uncovered, for 2 minutes. Add pork; heat through. Serve on buns.

1 sandwich: 460 cal., 16g fat (5g sat. fat), 81mg chol., 1018mg sod., 50g carb. (28g sugars, 1g fiber), 28g pro.

> **TEST KITCHEN TIP**
>
> If you'd like your sandwiches to look like basketballs, draw lines on top of the buns using a black food-safe marker. Visit *Wilton.com* to find FoodWriter edible markers, which are sold in a variety of colors.

MAPLE-BARBECUE
PORK SANDWICHES

MUSTARD PRETZEL DIP

This flavorful dip is addictive, so be careful! It's also delicious served with pita chips, crackers and fresh veggies.
—*Iola Egle, Bella Vista, AR*

Prep: 10 min. + chilling • **Makes:** 3½ cups

- 1 cup sour cream
- 1 cup mayonnaise
- 1 cup prepared mustard
- ½ cup sugar
- ¼ cup dried minced onion
- 1 envelope ranch salad dressing mix
- 1 Tbsp. prepared horseradish
  Sourdough pretzel nuggets

In a large bowl, combine first 7 ingredients. Cover and refrigerate for at least 30 minutes. Serve with pretzels. Refrigerate leftovers.

2 Tbsp.: 101 cal., 8g fat (2g sat. fat), 8mg chol., 347mg sod., 6g carb. (4g sugars, 0 fiber), 1g pro.

CHOCOLATE-PEANUT BUTTER CUP COOKIES

If you want to enjoy one of these soft, fully loaded treats the day after you make them, you'd better find a good hiding spot—because they'll get gobbled up fast!
—*Jennifer Krey, Clarence, NY*

Prep: 25 min. • **Bake:** 10 min./batch
Makes: 4 dozen

- 1 cup butter, softened
- ¾ cup creamy peanut butter
- 1 cup packed brown sugar
- ½ cup sugar
- 2 large egg yolks, room temperature
- ¼ cup 2% milk
- 2 tsp. vanilla extract
- 2⅓ cups all-purpose flour
- ⅓ cup baking cocoa
- 1 tsp. baking soda
- 1 cup milk chocolate chips
- 1 cup peanut butter chips
- 6 pkg. (1½ oz. each) peanut butter cups, chopped

1. Preheat the oven to 350°. In a large bowl, cream butter, peanut butter and sugars until light and fluffy, 5-7 minutes. Beat in egg yolks, milk and vanilla. Combine flour, cocoa and baking soda; gradually add to the creamed mixture and mix well. Stir in chips and peanut butter cups.

2. Drop heaping tablespoons 2 in. apart onto ungreased baking sheets. Bake until set (do not overbake), 8-10 minutes. Cool cookies for 2 minutes before removing from pans to wire racks. Store in an airtight container.

1 cookie: 170 cal., 10g fat (4g sat. fat), 20mg chol., 100mg sod., 18g carb. (12g sugars, 1g fiber), 3g pro.

SOUR CREAM SUGAR COOKIE CAKE

My husband requested a giant sugar cookie for his birthday. I wanted to do something a bit more exciting than birthday cookies, so I came up with this sugar cookie cake. The secret to a dense yet cakelike texture is to make sure you don't overbake the cake.
—*Carmell Childs, Orangeville, UT*

Prep: 20 min. • **Bake:** 20 min. + cooling
Makes: 20 servings

- ½ cup butter, softened
- 1½ cups sugar
- 2 large eggs, room temperature
- 1 tsp. vanilla extract
- 3 cups all-purpose flour
- ¾ tsp. salt
- ½ tsp. baking powder
- ½ tsp. baking soda
- 1 cup sour cream
- 1 can (16 oz.) vanilla frosting
  Optional: Coarse sugar, sprinkles and additional frosting

1. Preheat oven to 350°. In a large bowl, cream butter and sugar until light and fluffy, 5-7 minutes. Beat in the eggs and vanilla. In another bowl, whisk flour, salt, baking powder and baking soda; add to creamed mixture alternately with sour cream, beating after each addition just until combined. Spread into a greased 13x9-in. baking pan.

2. Bake until a toothpick inserted in center comes out clean, 20-25 minutes. Cool cake completely on a wire rack. Spread frosting over top. Decorate with optional toppings as desired.

1 piece: 295 cal., 11g fat (6g sat. fat), 34mg chol., 228mg sod., 46g carb. (29g sugars, 1g fiber), 3g pro.

SOUR CREAM
SUGAR COOKIE CAKE

MARCH MADNESS PARTY IDEAS

Kick off the Big Dance with a bash for sports lovers! Here are a few clever ideas to keep guests entertained.

SEND GAME BRACKETS AS PARTY INVITATIONS

Have guests fill out the brackets on the invitations before they arrive at the party so you will be able to start the fun with a basketball pool.

DECORATIONS

Orange and black are neutral basketball colors to use when decorating a March Madness party. If all your guests will be cheering for the same team, by all means, decorate accordingly.

USE A COOLER TO STORE DRINKS AT YOUR PARTY

In addition to serving soda, bottled water and beer, throw a couple of sports drinks like Gatorade in your cooler to create a game-time atmosphere.

DRESS THE PART

As the host, mix things up a bit by wearing a referee jersey and carrying a whistle.

WORLD'S GREATEST FAN

Create a basketball trivia game with questions about the teams playing in the games.

CRANK THE TUNES

Try something from the ESPN "Jock Jams" collection. These popular, catchy songs are designed to pump up fans during games.

PICKUP GAME

Guests won't mind helping pick up when you put a basketball hoop over your trash can.

CINCO DE MAYO FIESTA

On May 5th, say hola to a lineup of authentic Mexican flavors that will take you on a journey south of the border. Make your Cinco de Mayo fiesta unforgettable with sizzling fajitas, fruity margaritas, tres leches cake, homemade guac and other zesty, spicy and cheesy favorites. *Que deliciosos!*

Zesty Green Tomato Salsa (p. 177) **Mexican Steak Fajitas** (p. 178) **Tajin Limeade** (p. 177)

How to Plan a Cinco de Mayo Fiesta

As if you need an excuse to eat all the chips and guac! Use these easy entertaining ideas to inspire your Cinco de Mayo party this year.

SET THE SCENE

Festive decorations make the party. When it comes to Cinco de Mayo, the brighter and bolder the colors, the better (think hot pink, citrus orange, lime green and vibrant blue). Giant tissue paper flowers or traditional *papel picado* banners are great options. Along those same lines, coordinate your place settings with Mexican-themed cups, plates and napkins.

PICK THE PERFECT PINATA

Throw back to your childhood by hanging a pinata filled with a variety of candy and other small goodies. Buy a classic donkey from the party store or make your own with crepe paper and cardboard. Look for tutorials online.

BREAK OUT THE SALSA

And we aren't talking about pico de gallo (although that's a must, too!). Get your blood pumping by asking everyone to join you on the dance floor for a little fancy footwork. You can hire a professional salsa dancer to teach you all the moves or simply follow a tutorial on YouTube.

DON'T FORGET DESSERT

After salty chips and steak fajitas, guests are going to be craving a little something sweet. Treat them to an authentic Mexican dessert: tres leches cake (page 179). This cake is creamy and rich (and guests will be begging you for the recipe when the party is over).

TELL YOUR GUESTS "GRACIAS!"

The party doesn't have to stop when the night is over. Send each person home with a mini bottle of tequila —all they have to do is add lime and salt to make their own margaritas. Be an extra helpful host, and send them home with instructions on how to prep that perfect drink in their own kitchen. They are sure to love any of the recipes on pages 182-183.

GREEN TOMATO SALSA

ZESTY GREEN TOMATO SALSA

I came up with this fresh salsa so I could use all the green tomatoes from my garden when it started to get cold.
—*Vanessa Moon, Tucson, AZ*

- -

Prep: 20 min. + standing • **Cook:** 10 min.
Makes: 6 cups

- 1   medium green pepper
- 1   serrano pepper
- 5   medium green tomatoes or 5 large tomatillos, husked
- 1   medium onion, chopped
- 2   garlic cloves, minced
- ⅓   cup lime juice
- 2   Tbsp. olive oil
- 4   tsp. agave nectar
- 1   tsp. coarsely ground pepper
- ½   tsp. salt
- 3   Tbsp. fresh cilantro leaves
- 1   medium ripe avocado, peeled, pitted and quartered
     Tortilla chips

1. Preheat broiler. Place the peppers on a foil-lined baking sheet. Broil 3-4 in. from heat until skins blister, about 5 minutes. With tongs, rotate peppers a quarter turn. Broil and rotate until all sides are blistered and blackened. Immediately place in a bowl; let stand, covered, 20 minutes.
2. Using tongs, place tomatoes, a few at a time, in a pot of boiling water for 5 minutes. Remove tomatoes; cool slightly. Peel and finely chop tomatoes; place in a large bowl.
3. Remove the skin, stems and seeds from charred peppers. Finely chop peppers; add to tomatoes. Stir in onion and garlic.
4. Place all remaining ingredients except chips in a blender; cover and process until smooth. Add to tomato mixture, stirring to combine. Serve with chips.
¼ cup salsa: 27 cal., 2g fat (0 sat. fat), 0 chol., 50mg sod., 2g carb. (1g sugars, 1g fiber), 0 pro. **Diabetic exchanges:** 1 free food.

TAJIN LIMEADE

Tajin is a blend of chili peppers, salt and lime. I sprinkle it on a lot of food, but found it's also delicious in limeade.
—*Amanda Phillips, Portland, OR*

- -

Prep: 20 min. + freezing
Makes: 8 servings

- 3   Tbsp. Tajin seasoning, divided
- 1   cup plus 1 Tbsp. sugar, divided
- 4   cups water, divided
- 3   cups fresh lime juice
     Lime wedges, optional

1. Sprinkle 2 Tbsp. Tajin seasoning evenly in the bottom of 2 ice cube trays (16 ice cubes each). Fill with water and freeze.
2. In a saucepan, stir together 1 cup sugar and 1 cup water over medium-high heat. Bring to a boil, stirring frequently, until sugar dissolves. Remove from heat and let cool until room temperature.
3. In a large pitcher or bowl, stir together the lime juice, sugar mixture and remaining 3 cups water. On a small plate, combine remaining 1 Tbsp. Tajin seasoning and 1 Tbsp. sugar. Moisten rims of 8 tall glasses with the lime wedges; dip rims in Tajin mixture. Place 3-4 ice cubes in each glass; fill with limeade. Garnish with lime wedges if desired.
1 cup: 126 cal., 0 fat (0 sat. fat), 0 chol., 749mg sod., 34g carb. (28g sugars, 0 fiber), 0 pro.

MEXICAN STEAK FAJITAS

Strips of sirloin pick up plenty of spicy flavor from a marinade seasoned with cayenne pepper and cumin. These colorful fajitas are speedy and satisfying.
—*Shirley Hilger, Lincoln, NE*

Takes: 30 min. • **Makes:** 6 servings

- ¼ cup orange juice
- ¼ cup white vinegar
- 4 garlic cloves, minced
- 1 tsp. seasoned salt
- 1 tsp. dried oregano
- 1 tsp. ground cumin
- ¼ tsp. cayenne pepper
- 1 lb. beef top sirloin steak, cut into ¼-in. strips
- 1 medium onion, thinly sliced
- 1 medium green pepper, thinly sliced
- 1 medium sweet red pepper, thinly sliced
- 2 Tbsp. canola oil, divided
- 6 flour tortillas (10 in.)
  Optional: Shredded cheddar cheese, picante sauce and sour cream

1. In a large bowl, combine the orange juice, vinegar, garlic and seasonings; add the beef. Turn to coat; set aside. In a skillet, saute onion and peppers in 1 Tbsp. oil until crisp-tender; remove and set aside.
2. Drain and discard marinade. In the same skillet, cook beef in remaining 1 Tbsp. oil until it reaches desired doneness, 2-4 minutes. Return the vegetables to pan; heat through. Spoon meat and vegetables onto tortillas. If desired, top with cheese and serve with picante sauce and sour cream.
4 oz.-weight: 304 cal., 11g fat (2g sat. fat), 31mg chol., 425mg sod., 26g carb. (3g sugars, 5g fiber), 21g pro.

SALSA CORN CAKES

I whip up these corn patties to serve alongside nachos or tacos on hot summer evenings. The salsa is subtle but adds flavor. You can also use fresh corn when it is in season.
—*Lisa Boettcher, Rosebush, MI*

Takes: 20 min. • **Makes:** 8 servings

- 6 oz. cream cheese, softened
- ¼ cup butter, melted
- 6 large eggs
- 1 cup 2% milk
- 1½ cups all-purpose flour
- ½ cup cornmeal
- 1 tsp. baking powder
- 1 tsp. salt
- 1 can (15¼ oz.) whole kernel corn, drained
- ½ cup salsa, drained
- ¼ cup minced green onions
  Sour cream and additional salsa

1. In a large bowl, beat cream cheese and butter until smooth; add the eggs and mix well. Beat in the milk until smooth. Combine the flour, cornmeal, baking powder and salt; stir into cream cheese mixture just until moistened. Fold in the corn, salsa and onions.
2. Pour the batter by ¼ cupfuls into a large greased cast-iron skillet or hot griddle. Turn when bubbles form on top; cook until the second side is golden brown. Serve with sour cream and salsa.
1 serving: 324 cal., 15g fat (8g sat. fat), 191mg chol., 715mg sod., 34g carb. (5g sugars, 3g fiber), 11g pro.

PATIO PINTOS

Any time Mom had the gang over for dinner, she made these pinto beans. Once, she made a batch for my cousin's birthday and he ate the entire thing.
—*Joan Hallford, North Richland Hills, TX*

Prep: 25 min. • **Bake:** 1 hour
Makes: 10 servings

- ½ lb. bacon strips, chopped
- 1 large onion, chopped
- 2 garlic cloves, minced
- 6 cans (15 oz. each) pinto beans, rinsed and drained
- 4 cans (8 oz. each) tomato sauce
- 2 cans (4 oz. each) chopped green chiles
- ⅓ cup packed brown sugar
- 1 tsp. chili powder
- ¾ tsp. salt
- ½ tsp. dried oregano
- ¼ tsp. pepper

1. Preheat oven to 350°. In a Dutch oven, cook bacon over medium heat until crisp, stirring occasionally. Remove with a slotted spoon; drain on paper towels. Discard the drippings, reserving 2 Tbsp. in pan.
2. Add onion to drippings; cook and stir over medium heat 6-8 minutes or until tender. Add garlic; cook 1 minute longer. Stir in the beans, tomato sauce, green chiles, brown sugar and seasonings. Sprinkle top with bacon. Bake the bean mixture, covered, 60-70 minutes or until heated through.
Freeze option: Freeze cooled bean mixture in freezer containers. To use, partially thaw in refrigerator overnight. Heat through in a saucepan, stirring occasionally; add water if necessary.
¾ cup: 349 cal., 8g fat (2g sat. fat), 11mg chol., 1183mg sod., 55g carb. (13g sugars, 12g fiber), 17g pro.

MANGO & HABANERO GUACAMOLE

For the ultimate sweet-spicy combo, pair mango with fresh habanero chili peppers. Depending on your preferred taste, you can control the guac's heat with the number of pepper seeds you use.
—*Taste of Home Test Kitchen*

Takes: 15 min. • **Makes:** 6 servings

- 3 medium ripe avocados, peeled and cubed
- 2 to 3 Tbsp. fresh lime juice
- ½ to 1 tsp. kosher salt
- 1 medium mango, peeled and chopped
- ½ to 1 habanero pepper, seeded and chopped

In a bowl, mash the avocados until almost smooth. Stir in lime juice and ½ tsp. salt. Let stand 10 minutes to allow flavors to blend. Adjust seasoning with additional lime juice and salt if desired. Top with chopped mango and habanero.
¼ cup: 150 cal., 11g fat (2g sat. fat), 0 chol., 166mg sod., 15g carb. (8g sugars, 6g fiber), 2g pro. **Diabetic exchanges:** 2 fat, 1 starch.

Wear disposable gloves when cutting hot peppers; the oils can burn skin. Avoid touching your face.

BLUE-RIBBON
BEEF NACHOS

MARGARITA TRES LECHES CAKE

The first time I ever had tres leches cake I felt like I was in heaven. I have made it at home using several techniques and flavors, and this margarita twist on the classic is my favorite.
—*Laurie Lufkin, Essex, MA*

- -

Prep: 20 min. • **Bake:** 20 min. + chilling
Makes: 15 servings

- 4 large eggs, separated
- 1 cup sugar
- ½ cup tequila
- ½ cup butter, melted
- 6 Tbsp. key lime juice, divided
- 1 tsp. vanilla extract
- 1¾ cups all-purpose flour
- 1 tsp. baking soda
- ½ tsp. salt
- ½ cup confectioners' sugar
- 1 tsp. cream of tartar
- 1 can (14 oz.) sweetened condensed milk
- 1 cup 2% milk
- ½ cup evaporated milk
- ½ cup heavy whipping cream
  Optional: Whipped cream, and lime slices and zest

1. Place egg whites in a large bowl; let stand at room temperature for 30 minutes. Grease and flour a 13x9-in. baking pan; set aside. Preheat oven to 375°.
2. Beat sugar, tequila, butter, yolks, 3 Tbsp. lime juice and vanilla until well blended. Combine flour, baking soda and salt; gradually beat into yolk mixture until blended.
3. Add confectioners' sugar and cream of tarter to egg whites; beat with clean beaters until stiff peaks form. Fold into the batter. Transfer to prepared pan.
4. Bake until a toothpick inserted in the center comes out clean, 18-20 minutes. Place the pan on a wire rack. With a wooden skewer, poke holes in cake about ½ in. apart.
5. Beat condensed milk, 2% milk, evaporated milk, whipping cream and remaining lime juice until blended. Drizzle over cake; let stand for 30 minutes. Refrigerate the cake for 2 hours before serving.
6. Cut cake into squares. If desired, garnish with whipped cream, and lime slices and zest.
1 piece: 345 cal., 14g fat (8g sat. fat), 88mg chol., 282mg sod., 46g carb. (34g sugars, 0 fiber), 7g pro.

BLUE-RIBBON BEEF NACHOS

Chili powder and sassy salsa season a zesty mixture of ground beef and refried beans that's sprinkled with green onions, tomatoes and ripe olives.
—*Diane Hixon, Niceville, FL*

- -

Takes: 20 min. • **Makes:** 6 servings

- 1 lb. ground beef
- 1 small onion, chopped
- 1 can (16 oz.) refried beans
- 1 jar (16 oz.) salsa
- 1 can (6 oz.) pitted ripe olives, chopped
- ½ cup shredded cheddar cheese
- 1 green onion, chopped
- 2 Tbsp. chili powder
- 1 tsp. salt
  Tortilla chips
  Optional: Sliced ripe olives, chopped green onions and diced tomatoes

1. In a large skillet, cook the beef and onion over medium heat until meat is no longer pink; drain. Stir in next 7 ingredients; heat through.
2. Serve over tortilla chips. Top with olives, onions and tomatoes if desired.
1 serving: 294 cal., 14g fat (6g sat. fat), 53mg chol., 1353mg sod., 19g carb. (5g sugars, 9g fiber), 20g pro.

TEST KITCHEN TIP

There are plenty of other toppings you can add to nachos. Add a dollop of homemade guacamole or sour cream to this nacho recipe. If you like a little heat, try adding a few jalapeno slices on top. Don't have ground beef or cheddar cheese on hand? Use shredded chicken and Monterey Jack cheese instead.

FIESTA CORN

HEARTY CHICKEN ENCHILADAS

My husband and I love Mexican food, and this is our favorite dish. You can modify it to suit your taste by using corn tortillas or adding corn, rice or refried beans to the filling.
—*Jenny Miller, Raleigh, NC*

Prep: 6 hours 30 min. + simmering
Bake: 25 min.
Makes: 2 casseroles (2 servings each)

    1   lb. boneless skinless chicken breasts
    2   cans (15 oz. each) enchilada sauce
    1   can (4 oz.) chopped green chiles
    1   can (15 oz.) black beans, rinsed and
        drained
    8   flour tortillas (6 in.)
    1   cup shredded Mexican cheese blend
        Optional toppings: Sour cream,
        shredded lettuce, pico de gallo and
        sliced avocado

1. In a 3-qt. slow cooker, combine the chicken, enchilada sauce and chiles. Cover and cook on low for 6-8 hours or until meat is tender.
2. Remove chicken and shred with 2 forks. Reserve 1⅔ cups cooking juices. Pour the remaining cooking juices into a large bowl; add the beans and shredded chicken. Coat 2 freezer-safe 8-in. square baking dishes with cooking spray; add ½ cup reserved juices to each dish.
3. Place about ⅓ cup chicken mixture down the center of each tortilla. Roll up and place seam side down in prepared dishes. Pour remaining reserved juices over top; sprinkle with cheese.
4. Cover 1 dish and freeze for up to 3 months. Cover and bake the second dish at 350° for 20 minutes. Uncover; bake until cheese is lightly browned, about 5 minutes longer. Serve with toppings as desired.
Freeze option: To use frozen enchiladas, thaw in the refrigerator overnight. Remove from the refrigerator 30 minutes before baking. Bake enchiladas as directed.
2 enchiladas: 577 cal., 20g fat (4g sat. fat), 83mg chol., 1541mg sod., 57g carb. (8g sugars, 8g fiber), 46g pro.

FIESTA CORN

Corn with tomatoes and jalapenos is one of the first dishes I cooked for my husband. Don't like too much heat? Use green bell peppers instead of jalapenos.
—*Cassandra Ramirez, Bardstown, KY*

Takes: 25 min. • **Makes:** 8 servings

    ¼   cup butter, cubed
    1   small onion, chopped
    2   to 3 jalapeno peppers, seeded and
        chopped
    6   plum tomatoes, seeded and chopped
    5   cups fresh or frozen corn
    1½ tsp. salt
        Lime wedges, optional

1. In a 6-qt. stockpot, heat the butter over medium heat. Add the onion and jalapenos; cook and stir until the onion is crisp-tender, 3-4 minutes. Stir in the tomatoes; cook for 3 minutes longer.
2. Add corn; cook, uncovered, until tender, stirring occasionally, 8-10 minutes. Stir in salt. If desired, serve with lime wedges.
¾ cup: 142 cal., 7g fat (4g sat. fat), 15mg chol., 505mg sod., 20g carb. (7g sugars, 3g fiber), 4g pro.

FRESAS CON CREMA

This refreshing dessert is wonderful when berries are in season. Media crema is a rich, unsweetened cream found in the baking aisle or ethnic food section of most grocery stores. It's similar to creme fraiche and sour cream, although sour cream is quite a bit tangier.
—*Taste of Home* Test Kitchen

Takes: 10 min. • **Makes:** 4 servings

    1   can (7.6 oz.) media crema table
        cream
    3   Tbsp. sweetened condensed milk
    1   tsp. vanilla extract
    3   cups chopped fresh strawberries
        Fresh mint leaves, optional

In a small bowl, whisk crema, sweetened condensed milk and vanilla. Divide the strawberries among 4 serving dishes. Top with milk mixture. Garnish with fresh mint if desired.
¾ cup: 241 cal., 17g fat (10g sat. fat), 43mg chol., 58mg sod., 21g carb. (14g sugars, 2g fiber), 2g pro.

HEARTY CHICKEN
ENCHILADAS

Margarita Mania

Whether you love 'em on the rocks or blended to perfection, these tart and tangy refreshers turn any smiley, sunny day into a fiesta.

Shaken Margarita

Pour ingredients into a cocktail shaker. Fill shaker with ice; cover and shake until frost forms on outside of shaker, 15-20 seconds. Strain into prepared glass. Garnish if desired.

Classic Margarita: 1½ oz. blanco tequila; 1 oz. Triple Sec; ½ oz. freshly squeezed lime juice. **Garnish:** Lime wedge.

Melon Margarita: 1½ oz. blanco tequila; 1½ oz. melon liqueur; ½ oz. freshly squeezed lime juice. **Garnish:** Honeydew melon balls.

Caribbean Margarita: 1½ oz. blanco tequila; 1 oz. blue curacao; ½ oz. freshly squeezed lime juice. **Garnish:** Starfruit slice.

Amaretto Margarita: 1½ oz. blanco tequila; 1 oz. Triple Sec; ½ oz. freshly squeezed lime juice; ½ oz. amaretto. **Garnish:** Maraschino cherry.

Grapefruit Sunset Margarita: 1½ oz. blanco tequila; 1 oz. Triple Sec; 1 oz. ruby red grapefruit juice. **Garnish:** 1 tsp. grenadine syrup; grapefruit slice.

Frozen Margarita

Prepare glass as desired. Pour all ingredients into a blender; cover and process until smooth. Pour into glass. Garnish if desired.

Blueberry-Mint Frozen Margarita:
1 cup frozen unsweetened blueberries; 1½ oz. blanco tequila; 1 oz. Triple Sec; ½ oz. freshly squeezed lime juice; 4 fresh mint leaves. **Garnish:** Sugared rim; mint sprig.

Raspberry-Ginger Frozen Margarita:
1 cup frozen unsweetened raspberries; 1½ oz. blanco tequila; 1 oz. ginger liqueur; 1 oz. raspberry liqueur; ½ oz. freshly squeezed lime juice. **Garnish:** Sugared rim; strawberry; crystallized ginger slice.

Frozen Coconut Margarita: 1 cup crushed ice; 2 oz. cream of coconut; 1½ oz. blanco tequila; 1 oz. Triple Sec; ½ oz. freshly squeezed lime juice. **Garnish:** Chopped toasted shredded coconut on rim; toasted coconut slices.

Strawberry-Basil Frozen Margarita:
1 cup frozen unsweetened sliced strawberries; 1½ oz. blanco tequila; 1 oz. Triple Sec; ½ oz. freshly squeezed lime juice; 4 fresh basil leaves. **Garnish:** Sugared rim; strawberry; basil leaf.

Sriracha-Mango Frozen Margarita:
1 cup frozen mango chunks; 1½ oz. blanco tequila; 1 oz. mango nectar; ½ oz. freshly squeezed lime juice; ½ tsp. Sriracha chili sauce. **Garnish:** Sugared rim; mango slice.

JUNETEENTH

June 19, also known as Freedom Day or Emancipation Day, is an annual holiday generally commemorating the end of slavery in the United States. Celebrated since the late 1800s, the day is filled with fun community events and a lineup of barbecue-style foods. Use these recipes and ideas as inspiration for your own Juneteenth celebrations.

Watermelon Salad with Cinnamon Pretzel Crunch (p. 186)
Strawberry Cooler (p. 188) Smoked Brisket (p. 190)

WATERMELON SALAD WITH CINNAMON PRETZEL CRUNCH

This is a wonderful side dish during hot Texas summers. My family loves watermelon, fresh peaches and nectarines, and I made a pretzel crunch to give the salad a little bite.
—*Joan Hallford, North Richland Hills, TX*

Prep: 20 min. + chilling • **Bake:** 5 min. + cooling
Makes: 10 servings

- 2 cups chopped seedless watermelon
- 2 cups fresh blueberries
- 1 medium peach, chopped
- 1 medium nectarine, chopped
- 1 large kiwifruit, peeled and chopped
- ½ cup sweet white wine or grape juice
- 3 Tbsp. sugar

CRUNCH
- 1 cup chopped miniature pretzels
- ½ cup packed brown sugar
- ½ cup butter, melted
- ½ cup chopped pecans
- ¼ tsp. ground cinnamon

1. Preheat the oven to 425° In a large bowl, combine the watermelon, blueberries, peach, nectarine and kiwi. Drizzle with wine and sugar. Toss to coat. Cover and refrigerate for 1 hour.

2. Meanwhile, in a small bowl, combine pretzels, brown sugar, butter, pecans and cinnamon; toss to coat. Spread mixture evenly onto a parchment-lined 15x10x1-in. baking pan. Bake 5-7 minutes or until the mixture is bubbly and the sugar is dissolved. Cool completely. Break into small chunks.

3. Just before serving, gently stir half of the pretzel mixture into the fruit. Top with remaining pretzel mixture to serve.

¾ cup: 244 cal., 14g fat (6g sat. fat), 24mg chol., 146mg sod., 30g carb. (23g sugars, 2g fiber), 2g pro.

BOURBON CANDIED BACON DEVILED EGGS

At our house, it doesn't get any better than deviled eggs with bacon—bourbon candied bacon, that is. See if you can resist them. We certainly can't!
—*Colleen Delawder, Herndon, VA*

Prep: 20 min. • **Bake:** 25 min. + cooling
Makes: 2 dozen

- 2 Tbsp. brown sugar
- ¾ tsp. Dijon mustard
- ½ tsp. maple syrup
- ⅛ tsp. salt
- 2 tsp. bourbon, optional
- 4 thick-sliced bacon strips

EGGS
- 12 hard-boiled large eggs
- ¾ cup mayonnaise
- 1 Tbsp. maple syrup
- 1 Tbsp. Dijon mustard
- ¼ tsp. pepper
- ¼ tsp. ground chipotle pepper
  Minced fresh chives

1. Preheat oven to 350°. In a small bowl, mix brown sugar, ¾ tsp. mustard, ½ tsp. syrup and salt. If desired, stir in bourbon. Coat bacon with brown sugar mixture. Place on a rack in a foil-lined 15x10x1-in. baking pan. Bake 25-30 minutes or until crisp. Cool completely.
2. Cut eggs in half lengthwise. Remove yolks, reserving whites. In a small bowl, mash yolks. Add the mayonnaise, 1 Tbsp. syrup, 1 Tbsp. mustard and both types of pepper; stir until smooth. Chop bacon finely; fold half into egg yolk mixture. Spoon or pipe into egg whites. Sprinkle with remaining bacon and the chives. Refrigerate, covered, until serving.
1 stuffed egg half: 107 cal., 9g fat (2g sat. fat), 97mg chol., 142mg sod., 2g carb. (2g sugars, 0 fiber), 4g pro.

COLORFUL CORNBREAD SALAD

When my garden comes in, I harvest the veggies for potluck dishes. I live in the South, and we think bacon and cornbread make everything better—even salad!
—*Rebecca Clark, Warrior, AL*

Prep: 30 min. + chilling
Bake: 15 min. + cooling
Makes: 14 servings

- 1 pkg. (8½ oz.) cornbread/muffin mix
- 1 cup mayonnaise
- ½ cup sour cream
- 1 envelope ranch salad dressing mix
- 1 to 2 Tbsp. adobo sauce from canned chipotle peppers
- 4 to 6 cups torn romaine
- 4 medium tomatoes, chopped
- 1 medium green pepper, chopped
- 1 medium onion, chopped
- 1 lb. bacon strips, cooked and crumbled
- 4 cups shredded cheddar cheese

1. Preheat oven to 400°. Prepare cornbread batter according to package directions. Pour into a greased 8-in. square baking pan. Bake until a toothpick inserted in center comes out clean, 15-20 minutes. Cool completely in pan on a wire rack.
2. Coarsely crumble cornbread into a large bowl. In a small bowl, mix mayonnaise, sour cream, salad dressing mix and adobo sauce.
3. In a 3-qt. trifle bowl or glass bowl, layer a third of the cornbread and half of each of the following: romaine, tomatoes, pepper, onion, bacon, cheese and the mayonnaise mixture. Repeat layers. Top with remaining cornbread and, if desired, additional chopped tomato and bacon. Refrigerate, covered, 2-4 hours before serving.
¾ cup: 407 cal., 31g fat (11g sat. fat), 61mg chol., 821mg sod., 18g carb. (6g sugars, 2g fiber), 14g pro.

STRAWBERRY COOLER

This refreshing beverage is easy to double. Just make two batches ahead of time, and add ginger ale and ice when you're ready for more!
—*Judy Robertson, Southington, CT*

Takes: 10 min. • **Makes:** 8 servings

- 3 cups water
- 5 cups sliced fresh strawberries
- ¾ to 1 cup sugar
- ¼ cup lemon juice
- 2 tsp. grated lemon zest
- 1 cup ginger ale
  Crushed ice
  Additional strawberries, optional

In a blender, process the water, sliced fresh strawberries, sugar, and lemon juice and zest in batches until smooth. Strain the berry seeds if desired. Pour mixture into a pitcher; stir in the ginger ale. Serve in chilled glasses over ice. If desired, garnish with strawberries.
1 cup: 116 cal., 0 fat (0 sat. fat), 0 chol., 3mg sod., 29g carb. (26g sugars, 2g fiber), 1g pro.

TANGIER ISLAND VIRGINIA CRAB CAKES

I grew up eating these crab cakes, which are crisp on the outside and tender on the inside. They're absolutely delicious every time!
—*Ann Girucky, Norfolk, VA*

Prep: 20 min. • **Cook:** 5 min./batch
Makes: 12 crab cakes

- 1 large egg, beaten
- 1 Tbsp. mayonnaise
- 1 tsp. ground mustard
- 1 tsp. seafood seasoning
- 1 tsp. prepared mustard
- 1 tsp. minced fresh parsley
- ½ tsp. salt
- ¼ tsp. pepper
- 1 lb. lump crabmeat, drained
- 2 slices white bread, finely crumbled (about 1½ cups)
- 3 Tbsp. canola oil

1. In a large bowl, mix the first 8 ingredients until blended. Fold in crab until well coated. Gently stir in bread crumbs until well blended. Shape into twelve ½-in.-thick patties.
2. In a large cast-iron or other heavy skillet, heat oil over medium-high heat. Add crab cakes in batches; cook until dark golden brown, 2-3 minutes on each side.
1 crab cake: 90 cal., 5g fat (1g sat. fat), 52mg chol., 407mg sod., 3g carb. (0 sugars, 0 fiber), 8g pro.

SOUTHERN BLACK-EYED PEAS

What's the secret to a good black-eyed pea recipe? The pork! After the first bite, you'll be glad you added this ingredient.
—*Emory Doty, Jasper, GA*

Prep: 20 min. + soaking • **Cook:** 45 min.
Makes: 6 servings

- 1 lb. dried black-eyed peas, sorted and rinsed
- 1 large onion, chopped
- 2 Tbsp. olive oil
- 2 oz. sliced salt pork belly, chopped
- 6 garlic cloves, minced
- 2 bay leaves
- 1 Tbsp. minced fresh thyme or 1 tsp. dried thyme
- ¼ tsp. crushed red pepper flakes
- ¼ tsp. pepper
- 1 carton (32 oz.) reduced-sodium chicken broth
- 2 smoked ham hocks

1. Place the peas in a Dutch oven; add water to cover by 2 in. Bring to a boil; boil peas for 2 minutes. Remove from the heat; cover and let stand for 1 hour. Drain and rinse peas, discarding liquid; set aside.
2. In the same pan, saute onion in oil until tender. Add the pork belly, garlic, bay leaves, thyme, pepper flakes and pepper; cook for 1 minute longer.
3. Add chicken broth, ham hocks and peas; bring to a boil. Reduce the heat; simmer, uncovered, for 35-40 minutes or until the peas are tender, stirring occasionally and adding more water if desired.
4. Discard bay leaves. Remove ham hocks; cool slightly. Remove meat from the bones if desired; finely chop and return to pan. Discard bones. If desired, top with additional minced fresh thyme.
¾ cup: 359 cal., 11g fat (3g sat. fat), 5mg chol., 788mg sod., 48g carb. (9g sugars, 14g fiber), 20g pro.

BACON COLLARD GREENS

Collard greens are a staple vegetable of southern cuisine. This side dish is often made with smoked or salt-cured meats, such as ham hocks, pork or fatback.
—*Marsha Ankeney, Niceville, FL*

Prep: 25 min. • **Cook:** 55 min.
Makes: 9 servings

- 2 lbs. collard greens
- 4 thick-sliced bacon strips, chopped
- 1 cup chopped sweet onion
- 5 cups reduced-sodium chicken broth
- 1 cup sun-dried tomatoes (not packed in oil), chopped
- ½ tsp. garlic powder
- ¼ tsp. salt
- ¼ tsp. crushed red pepper flakes

1. Trim thick stems from the collard greens; coarsely chop leaves. In a Dutch oven, saute bacon for 3 minutes. Add onion; cook until onion is tender and bacon is crisp, 8-9 minutes longer. Add greens; cook just until wilted.
2. Stir in remaining ingredients. Bring to a boil. Reduce heat; cover and simmer until greens are tender, 45-50 minutes.
¾ cup: 157 cal., 10g fat (4g sat. fat), 12mg chol., 651mg sod., 11g carb. (4g sugars, 5g fiber), 7g pro.

MARINATED
SWEET POTATO
SALAD

MARINATED SWEET POTATO SALAD

My family has been growing sweet potatoes for over 20 years. This family recipe is a terrific way to serve our favorite vegetable.
—*Tim Jack Edmondson, Vardaman, MS*

Prep: 40 min. + chilling • **Makes:** 12 servings

- 8 medium sweet potatoes (about 4 lbs.)
- 1 cup tarragon vinegar
- ½ cup vegetable oil
- 1 Tbsp. honey
- 2 garlic cloves, minced
- 2 bay leaves
- ½ tsp. salt
- ¼ tsp. pepper
- ¼ tsp. dried oregano
- ¼ tsp. dried thyme
- 1 medium onion, quartered and thinly sliced
- 1 medium green pepper, julienned and cut into 1-in. pieces.

1. Place sweet potatoes in a large saucepan or Dutch oven; cover with water. Bring to a boil. Reduce heat; cover and cook just until tender, 20-23 minutes. Drain; cool slightly and peel.
2. Meanwhile, in a jar with a tight-fitting lid, combine the next 9 ingredients; shake well.
3. Cut potatoes in half lengthwise. In a large bowl, slice potato halves into ¼-in. slices. Add the onion and green pepper. Shake dressing; drizzle over potato mixture and gently toss to coat. Cover and refrigerate for at least 3 hours. Discard bay leaves.
¾ cup: 222 cal., 9g fat (1g sat. fat), 0 chol., 112mg sod., 33g carb. (15g sugars, 4g fiber), 2g pro. **Diabetic exchanges:** 2 starch, 2 fat.

DID YOU KNOW?

Sweet potatoes are a low-calorie, high-fiber food that's packed full of vitamins and minerals. Every cup of baked sweet potato (with the skin on) contains a whopping 769% of the recommended daily value of vitamin A, along with vitamins C and B6, manganese and potassium.

What Is Juneteenth?

Celebrated on June 19, the holiday remembers the emancipation of enslaved people in the United States. Here's a brief history and some tips for how to plan your celebration.

WHAT'S THE HISTORY BEHIND JUNETEENTH?

On June 19, 1865, shortly after the end of the Civil War, Union troops arrived to take control of Galveston, Texas. This is when the remaining enslaved Blacks in Texas finally learned of their freedom, more than two years after the Emancipation Proclamation. The day became a holiday known as Juneteenth, a portmanteau of "June" and "19th."

In 1872, a group of Black ministers and businessmen in Houston, Texas, purchased 10 acres of land and created Emancipation Park for the annual Juneteenth gathering.

Over the years, Juneteenth continued to be celebrated in Texas and spread throughout the South. But the day is becoming increasingly well known across the country, and many state and local governments now recognize Juneteenth as an official holiday.

HOW IS JUNETEENTH CELEBRATED?

To commemorate Emancipation Day, friends and family gather to celebrate the legacy of resilience and acknowledge the ongoing struggle through marches, prayers and other remembrances. During gatherings, participants often picnic with a variety of traditional soul food dishes, one of the nation's most identifiable culinary traditions.

WHAT KIND OF FOOD IS SERVED?

The red trinity—barbecue, watermelon and a red beverage—is at the heart of the meal. But no Juneteenth menu is complete without traditional side dishes and desserts like collard greens, potato salad, cornbread pudding, peach cobbler and banana pudding.

This traditional cooking is an ode to history and heritage. Perhaps no region has had more impact on America's culinary history than the South.

THE BEST BABY BACK RIBS

I marinate racks of ribs before adding my zesty spice rub. Then I grill them to perfection. They always turn out juicy and loaded with flavor.
—*Iola Egle, Bella Vista, AR*

Prep: 10 min. + marinating • **Grill:** 80 min.
Makes: 6 servings

- 2 racks baby back ribs (about 4½ lbs.)
- ¾ cup chicken broth
- ¾ cup soy sauce
- 1 cup sugar, divided
- 6 Tbsp. cider vinegar
- 6 Tbsp. olive oil
- 3 garlic cloves, minced
- 2 tsp. salt
- 1 Tbsp. paprika
- ½ tsp. chili powder
- ½ tsp. pepper
- ¼ tsp. garlic powder
    Dash cayenne pepper
    Barbecue sauce, optional

1. If necessary, remove thin membrane from ribs and discard. Combine broth, soy sauce, ½ cup sugar, vinegar, olive oil and garlic. Place ribs in a shallow baking dish; pour two-thirds of the marinade over the ribs. Turn to coat; refrigerate overnight, turning occasionally. Cover and refrigerate remaining marinade.
2. Drain ribs, discarding marinade. Combine remaining sugar, salt and seasonings; rub over both sides of ribs.
3. Grill the ribs, covered, on an oiled rack over indirect medium heat for 30 minutes on each side.
4. Baste with the reserved marinade, or, if desired, barbecue sauce. Move ribs to direct medium heat and cook 20-40 minutes longer or until pork is tender, turning and basting the ribs occasionally.
1 serving: 647 cal., 41g fat (13g sat. fat), 123mg chol., 2345mg sod., 30g carb. (29g sugars, 1g fiber), 37g pro.

SMOKED BRISKET

This is always a crowd favorite—it melts in your mouth! Make sure to prep the brisket at least one day in advance of serving.
—*Jodi Abel, La Jolla, CA*

Prep: 20 min. + marinating
Grill: 8 hours + standing
Makes: 20 servings

- 2 Tbsp. olive oil
- 1 fresh beef brisket (7 to 8 lbs.), flat cut

RUB
- 2 Tbsp. garlic powder
- 2 Tbsp. onion powder
- 2 Tbsp. chili powder
- 1 Tbsp. ground mustard
- 1 Tbsp. ground cumin
- 1 Tbsp. paprika
- 1 Tbsp. smoked sea salt

MOP SAUCE
- 2 cups beef broth
- ¼ cup olive oil
- 2 Tbsp. Worcestershire sauce
- 2 Tbsp. hickory-flavored liquid smoke

1. Brush olive oil over brisket. Combine rub ingredients; rub over both sides of beef. Place the brisket on a rimmed baking sheet. Cover and refrigerate overnight or up to 2 days. Meanwhile, in a small saucepan, combine the mop sauce ingredients. Simmer 15 minutes, stirring occasionally. Refrigerate until ready to grill.
2. Soak hickory and mesquite chips or pellets; add to smoker according to manufacturer's directions. Heat to 225°. Uncover brisket. Place brisket in the smoker fat side up; smoke 2 hours. Brush generously with mop sauce; turn the meat. Smoke 2 more hours; brush generously with mop sauce again. Wrap the brisket securely in heavy-duty aluminum foil; smoke until a thermometer inserted in beef reads 190°, 4-5 more hours.
3. Let beef stand 20-30 minutes before slicing; cut diagonally across the grain into thin slices.
Note: This is a fresh beef brisket, not corned beef.
4 oz. cooked beef: 252 cal., 11g fat (3g sat. fat), 68mg chol., 472mg sod., 2g carb. (0 sugars, 1g fiber), 33g pro. **Diabetic exchanges:** 4 lean meat.

SMOKED BRISKET

LISA'S ALL-DAY SUGAR & SALT PORK ROAST

My family loves this tender and juicy roast, so we eat it a lot. The salty crust is so delicious mixed into the pulled pork.
—*Lisa Allen, Joppa, AL*

Prep: 15 min. + marinating • **Cook:** 6¼ hours
Makes: 12 servings

- 1 cup plus 1 Tbsp. sea salt, divided
- 1 cup sugar
- 1 bone-in pork shoulder butt roast (6 to 8 lbs.)
- ¼ cup barbecue seasoning
- ½ tsp. pepper
- ½ cup packed brown sugar
- 12 hamburger buns or kaiser rolls, split

1. Combine 1 cup sea salt and granulated sugar; rub onto all sides of roast. Place in a shallow dish; refrigerate, covered, overnight.
2. Preheat oven to 300°. Using a kitchen knife, scrape the salt and sugar coating from roast; discard any accumulated juices. Transfer pork to a large shallow roasting pan. Rub with the barbecue seasoning; sprinkle with pepper. Roast until tender, 6-8 hours.
3. Increase oven temperature to 500°. Combine brown sugar and 1 Tbsp. sea salt; sprinkle over cooked pork. Return pork to oven and roast 10-15 minutes or until a crisp crust forms. Remove; when cool enough to handle, shred meat with 2 forks. Serve warm on fresh buns or rolls.

Freeze option: Freeze cooled meat with some of the juices in freezer containers. To use, partially thaw in refrigerator overnight. Heat through in a saucepan, stirring occasionally; add water if necessary.

1 sandwich: 534 cal., 24g fat (9g sat. fat), 135mg chol., 2240mg sod., 33g carb. (14g sugars, 1g fiber), 43g pro.

PEACH UPSIDE-DOWN
CHEESECAKE

PEACH UPSIDE-DOWN CHEESECAKE

I make this every summer when peaches are ripe. Each year I improve it with a few slight tweaks. This version is the best one yet.
—*Kristin Renee Olbert, Richmond, VA*

Prep: 30 min. • **Bake:** 65 min. + chilling
Makes: 16 servings

- ¼ cup butter, melted
- ½ cup packed brown sugar
- 3 medium peaches, divided
- 3 pkg. (8 oz. each) cream cheese, softened
- 1 cup sugar
- 1 cup sour cream
- 1 tsp. vanilla extract
- 4 large eggs, room temperature, lightly beaten

1. Preheat oven to 350°. Line the bottom and sides of a 9-in. round baking pan with parchment. Pour butter into prepared pan; sprinkle with brown sugar. Slice 2 peaches and arrange in a single layer over brown sugar.
2. In a large bowl, beat cream cheese and sugar until smooth. Beat in sour cream and vanilla. Add eggs; beat on low speed just until blended. Chop remaining peach; fold into batter. Spoon over peach slices. Place cake pan in a larger baking pan; add 1 in. of hot water to larger pan.
3. Bake until center is just set and top appears dull, 65-75 minutes. Remove the cake pan from the water bath. Cool cheesecake on a wire rack 10 minutes. Loosen sides from pan with a knife. Cool 1 hour longer. Refrigerate overnight, covering when completely cooled. Invert onto a serving plate.
1 piece: 309 cal., 22g fat (13g sat. fat), 101mg chol., 181mg sod., 25g carb. (24g sugars, 0 fiber), 5g pro.

TEST KITCHEN TIP

To make slicing easier, run warm water over a thin, sharp knife, dry and immediately slice. Then, wipe off excess cheesecake and repeat.

If you want to pre-slice the entire cheesecake, take parchment and fold it in half so it is the same height as the cheesecake. Place your knife inside of the fold and using the knife, press the paper into each cut.

RED VELVET POUND CAKE

This delicious red velvet pound cake is the perfect combination of flavors. Make sure the cake has cooled before icing it. For extra crunch, sprinkle some roasted pecans on top.
—*Robin Smith, Old Fort, NC*

Prep: 30 min. • **Bake:** 70 min. + cooling
Makes: 16 servings

- 1 cup butter, softened
- ½ cup shortening
- 3 cups sugar
- 6 large eggs, room temperature
- 2 bottles (1 oz. each) red food coloring
- 1 tsp. lemon extract
- 1 tsp. vanilla extract
- 3¼ cups all-purpose flour
- 1 Tbsp. baking cocoa
- ½ tsp. baking powder
- ½ tsp. salt
- ¾ cup 2% milk

ICING
- 1 pkg. (8 oz.) cream cheese, softened
- ¼ cup butter or margarine, softened
- ½ tsp. vanilla extract
- 3¾ cups confectioners' sugar
- ½ cup chopped pecans, toasted

1. Preheat oven to 325°. Grease and flour a 10-in. fluted tube pan.
2. In a large bowl, cream butter, shortening and sugar until light and fluffy, 5-7 minutes. Add eggs, 1 at a time, beating well after each addition. Beat in food coloring and extracts (mixture may appear curdled). In another bowl, whisk the flour, baking cocoa, baking powder and salt; add to creamed mixture alternately with milk, beating after each addition just until combined.
3. Transfer to prepared pan. Bake until a toothpick inserted in center comes out clean, 70-75 minutes. Cool in pan 15 minutes before removing to a wire rack to cool completely.
4. For icing, in a large bowl, beat the cream cheese and butter until creamy. Beat in vanilla. Gradually beat in confectioners' sugar until smooth. Spread over cake; sprinkle with pecans. Store in refrigerator.
1 piece: 639 cal., 30g fat (14g sat. fat), 123mg chol., 281mg sod., 87g carb. (67g sugars, 1g fiber), 7g pro.

PECAN PIE COBBLER

I had an idea for a dessert in my head, but couldn't find a recipe. So I got creative and devised this recipe that combines the ease of a cobbler and the rich taste of pecan pie. It tastes even better with ice cream or freshly whipped cream.
—*Willa Kelley, Edmond, OK*

Prep: 20 min. • **Bake:** 30 min. + cooling
Makes: 12 servings

- ½ cup butter, cubed
- 1 cup plus 2 Tbsp. all-purpose flour
- ¾ cup sugar
- 3 tsp. baking powder
- ¼ tsp. salt
- ⅔ cup 2% milk
- 1 tsp. vanilla extract
- 1½ cups coarsely chopped pecans
- 1 cup packed brown sugar
- ¾ cup brickle toffee bits
- 1½ cups boiling water
  Vanilla ice cream, optional

1. Preheat oven to 350°. Place butter in a 13x9-in. baking pan; heat pan in oven until butter is melted, 3-5 minutes. Meanwhile, combine the flour, sugar, baking powder and salt. Stir in milk and vanilla until combined.
2. Remove baking pan from oven; add batter. Sprinkle with pecans, brown sugar and toffee bits. Slowly pour boiling water over top (do not stir). Bake, uncovered, until golden brown, 30-35 minutes. Cool on wire rack for 30 minutes (cobbler will thicken upon cooling). Serve cobbler warm, with ice cream if desired.
1 serving: 411 cal., 23g fat (8g sat. fat), 26mg chol., 327mg sod., 51g carb. (41g sugars, 2g fiber), 3g pro.

FIREWORKS-WATCHING PARTY

Get ready for a sky-high celebration! Grab your favorite blanket and a basket or cooler packed with these patriotic treats. This festive, fun spread is so good you just might forget to look up after the sun goes down.

SUMMER FRESH PASTA SALAD

I made this fast and easy salad for dinner while preparing lunch. We love it best with fresh fruits and veggies that are in season. I serve this salad with almond crackers and sharp cheddar slices. So tasty!
—*Cathy Orban, Chandler, AZ*

Prep: 20 min. + chilling • **Makes:** 12 servings

- 4 cups uncooked campanelle or spiral pasta
- 2 medium carrots, finely chopped
- 2 medium peaches, chopped
- 1 pouch (11 oz.) light tuna in water
- ½ cup sliced celery
- ½ cup julienned cucumber
- ½ cup julienned zucchini
- ½ cup fresh broccoli florets, chopped
- ½ cup grated red cabbage
- ½ tsp. salt
- ½ tsp. pepper
- 2 cups Caesar salad dressing

Cook pasta according to package directions for al dente. Drain; rinse with cold water and drain well. Transfer to a large bowl. Add the carrots, peaches, tuna, celery, cucumber, zucchini, broccoli, cabbage, salt and pepper. Drizzle salad with dressing and toss to coat. Refrigerate salad, covered, at least 3 hours before serving.

¾ cup: 357 cal., 23g fat (4g sat. fat), 25mg chol., 651mg sod., 26g carb. (5g sugars, 2g fiber), 10g pro.

SUMMER FRESH PASTA SALAD

LAYERED AVOCADO BEAN DIP

I grew up in Northern California and miss the flavors from home. I created this dip that combines some of my favorite ingredients—avocados, artichokes and almonds. I serve the dip with sourdough bread, another California favorite, but it works well with pita chips or tortilla chips, too.
—*Elisabeth Larsen, Pleasant Grove, UT*

Takes: 15 min.
Makes: 16 servings

- 1 can (15 oz.) cannellini or great northern beans, rinsed and drained
- 2 Tbsp. olive oil
- 2 Tbsp. lemon juice
- ¼ tsp. pepper
- ½ tsp. salt, divided
- 3 medium ripe avocados, peeled
- ½ cup marinated quartered artichoke hearts, chopped
- ½ cup shredded Monterey Jack cheese
- ½ cup julienned soft sun-dried tomatoes (not packed in oil), chopped
- ¼ cup sliced ripe olives
- ¼ cup sliced almonds, toasted
  Sourdough baguette slices, toasted, or baked pita chips

1. Place beans, oil, lemon juice, pepper and ¼ tsp. salt in a food processor; process until creamy. Spread onto the bottom of a 9-in. pie plate.
2. In a large bowl, mash the avocados with remaining salt; spread over bean mixture. Layer with the artichoke hearts, cheese, tomatoes, olives and almonds. Serve with baguette slices.

¼ cup: 125 cal., 9g fat (2g sat. fat), 3mg chol., 240mg sod., 9g carb. (2g sugars, 4g fiber), 3g pro.

> ### TEST KITCHEN TIP
>
> The recipe for this bean dip was tested with sun-dried tomatoes that can be used without soaking. When using sun-dried tomatoes that are not oil-packed, cover with boiling water and let stand until soft. Drain before using.

CHEESE-STUFFED CHERRY TOMATOES
(PICTURED ON COVER)

We grow plenty of tomatoes, so my husband and I often handpick enough cherry tomatoes for these easy-to-fix appetizers. This is one of our favorite recipes, and it's impossible to eat just one.
—*Mary Lou Robison, Greensboro, NC*

Prep: 15 min. + chilling • **Makes:** 1 dozen

- 1 pint cherry tomatoes
- 1 pkg. (4 oz.) crumbled feta cheese
- ½ cup finely chopped red onion
- ½ cup olive oil
- ¼ cup red wine vinegar
- 1 Tbsp. dried oregano
  Salt and pepper to taste

1. Cut a thin slice off the top of each tomato. Scoop out and discard pulp. Invert tomatoes onto paper towels to drain. Combine cheese and onion; spoon into tomatoes.
2. In a small bowl, whisk oil, vinegar, oregano, salt and pepper. Spoon over tomatoes. Cover and refrigerate for 30 minutes or until ready to serve.

1 tomato: 111 cal., 11g fat (2g sat. fat), 5mg chol., 93mg sod., 2g carb. (1g sugars, 1g fiber), 2g pro.

DILLY CHICKPEA SALAD SANDWICHES

CHERRY RIBBON SALAD

Filled with pineapple, pecans and cherry pie filling, this colorful salad mold adds fun, fruity flavor to any potluck menu.
—*Virginia Luke, Red Level, AL*

- -

Prep: 10 min. + chilling • **Makes:** 12 servings

1	pkg. (3 oz.) cherry gelatin
2¼	cups boiling water, divided
1	can (21 oz.) cherry pie filling
1	pkg. (3 oz.) orange gelatin
1	can (8 oz.) crushed pineapple, undrained
1	cup whipped topping
⅓	cup mayonnaise
¼	cup chopped pecans, optional

1. In a large bowl, dissolve cherry gelatin in 1¼ cups boiling water. Stir in pie filling. Pour into a 7-cup ring mold coated with cooking spray; refrigerate for about 1 hour or until thickened but not set.

2. In a large bowl, dissolve orange gelatin in remaining boiling water. Stir in pineapple. Chill gelatin for about 1 hour or until thickened but not set.

3. Combine the whipped topping, mayonnaise and, if desired, pecans; fold into the orange mixture. Spoon over cherry layer. Refrigerate for at least 1 hour or until firm. Unmold onto a serving plate.

1 piece: 184 cal., 6g fat (2g sat. fat), 2mg chol., 75mg sod., 31g carb. (28g sugars, 0 fiber), 2g pro.

DILLY CHICKPEA SALAD SANDWICHES

This chickpea salad is super flavorful and contains less fat and cholesterol than chicken salad. These sandwiches are great for picnics, potlucks or any outdoor gathering.
—*Deanna Wolfe, Muskegon, MI*

- -

Takes: 15 min. • **Makes:** 6 servings

1	can (15 oz.) chickpeas or garbanzo beans, rinsed and drained
½	cup finely chopped onion
½	cup finely chopped celery
½	cup reduced-fat mayonnaise or vegan mayonnaise
3	Tbsp. honey mustard or Dijon mustard
2	Tbsp. snipped fresh dill
1	Tbsp. red wine vinegar
¼	tsp. salt
¼	tsp. paprika
¼	tsp. pepper
12	slices multigrain bread
	Optional: Romaine leaves, tomato slices, dill pickle slices and sweet red pepper rings

Place chickpeas in a large bowl; mash to desired consistency. Stir in onion, celery, mayonnaise, mustard, dill, vinegar, salt, paprika and pepper. Spread over each of 6 bread slices; layer with toppings of your choice and remaining bread.

1 sandwich: 295 cal., 11g fat (2g sat. fat), 7mg chol., 586mg sod., 41g carb. (9g sugars, 7g fiber), 10g pro.

Let the Fun Times Ring!

To pass time until the main event, line up bottles (full or empty) of your favorite sipper in a wooden crate, and get to tossing! Mason jar rings wrapped with yarn are an easy craft—and perfect for making soft landings. Fire away!

CHOCOLATE CHIP
ZUCCHINI COOKIES

Bowl Covers

WHAT YOU'LL NEED
- ☐ 3 cotton bandannas
- ☐ Iron-on vinyl sheet
- ☐ 3 yd. extra-wide double-fold bias tape in coordinating color
- ☐ 9-ft. 3mm elastic cord
- ☐ Scissors
- ☐ Iron
- ☐ Straight pins
- ☐ Large blunt needle

DIRECTIONS
1. Wash and dry bandannas.
2. Cut a circle from each bandanna to a diameter to fit desired bowls—standard sizes are 11-, 13- and 15-in.
3. Cut a coordinating piece of iron-on vinyl for each circle and apply it to 1 side of each circle according to the manufacturer's instructions.
4. Fold bias tape around outer edge of circle, overlapping ends 1 in. Pin in place. Topstitch bias tape around the circle, leaving a 1½-in. opening to insert elastic.
5. Cut a length of elastic 2 in. longer than the circumference of the circle. Insert elastic through bias tape, using blunt needle, carefully working elastic around the circle. Cinch elastic to fit bowl and tie ends together in a secure square knot. Stitch opening closed.
6. Repeat the process with remaining 2 bandanna circles.
7. To clean bowl covers, wipe with a damp cloth or hand-wash in cold water and hang to dry.

CHOCOLATE CHIP ZUCCHINI COOKIES

I love cooking and baking with zucchini in the summertime. Unfortunately my garden did not produce any—but my neighbor's garden did! These remind me of a zucchini bread my aunt makes, but I wanted to make cookies for a family get-together because they would be easier to grab and eat. These taste better if you make them the day before.
—*Melissa Obernesser, Oriskany, NY*

Prep: 15 min. • **Bake:** 12 min./batch + cooling
Makes: 4 dozen

- ½ cup unsalted butter, softened
- ½ cup sugar
- ⅓ cup packed brown sugar
- 1 large egg, room temperature
- 1½ tsp. vanilla extract
- 1 cup all-purpose flour
- ½ cup whole wheat flour
- 1 tsp. ground cinnamon
- ½ tsp. baking soda
- ¼ tsp. salt
- 1½ cups shredded zucchini
- 1 cup quick-cooking oats
- 1 cup semisweet chocolate chips
- ¾ cup chopped pecans, toasted

1. Preheat the oven to 350°. In a large bowl, cream butter and sugars until light and fluffy, 5-7 minutes. Beat in the egg and vanilla. In another bowl, whisk flours, cinnamon, baking soda and salt; gradually beat into creamed mixture. Stir in remaining ingredients.
2. Drop dough by tablespoonfuls 2 in. apart onto greased baking sheets. Bake until edges start to brown, 12-14 minutes. Cool on pans 2 minutes. Remove to wire racks to cool. Store between pieces of waxed paper in an airtight container.

1 cookie: 79 cal., 4g fat (2g sat. fat), 9mg chol., 27mg sod., 10g carb. (6g sugars, 1g fiber), 1g pro.

RHUBARB BERRY BARS

Our calendar always fills up fast with potlucks and picnics to see family and friends, and this is a dessert they look forward to every year. If you're lucky enough to have one or two left, try warming up a piece in the microwave and topping it with vanilla ice cream.
—*Jennifer Pelzel, Spring Valley, WI*

Prep: 30 min. • **Bake:** 30 min. + cooling
Makes: 1½ dozen

- 1½ cups all-purpose flour
- 1½ cups quick-cooking oats
- ½ cup packed brown sugar
- 1 tsp. ground cinnamon
- ½ tsp. baking soda
- ½ tsp. salt
- ¾ cup butter, melted

FILLING
- 3 cups diced fresh or frozen rhubarb
- 1½ cups sugar
- ¼ cup water
- 3 Tbsp. cornstarch
- 1½ cups fresh or frozen unsweetened raspberries, thawed
- 1 tsp. vanilla extract

1. Preheat oven to 375°. Combine the first 6 ingredients in a large bowl. Add butter; mix well. Set aside 1 cup for topping; press the remaining crumb mixture onto the bottom of a greased 13x9-in. baking pan. Bake until crust is lightly browned, about 10 minutes.
2. Combine the diced rhubarb, sugar, water and cornstarch in a large saucepan. Bring to a boil; cook and stir until the sauce is thickened, 3-5 minutes.
3. Remove from the heat; stir in raspberries and vanilla. Cool slightly. Spread filling over crust; sprinkle with reserved crumb mixture.
4. Bake until golden brown, 30-35 minutes. Cool on a wire rack. Cut into bars.
1 bar: 235 cal., 8g fat (5g sat. fat), 20mg chol., 165mg sod., 39g carb. (24g sugars, 2g fiber), 2g pro.

WATERMELON & BLACKBERRY SANGRIA

This recipe is deliciously pink! Living in the zinfandel wine country of Northern California's Gold Country, I use our local fare in my recipes often. Our scorching summer months of July and August inspired this refreshing, light style of sangria. I garnish it with sprigs of mint or basil for personal flair. This easy recipe is perfect for entertaining, and it's especially brunch friendly.
—*Carolyn Kumpe, El Dorado, CA*

Prep: 5 min. + chilling • **Makes:** 8 servings

- 1 bottle (750 ml) white zinfandel or rose wine, chilled
- ¼ cup watermelon schnapps liqueur
- 1½ cups cubed seedless watermelon (½-in. cubes)
- 1 medium lime, thinly sliced
- ½ to 1 cup fresh blackberries, halved
- 1 can (12 oz.) lemon-lime soda, chilled
  Ice cubes
  Fresh basil or mint leaves

In a large pitcher, stir together the wine and schnapps; add the watermelon, lime and blackberries. Chill at least 2 hours. Just before serving, stir in soda. Serve over ice. Garnish with basil or mint.
¾ cup: 119 cal., 0 fat (0 sat. fat), 0 chol., 10mg sod., 12g carb. (8g sugars, 1g fiber), 0 pro.

ULTIMATE CLUB
ROLL-UPS

ULTIMATE CLUB ROLL-UPS

Packed with meat, cheese and olives, these roll-ups are always a hit at parties. Experiment with different lunchmeat, shredded cheese and salad dressing flavors.
—*Linda Searl, Pampa, TX*

Takes: 25 min. • **Makes:** 8 servings

- 3 oz. cream cheese, softened
- ½ cup ranch salad dressing
- 2 Tbsp. ranch salad dressing mix
- 8 bacon strips, cooked and crumbled
- ½ cup finely chopped onion
- 1 can (2¼ oz.) sliced ripe olives, drained
- 1 jar (2 oz.) diced pimientos, drained
- ¼ cup diced canned jalapeno peppers
- 8 flour tortillas (10 in.), room temperature
- 8 thin slices deli ham
- 8 thin slices deli turkey
- 8 thin slices deli roast beef
- 2 cups shredded cheddar cheese

1. In a small bowl, beat the cream cheese, ranch dressing and dressing mix until well blended. In another bowl, combine bacon, onion, olives, pimientos and jalapenos.
2. Spread cream cheese mixture over tortillas; layer with the deli ham, turkey and roast beef. Sprinkle with the bacon mixture and cheddar cheese; roll up.
1 roll-up: 554 cal., 29g fat (12g sat. fat), 80mg chol., 1802mg sod., 39g carb. (2g sugars, 7g fiber), 27g pro.

Utensil Holder

A convenient carrier corrals napkins and utensils when you're on the go. Pop in a mini flag for some extra fun!

Flag Wall Hanging

WHAT YOU'LL NEED
- ☐ Four 22-in.-sq. red bandannas
- ☐ Three 22-in.-sq. white bandannas
- ☐ One 22-in.-sq. blue bandanna
- ☐ Coordinating thread
- ☐ 26-in. dowel rod
- ☐ Twine
- ☐ 13 star-shaped lapel pins
- ☐ Scissors
- ☐ Sewing machine
- ☐ Straight pins
- ☐ Iron

DIRECTIONS
1. Wash and dry bandannas.
2. Cut red and white bandannas into 5-in.-wide strips. Sew 2 red strips together at short end. Repeat with remaining red pieces for 7 long red strips. Repeat with white pieces for 6 long strips.
3. Fold 1½ in. of raw edge of each strip to back and press in place, leaving 2-in.-wide strip.
4. Fold 3 in. of each strip over the dowel rod and pin in place with the straight pins, alternating red and white stripes.
5. Fold blue bandanna to match width of 7 stripes (approximately 14 in.). Fold over dowel, covering left 7 stripes and adjusting to desired length. Secure with straight pins.
6. Cut 30 in. of twine and tie around ends of dowel to hang.
7. Once hanging, insert star-shaped pins at the top of each stripe to secure. Remove straight pins.

PEANUT BUTTER CUPCAKES

Peanut butter lovers can double their pleasure with these tender treats. I use the popular ingredient in the cupcakes as well as in the creamy homemade frosting.
—*Ruth Hutson, Westfield, IN*

Prep: 20 min. • **Bake:** 20 min. + cooling
Makes: about 1½ dozen

- ⅓ cup butter, softened
- ½ cup peanut butter
- 1¼ cups packed brown sugar
- 1 large egg, room temperature
- 1 tsp. vanilla extract
- 2 cups all-purpose flour
- ½ tsp. salt
- ½ tsp. baking powder
- ½ tsp. baking soda
- ¼ tsp. ground cinnamon
- ¾ cup 2% milk

FROSTING
- ⅓ cup peanut butter
- 2 cups confectioners' sugar
- 2 tsp. honey
- 1 tsp. vanilla extract
- 3 to 4 Tbsp. 2% milk

1. Preheat the oven to 350°. In a large bowl, cream the butter, peanut butter and brown sugar until light and fluffy, 5-7 minutes. Beat in egg and vanilla. Combine the dry ingredients; add to creamed mixture alternately with milk, beating well after each addition.
2. Fill paper-lined muffin cups two-thirds full. Bake at 350° for 18-22 minutes or until a toothpick inserted in the center comes out clean. Cool for 10 minutes before removing from pans to wire racks to cool completely.
3. For frosting, in a small bowl, cream peanut butter and sugar 5-7 minutes or until light and fluffy. Beat in the honey and vanilla. Beat in enough milk to reach a spreading consistency. Frost cupcakes.
Note: Reduced-fat peanut butter is not recommended for this recipe.
1 cupcake: 276 cal., 10g fat (4g sat. fat), 20mg chol., 206mg sod., 43g carb. (31g sugars, 1g fiber), 5g pro.

CHOCOLATE-COVERED STRAWBERRY SNACK MIX

I love chocolate-covered strawberries but reserve them for special occasions. With a little experimenting, I captured the same flavor in a treat I can take anywhere. This snack mix is great for picnics, tailgates or road trips. A dash of patriotic sprinkles makes it feel festive for the Fourth of July.
—*TerryAnn Moore, Vineland, NJ*

Prep: 15 min. + standing • **Makes:** 2 qt.

- 6 cups Rice Chex
- 2 cups Chocolate Chex
- 1 cup semisweet chocolate chips
- ½ cup seedless strawberry jam
- 3 Tbsp. butter
- 1 tsp. almond extract
- 2 cups ground almonds
- 1 cup white baking chips
  Sprinkles, optional

1. In a large bowl, combine the cereals. In a microwave, melt the chocolate chips, jam and butter; stir until smooth. Add extract. Pour over cereal mixture and toss to coat. Sprinkle with almonds; toss to coat.
2. Immediately spread onto waxed paper. In a microwave, melt white chips; stir until smooth. Drizzle over the cereal mixture. If desired, add sprinkles. Let stand until set. Break into pieces. Store snack mix in an airtight container.
¾ cup: 443 cal., 24g fat (9g sat. fat), 11mg chol., 231mg sod., 55g carb. (33g sugars, 3g fiber), 7g pro.

TEST KITCHEN TIP

It's easy to overcook chocolate in a microwave. (This is truer still for white chocolate.) When exposed to too much heat too fast, chocolate gets an icky, grainy texture—or worse, it can burn entirely. When melting chocolate, cook in 30-second increments and stir frequently to keep any sections (often along the edges of the bowl) from overheating. And because each microwave behaves differently, keep a careful eye on your chocolate.

CHOCOLATE-COVERED
STRAWBERRY SNACK MIX

COPYCAT STREET FOODS

Food trucks, pushcarts and even the back of a bicycle—these mobile food wagons have folks lining up for decadent grab-and-go fare. Now you no longer have to take to the streets to savor these culinary wonders. Whether you're hungry for global comfort food or a classic corn dog, make your favorites right at home.

Corn Dogs (p. 207)

SOUVLAKI PITA POCKETS

This is a favorite at our house, especially in summer. A quick trip to the market for a few ingredients results in gourmet-style Greek sandwiches we often enjoy outdoors. A simple Greek salad on the side is a nice addition.
—*Becky Drees, Pittsfield, MA*

Prep: 20 min. + marinating • **Grill:** 10 min.
Makes: 6 servings

- 4 medium lemons, divided
- 4 Tbsp. olive oil
- 4 garlic cloves, minced
- 2 tsp. dried oregano
- ½ tsp. salt
- ¼ tsp. pepper
- 2 lbs. boneless skinless chicken breasts, cut into 1-in. pieces
- 12 pita pocket halves
- 1 carton (8 oz.) refrigerated tzatziki sauce
  Optional toppings: Chopped tomatoes, sliced cucumber and sliced red onion

1. Cut 3 lemons crosswise in half; squeeze juice from lemons. Transfer to a large bowl or shallow dish. Whisk in oil, garlic, oregano, salt and pepper. Add chicken; turn to coat. Refrigerate 1 hour.
2. Drain chicken, discarding marinade. Thinly slice remaining lemon. On 6 metal or soaked wooden skewers, alternately thread chicken and lemon slices. Grill kabobs, covered, over medium heat or broil 4 in. from heat until chicken is no longer pink, turning occasionally. Remove chicken from kabobs; discard lemon slices. Serve chicken in pita pockets with tzatziki sauce and desired toppings.
2 filled pita halves: 369 cal., 8g fat (2g sat. fat), 90mg chol., 462mg sod., 34g carb. (2g sugars, 1g fiber), 37g pro. **Diabetic exchanges:** 5 lean meat, 2 starch, 1 fat.

CORN DOGS
(PICTURED ON PAGE 205)
It's easy to make homemade corn dogs that taste just like those sold at carnivals, fairs and on food trucks.
—*Ruby Williams, Bogalusa, LA*

Takes: 25 min. • **Makes:** 10 servings

- ¾ cup yellow cornmeal
- ¾ cup self-rising flour
- 1 large egg, lightly beaten
- ⅔ cup 2% milk
- 10 pop sticks
- 10 hot dogs
  Oil for deep-fat frying

1. In a large bowl, combine cornmeal, flour and egg. Stir in milk to make a thick batter; let stand 4 minutes. Insert sticks into hot dogs; dip into batter.
2. In an electric skillet or deep-fat fryer, heat oil to 375°. Fry the corn dogs, a few at a time, until golden brown, 6-8 minutes, turning occasionally. Drain on paper towels.
1 corn dog: 316 cal., 23g fat (7g sat. fat), 45mg chol., 588mg sod., 18g carb. (2g sugars, 1g fiber), 8g pro.
Note: To help the batter stick to the hot dog, make sure the dogs are thoroughly dry before dipping them. The batter won't adhere to any part that's wet.

GREEN CHILE ADOBADO POUTINE

A Canadian comfort-food classic is even better when served southwestern-style, as either an appetizer or an entree. Although the ribs are done here without fuss in a slow cooker, you can also bake them at 325°, covered with foil, about 45 minutes. Then uncover and bake for another 20 minutes.
—*Johnna Johnson, Scottsdale, AZ*

Prep: 50 min. • **Cook:** 3 hours
Makes: 8 servings

- 3 garlic cloves, unpeeled
- 4 dried guajillo or ancho chiles, stemmed and seeded
- 1 can (10 oz.) enchilada sauce, divided
- 3 cans (4 oz. each) chopped green chiles, divided
- 1 Tbsp. cider vinegar
- 2 tsp. dried oregano
- ½ tsp. ground cumin
- ½ tsp. salt
- ½ tsp. pepper
- ⅛ tsp. ground cinnamon
- 2 lbs. boneless country-style pork ribs, cut into 2-in. pieces
- 1 pkg. (32 oz.) frozen french-fried potatoes
- 1 cup queso fresco
  Pico de gallo, optional

1. Lightly smash garlic cloves with the bottom of a heavy skillet to flatten. Cook in a large skillet over medium-low heat until garlic is softened and browned, about 10 minutes. Cool and peel.
2. In same skillet at the same time, cook dried chiles, pressing them against the bottom with a spatula or tongs until lightly toasted and fragrant, 1-2 minutes. Transfer to a bowl. Pour boiling water over chilies to cover; let stand 15 minutes. Drain.

3. Place chiles and garlic in a food processor. Add ½ cup enchilada sauce, 2 cans green chiles, vinegar, oregano, cumin, salt, pepper and cinnamon; process until blended. Stir in remaining enchilada sauce and green chiles. Transfer to a 5- or 6-qt. slow cooker. Add ribs; turn to coat. Cover and cook on high until meat is tender, 3-4 hours. During the final 30 minutes, cook fries according to package directions.
4. Remove pork; shred with 2 forks. Top fries with meat, queso fresco, enchilada gravy and, if desired, pico de gallo.
1 serving: 434 cal., 19g fat (7g sat. fat), 75mg chol., 1065mg sod., 31g carb. (2g sugars, 5g fiber), 28g pro.

TEST KITCHEN TIP

Created in Quebec, Canada, in the 1950s, poutine is a decadent concoction of crispy french fries and white cheese curds smothered in hot gravy. To enjoy this specialty in its most authentic form, use room temperature cheese curds and make sure the gravy is hot so the cheese will melt while still maintaining its shape. Over the years, many fun twists and toppings have been incorporated in this dish. You can add sauteed mushrooms, crumbled bacon, pulled pork, lobster, smoked meats, scallions or other toppings to make it your own.

**JALAPENO POPPER
MEXICAN STREET CORN**

FALAFEL CHICKEN BURGERS WITH LEMON SAUCE

Falafel burgers with a lemon yogurt sauce mark the first recipe I created myself. Use leftover falafel mix to bread fish, chicken and veggies or use in meatballs.
—*Nicole Mederos, Hoboken, NJ*

- -

Prep: 35 min. • **Cook:** 10 min.
Makes: 4 servings

  4 frozen onion rings, optional
SAUCE
  1 carton (5.3 oz.) fat-free lemon
     Greek yogurt
  ¼ tsp. ground cumin
  ¼ tsp. dill weed
  ⅛ tsp. salt
  ⅛ tsp. paprika
BURGERS
  ¼ cup minced fresh parsley
  3 Tbsp. crumbled cooked bacon
  3 garlic cloves, minced
  ¾ tsp. salt
  ¾ tsp. curry powder
  ½ tsp. pepper
  ¼ tsp. ground cumin
  1 lb. ground chicken
  1 pkg. (6 oz.) falafel mix
  4 tsp. canola oil
  4 sesame seed hamburger buns, split
  1 cup fresh arugula or baby spinach
     Sliced tomato and cucumber

JALAPENO POPPER MEXICAN STREET CORN

One of the best things about summer is fresh sweet corn, and this recipe is a definite standout. We love the creamy dressing, crunchy panko coating and spicy jalapeno kick. If you're really feeling wild, sprinkle these with a bit of cooked and crumbled bacon!
—*Crystal Schlueter, Northglenn, CO*

- -

Takes: 30 min. • **Makes:** 4 servings

  4 ears fresh sweet corn
  2 jalapeno peppers
  3 Tbsp. canola oil, divided
  ¾ tsp. salt, divided
  ¼ cup panko bread crumbs
  ½ tsp. smoked paprika
  ½ tsp. dried Mexican oregano
  4 oz. cream cheese, softened
  ¼ cup media crema table cream or sour
     cream thinned with 1 tsp. 2% milk
  2 Tbsp. lime juice
     Ground chipotle pepper or chili
     powder
     Optional: Chopped fresh cilantro and
     lime wedges

1. Husk corn. Rub corn and jalapenos with 2 Tbsp. canola oil. Grill, covered, on a greased grill rack over medium-high direct heat until lightly charred on all sides, 10-12 minutes. Remove from heat. When jalapenos are cool enough to handle, remove skin, seeds and membranes; chop finely. Set aside.
2. Sprinkle corn with ½ tsp. salt. In a small skillet, heat remaining oil over medium heat. Add the panko; cook and stir until starting to brown. Add paprika and oregano; cook until crumbs are toasted and fragrant.
3. Meanwhile, combine cream cheese, crema, lime juice and remaining salt; spread over corn. Sprinkle with bread crumbs, jalapenos and chipotle pepper. If desired, sprinkle with cilantro and serve with lime wedges.
1 ear of corn: 339 cal., 26g fat (9g sat. fat), 39mg chol., 568mg sod., 25g carb. (8g sugars, 3g fiber), 6g pro.

1. If desired, prepare onion rings according to package directions.
2. Meanwhile, in a small bowl, mix sauce ingredients. In a large bowl, mix the first 7 burger ingredients. Add chicken; mix lightly but thoroughly. Shape into four ½-in.-thick patties. Place ½ cup falafel mix in a shallow bowl (save remaining mix for another use). Press patties into falafel mix, patting to help coating adhere.
3. In a large nonstick skillet, heat oil over medium-high heat. Add burgers; cook until a thermometer reads 165°, 4-5 minutes on each side. Serve burgers on buns with sauce and arugula; add sliced tomato, cucumber slices and, if desired, an onion ring to each.
1 burger: 435 cal., 22g fat (5g sat. fat), 86mg chol., 1036mg sod., 33g carb. (9g sugars, 3g fiber), 32g pro.

FALAFEL CHICKEN
BURGERS WITH
LEMON SAUCE

LOADED PULLED PORK CUPS

Potato nests are easy to make and surprisingly handy for pulled pork, cheese, sour cream and other fun toppings. Make, bake and collect the compliments.
—*Melissa Sperka, Greensboro, NC*

Prep: 40 min. • **Bake:** 25 min.
Makes: 1½ dozen

- 1 pkg. (20 oz.) refrigerated shredded hash brown potatoes
- ¾ cup shredded Parmesan cheese
- 2 large egg whites, beaten
- 1 tsp. garlic salt
- ½ tsp. onion powder
- ¼ tsp. pepper
- 1 carton (16 oz.) refrigerated fully cooked barbecued shredded pork
- 1 cup shredded Colby-Monterey Jack cheese
- ½ cup sour cream
- 5 bacon strips, cooked and crumbled
  Minced chives

1. Preheat oven to 450°. In a large bowl, mix hash browns, Parmesan cheese, egg whites and seasonings until blended. Divide potato mixture among 18 well-greased muffin cups; press on the bottoms and up the sides to form cups.
2. Bake until edges are dark golden brown, 22-25 minutes. Carefully run a knife around sides of each cup. Cool 5 minutes before removing from pans to a serving platter. Meanwhile, heat pulled pork according to package directions.
3. Sprinkle cheese into cups. Top with pork, sour cream and bacon; sprinkle with chives. Serve warm.
1 hash brown cup: 129 cal., 6g fat (3g sat. fat), 19mg chol., 439mg sod., 11g carb. (4g sugars, 0 fiber), 8g pro.

DEEP-FRIED COOKIES

My kids love this indulgent treat. I give the batter a kick by adding a pinch of cinnamon and a teaspoon of vanilla extract.
—*Margarita Torres, Bayamon, PR*

Prep: 10 min. + freezing • **Cook:** 15 min.
Makes: 1½ dozen

- 18 Oreo cookies
  Oil for deep-fat frying
- 1 cup biscuit/baking mix
- 1 large egg
- ½ cup 2% milk
  Confectioners' sugar

1. On each of eighteen 4-in. wooden skewers, thread 1 cookie, inserting pointed end of skewer into filling. Freeze until firm, about 1 hour.
2. In a deep cast-iron skillet or deep fryer, heat oil to 375°. Place biscuit mix in a shallow bowl. In another bowl, combine egg and milk; whisk into biscuit mix just until moistened.
3. Holding skewer, dip cookie into biscuit mixture to coat both sides; shake off excess.
4. Fry cookies, a few at a time, until golden brown, 1-2 minutes on each side. Drain on paper towels. Dust with confectioners' sugar before serving.
1 cookie: 100 cal., 5g fat (1g sat. fat), 11mg chol., 123mg sod., 13g carb. (5g sugars, 1g fiber), 1g pro.

FUNNEL CAKES

FUNNEL CAKES

These funnel cakes are easier to make than doughnuts, and they're just as good. Funnel cakes have been a favorite of ours since we first tried them while living in the Ozarks.
—*Mary Faith Yoder, Unity, WI*

Prep: 15 min. • **Cook:** 5 min./batch
Makes: 8 funnel cakes

- 2   large eggs, room temperature
- 1   cup 2% milk
- 1   cup water
- ½   tsp. vanilla extract
- 3   cups all-purpose flour
- ¼   cup sugar
- 3   tsp. baking powder
- ¼   tsp. salt
     Oil for deep-fat frying
     Confectioners' sugar

1. In a large bowl, beat eggs. Add milk, water and vanilla until well blended. In another bowl, whisk flour, sugar, baking powder and salt; beat into egg mixture until smooth. In a deep cast-iron or electric skillet, heat oil to 375°.
2. Cover the bottom of a funnel spout with your finger; ladle ½ cup batter into the funnel. Holding the funnel several inches above the oil, release your finger and move the funnel in a spiral motion until all the batter is released, scraping with a rubber spatula if needed.
3. Fry until golden brown, 2 minutes on each side. Drain on paper towels. Dust cakes with confectioners' sugar; serve warm.
1 funnel cake: 316 cal., 12g fat (2g sat. fat), 50mg chol., 256mg sod., 44g carb. (8g sugars, 1g fiber), 7g pro.

← Funnel cakes are delicious with just powdered sugar, or go all out with tons of toppings. Go for a sundae feel with chocolate syrup, chopped peanuts, cherries and whipped cream. If you add some cinnamon and sugar while warm, you'll get a fun twist on homemade churros.

CHICKEN SKEWERS WITH COOL AVOCADO SAUCE

I'm always looking for lighter recipes to take on tailgate outings—and this chicken is great for grilling. You can whip up the sauce ahead of time. It's so easy to pack it all in a cooler and tote to the pregame festivities.
—*Veronica Callaghan, Glastonbury, CT*

Prep: 25 min. + marinating • **Grill:** 10 min.
Makes: 16 skewers (¾ cup sauce)

- 1 lb. boneless skinless chicken breasts
- ½ cup lime juice
- 1 Tbsp. balsamic vinegar
- 2 tsp. minced chipotle pepper in adobo sauce
- ½ tsp. salt

SAUCE
- 1 medium ripe avocado, peeled and pitted
- ½ cup fat-free sour cream
- 2 Tbsp. minced fresh cilantro
- 2 tsp. lime juice
- 1 tsp. grated lime zest
- ¼ tsp. salt

1. Flatten chicken to ¼-in. thickness; cut lengthwise into sixteen 1-in.-wide strips. In a large bowl, combine the lime juice, vinegar, chipotle pepper and salt; add the chicken to the marinade and turn to evenly coat. Cover and refrigerate for 30 minutes.
2. Meanwhile, for the sauce, place remaining ingredients in a food processor; cover and process until blended. Transfer to a serving bowl; cover and refrigerate until serving.
3. Drain the chicken, discarding marinade. Thread meat onto 4 metal or soaked wooden skewers. On a lightly oiled rack, grill skewers, covered, over medium heat or broil 4 in. from the heat for 8-12 minutes or until no longer pink, turning frequently. Serve with sauce.
1 skewer with about 2 tsp. sauce: 59 cal., 3g fat (0 sat. fat), 17mg chol., 74mg sod., 3g carb. (1g sugars, 1g fiber), 6g pro. **Diabetic exchanges:** 1 lean meat, ½ fat.

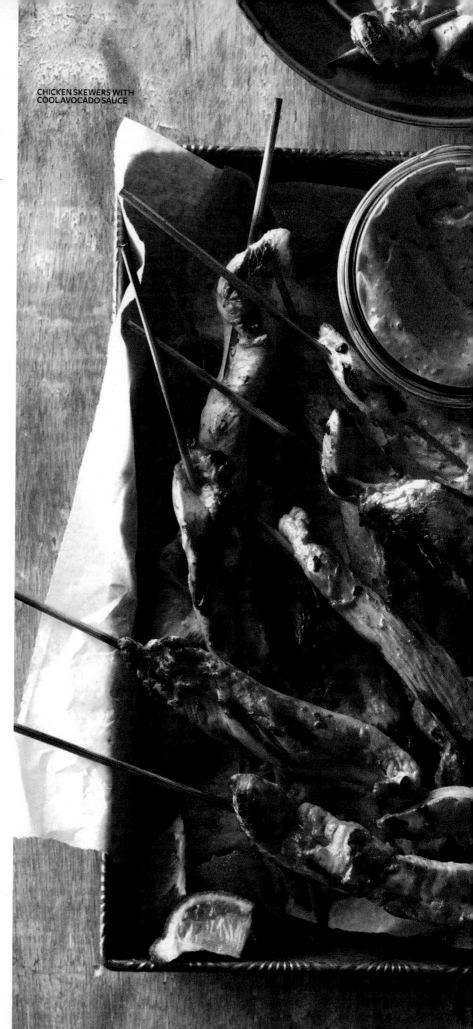

CHICKEN SKEWERS WITH
COOL AVOCADO SAUCE

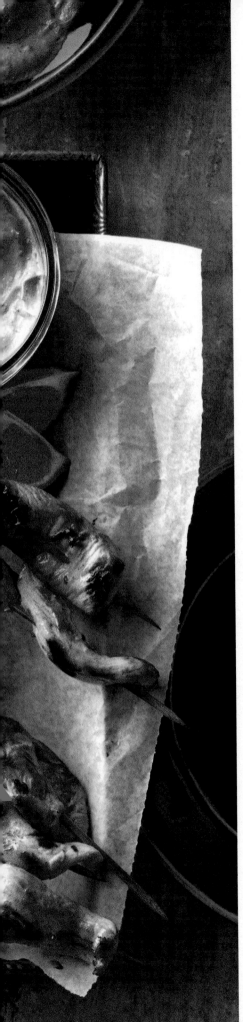

FANTASTIC FISH TACOS

I came up with these crispy, crunchy fish tacos while in search of a lighter alternative to ones that feature deep-fried fish. They're a hit with family and friends.
—*Jennifer Palmer, Rancho Cucamonga, CA*

Takes: 30 min. • **Makes:** 4 servings

- ½ cup fat-free mayonnaise
- 1 Tbsp. lime juice
- 2 tsp. fat-free milk
- 1 large egg
- 1 tsp. water
- ⅓ cup dry bread crumbs
- 2 Tbsp. salt-free lemon-pepper seasoning
- 1 lb. mahi mahi or cod fillets, cut into 1-in. strips
- 4 corn tortillas (6 in.), warmed

TOPPINGS

- 1 cup coleslaw mix
- 2 medium tomatoes, chopped
- 1 cup shredded reduced-fat Mexican cheese blend
- 1 Tbsp. minced fresh cilantro

1. For sauce, in a small bowl, mix mayonnaise, lime juice and milk; refrigerate until serving.
2. In a shallow bowl, whisk together egg and water. In another shallow bowl, toss bread crumbs with lemon pepper. Dip fish in egg mixture, then in crumb mixture, patting to help coating adhere.
3. Place a large nonstick skillet over medium-high heat. Add fish; cook 2-4 minutes per side or until golden brown and fish just begins to flake easily with a fork. Serve in tortillas with toppings and sauce.
1 taco: 321 cal., 10g fat (5g sat. fat), 148mg chol., 632mg sod., 29g carb. (5g sugars, 4g fiber), 34g pro. **Diabetic exchanges:** 4 lean meat, 2 starch.

TOASTED COCONUT MILK SHAKES

I created this recipe as a tribute to my oldest brother, Brad, who was a picky eater but loved any dessert with coconut. It has a short list of ingredients, but it's tall on coconut flavor!
—*Laurie Hudson, Westville, FL*

Takes: 15 min. • **Makes:** 4 servings

- ½ cup flaked coconut
- ⅔ cup coconut milk, stirred before measuring then chilled
- ½ cup cream of coconut, stirred before measuring then chilled
- 4 cups vanilla ice cream
  Sweetened whipped cream

1. In a small skillet, cook and stir coconut over medium-low heat until toasted, 6-8 minutes. Cool completely.
2. Place coconut milk, cream of coconut, ¼ cup toasted coconut and ice cream in a blender; cover and process until blended.
3. Pour into 4 glasses. Top with whipped cream; sprinkle with remaining coconut. Serve immediately.
1 cup: 502 cal., 30g fat (23g sat. fat), 58mg chol., 161mg sod., 54g carb. (51g sugars, 1g fiber), 6g pro.

BABY SHARK BIRTHDAY PARTY

Get ready for some under-the-sea fun! Baby sharks—and Mommy, Daddy, Grandma and Grandpa sharks, too!—won't be able to wait to take a big bite out of these yummy party foods. There are so many fun and creative things you can do (do do do) to make this a birthday that everyone will remember!

Beach Ball Cookies (p. 219) **Baby Shark Birthday Cake** (p. 222) **Ocean Punch** (p. 217)

OCEAN PUNCH

OCEAN PUNCH

This berry-flavored punch is refreshing and not overly sweet. Use your favorite Kool-Aid mix to switch up the taste and color for every season and occasion.
—*Elizabeth LeBlanc, Bourg, LA*

Prep: 10 min. + chilling
Makes: 18 servings (about 4½ qt.)

- 1 envelope unsweetened mixed berry Kool-Aid mix
- 2 qt. water
- ¾ cup sugar
  Swedish Fish candies, optional
- 1 can (46 oz.) pineapple juice, chilled
- 1 liter ginger ale, chilled

In a large pitcher, combine the Kool-Aid mix, water and sugar. Stir until mix is dissolved; refrigerate. If desired, dip Swedish Fish in water and adhere to the sides of an empty punch bowl; let stand until set. Just before serving, pour mixture into punch bowl; add pineapple juice and ginger ale.

1 cup: 94 cal., 0 fat (0 sat. fat), 0 chol., 7mg sod., 24g carb. (21g sugars, 0 fiber), 0 pro.

PEANUT BUTTER & JELLY FINGER SANDWICHES

Peanut butter and jelly sandwiches were my favorite food when I was a kid. My dad and I used to make PB&J crackers for an evening snack. And we usually had cinnamon-raisin bread in the house, so this version was a natural favorite.
—*Erica Allen, Tuckerton, NJ*

Takes: 20 min. • **Makes:** 2 dozen

- 6 Tbsp. creamy peanut butter
- 12 slices cinnamon-raisin bread, lightly toasted
- 6 Tbsp. whipped cream cheese
- 6 Tbsp. strawberry jelly

Spread peanut butter over each of 6 bread slices. Spread cream cheese, then jelly, over remaining 6 bread slices. Top with peanut butter bread slices. Cut each sandwich into 4 triangles.

1 triangle: 80 cal., 3g fat (1g sat. fat), 3mg chol., 60mg sod., 12g carb. (5g sugars, 1g fiber), 3g pro.

CHICKEN BITES WITH APRICOT SAUCE

CHICKEN BITES WITH APRICOT SAUCE

Satisfying a hungry crowd is simple with these oven-baked morsels. The bite-sized chicken pieces are served with an incredibly easy sauce that combines apricot preserves and mustard.
—*Michelle Krzmarzick, Redondo Beach, CA*

Prep: 25 min. • **Bake:** 15 min.
Makes: 2 dozen (1 cup sauce)

- ¾ cup all-purpose flour
- ½ cup buttermilk, divided
- 2 large eggs
- 2 cups crushed cornflakes
- ½ tsp. onion powder
- ½ tsp. garlic salt
- ¼ tsp. salt
- ¼ tsp. dried oregano
- ⅛ tsp. pepper
- 1 lb. boneless skinless chicken breasts, cut into 1-in. cubes
- 1 cup apricot preserves
- 2 Tbsp. prepared mustard

1. Preheat oven to 350°. Place flour and ¼ cup buttermilk in separate shallow bowls. In another shallow bowl, whisk eggs and remaining ¼ cup buttermilk. In a fourth shallow bowl, combine cornflakes, onion powder, garlic salt, salt, oregano and pepper. Dip chicken in buttermilk, then dip in flour to coat all sides; shake off excess. Dip in the egg mixture and then cornflake mixture, patting to help coating adhere. Arrange chicken in a greased 15x10x1-in. baking pan.
2. Bake until juices run clear, 15-18 minutes. In a small bowl, combine apricot preserves and mustard. Serve with chicken.

1 piece with 2 tsp. sauce: 102 cal., 1g fat (0 sat. fat), 26mg chol., 163mg sod., 18g carb. (7g sugars, 0 fiber), 6g pro.

SEASONED FISH CRACKERS

These zesty, easy-to-fix bites are irresistible. Once you start snacking on them, you'll have a difficult time stopping. For parties, I double the recipe. Even then, I never have enough!
—Deanne Causey, Midland, TX

Prep: 10 min. • **Bake:** 15 min. + cooling
Makes: about 2½ qt.

- 3 pkg. (6.6 oz. each) Goldfish cheddar crackers
- 1 envelope ranch salad dressing mix
- 3 tsp. dill weed
- ½ tsp. garlic powder
- ½ tsp. lemon-pepper seasoning
- ¼ tsp. cayenne pepper
- ⅔ cup canola oil

1. Preheat oven to 250°. Place crackers in a large bowl. Combine remaining ingredients; drizzle over crackers and toss to coat evenly. Transfer crackers to 2 ungreased 15x10x1-in. baking pans.
2. Bake 15-20 minutes, stirring occasionally. Cool completely in pans. Store crackers in an airtight container.
¼ cup: 117 cal., 7g fat (1g sat. fat), 2mg chol., 197mg sod., 10g carb. (0 sugars, 0 fiber), 2g pro.

MOM'S COLESLAW

Our family loves this crisp, refreshing salad any time of year. With a tangy vinegar and oil dressing, it has wonderful homemade flavor. When Mom made it years ago for our family of seven, it was rare to have leftovers.
—Teresa Ingebrand, Perham, MN

Prep: 10 min. + chilling • **Makes:** 12 servings

- 1 large head cabbage, shredded
- 2 medium carrots, shredded
- 1 tsp. celery seed
- 1 cup vegetable oil
- 1 cup sugar
- ½ cup white vinegar
- 1 tsp. salt
- 1 tsp. ground mustard
- 1 medium onion, quartered

In a large bowl, toss the cabbage, carrots and celery seed. Place the remaining ingredients in a blender; cover and process until combined. Pour over cabbage mixture and toss to coat. Cover and refrigerate for at least 2 hours. Serve with a slotted spoon.
½ cup: 262 cal., 19g fat (2g sat. fat), 0 chol., 220mg sod., 25g carb. (20g sugars, 3g fiber), 2g pro.

SOUTHWESTERN SEASHELL SALAD

Serve up southwestern flavor with this quick and lovely pasta salad. It's an excellent dish for picnics since no ingredients will sour. Mix it ahead for convenience, then toss with the dressing just before serving.
—Marguerite Shaeffer, Sewell, NJ

Takes: 25 min. • **Makes:** 10 servings

- 8 oz. uncooked small pasta shells
- 1 cup frozen corn, thawed
- 1 can (15 to 16 oz.) kidney or black beans, rinsed and drained
- 1 medium sweet yellow pepper, chopped
- 1 medium tomato, chopped
- ½ cup chopped red onion
- ¼ cup sliced pimiento-stuffed olives
- 3 Tbsp. lemon juice
- 2 Tbsp. minced fresh cilantro
- 2 tsp. ground cumin
- 2 tsp. olive oil
- ½ tsp. salt
- ½ tsp. pepper

1. Cook pasta according to the package directions, adding corn during the last 2 minutes. Drain and rinse in cold water.
2. Place the pasta and corn in a large bowl; add beans, yellow pepper, tomato, onion and olives. In a small bowl, whisk the lemon juice, cilantro, cumin, oil, salt and pepper. Pour over salad and toss to coat. Serve immediately.
¾ cup: 164 cal., 2g fat (0 sat. fat), 0 chol., 263mg sod., 30g carb. (3g sugars, 4g fiber), 7g pro.

BEACH BALL COOKIES

BEACH BALL COOKIES

These cookies are as colorful as beach balls and just as fun. They're delightful for kids' parties, school bake sales or when you just want a playful treat. Use bright, bold colors, or soft pastels for springtime.
—*Darlene Brenden, Salem, OR*

Prep: 45 min. • **Bake:** 10 min./batch
Makes: 2 dozen

½	cup butter, softened
½	cup sugar
½	cup confectioners' sugar
1	large egg, room temperature
½	cup canola oil
1	tsp. vanilla extract
2½	cups all-purpose flour
½	tsp. baking soda
½	tsp. cream of tartar
¼	tsp. salt
	Assorted food coloring

1. Preheat oven to 350°. In a large bowl, cream butter and sugars until light and fluffy, 5-7 minutes. Beat in egg, canola oil and vanilla. In another bowl, whisk flour, baking soda, cream of tartar and salt; gradually beat into creamed mixture.
2. Divide dough into 5 equal portions. Tint each portion a different color with food coloring. Divide each portion into 24 equal pieces; roll each piece into a ball. Gently press together 1 ball of each color to form a larger ball; place 1 in. apart on greased baking sheets. Flatten slightly with bottom of a glass.
3. Bake until bottoms are lightly browned, 10-12 minutes. Remove from pans to wire racks to cool.
1 cookie: 152 cal., 9g fat (3g sat. fat), 18mg chol., 85mg sod., 17g carb. (7g sugars, 0 fiber), 2g pro.

HOMEMADE
SLOPPY JOES

HOMEMADE SLOPPY JOES

I simmer a big batch of this hot and tangy sandwich filling, then freeze the extras. Just thaw and reheat it for a quick dinner.
—*Sandra Castillo, Janesville, WI*

Prep: 10 min. • **Cook:** 30 min.
Makes: 12 servings

- 2 lbs. ground beef
- 2 medium onions, chopped
- 2 to 3 garlic cloves, minced
- 2 cups ketchup
- 1 cup barbecue sauce
- ¼ cup packed brown sugar
- ¼ cup cider vinegar
- 2 Tbsp. prepared mustard
- 1 tsp. Italian seasoning
- 1 tsp. onion powder
- ½ tsp. pepper
- 12 hamburger buns, split

In a large skillet, cook beef, onions and garlic over medium heat until the meat is no longer pink, breaking meat into crumbles; drain. Stir in ketchup, barbecue sauce, brown sugar, vinegar, mustard, Italian seasoning, onion powder and pepper. Bring to a boil. Reduce heat; simmer, uncovered, for 20 minutes. Serve on buns.

Freeze option: Freeze cooled meat mixture in freezer containers. To use, partially thaw in the refrigerator overnight. Heat through in a saucepan, stirring occasionally; add a little water if necessary.

1 sandwich: 368 cal., 11g fat (4g sat. fat), 47mg chol., 1029mg sod., 49g carb. (27g sugars, 1g fiber), 18g pro.

PIZZA STROMBOLI

I used to own a bakery, and this bread was one of our customers' favorites. Once they smelled the aroma of pizza and sampled these tempting spiral slices, they just couldn't resist taking some home.
—*John Morcom, Oxford, MI*

Prep: 25 min. + rising • **Bake:** 25 min.
Makes: 1 loaf (12 pieces)

- 1 pkg. (¼ oz.) active dry yeast
- ¾ cup warm water (110° to 115°)
- 4½ tsp. honey
- 1 Tbsp. nonfat dry milk powder
- 2 cups bread flour
- ½ cup whole wheat flour
- 2 tsp. Italian seasoning
- 1 tsp. salt
- 4½ tsp. pizza sauce
- ¾ cup chopped pepperoni
- ½ cup shredded cheddar cheese, divided

- ¼ cup shredded Parmesan cheese
- ¼ cup shredded part-skim mozzarella cheese, divided
- 2 Tbsp. finely chopped onion
- 1 Tbsp. each chopped ripe olives, chopped pimiento-stuffed olives and chopped canned mushrooms

1. In a large bowl, dissolve yeast in warm water. Stir in honey and milk powder until well blended. In a small bowl, combine 1 cup bread flour, whole wheat flour, seasoning and salt. Add to yeast mixture; beat until smooth. Stir in pizza sauce. Stir in enough remaining bread flour to form a soft dough.

2. Turn onto a floured surface; knead until smooth and elastic, 6-8 minutes. Place in a greased bowl, turning once to grease top. Cover; let rise in a warm place until doubled, about 1 hour.

3. Preheat oven to 350°. Punch dough down. Turn onto a lightly floured surface; roll into a 14x12-in. rectangle. Sprinkle pepperoni, ¼ cup cheddar cheese, Parmesan cheese, 2 Tbsp. mozzarella cheese, onion, stuffed olives and mushrooms to within ½ in. of edges.

4. Roll up jelly-roll style, starting with a long side; pinch seam to seal and tuck ends under. Place seam side down on a greased baking sheet. Cover and let rise for 45 minutes.

5. Sprinkle with the remaining cheddar and mozzarella cheeses. Bake until golden brown, 25-30 minutes. Remove from pan to a wire rack. Serve warm. Refrigerate leftovers.

1 piece: 192 cal., 7g fat (3g sat. fat), 15mg chol., 478mg sod., 24g carb. (3g sugars, 1g fiber), 8g pro.

**BABY SHARK
BIRTHDAY CAKE**

BABY SHARK
BIRTHDAY CAKE

It doesn't take much to add a fun theme to
a birthday party. This delightfully decorated
cake, plus a few colorful frills, will bring a baby
shark theme to life.
—Taste of Home *Test Kitchen*

- -

Prep: 1 hour • **Bake:** 25 min. + cooling
Makes: 16 servings

1	cup butter, softened
2½	cups sugar
4	large eggs, room temperature
4	cups all-purpose flour
3	tsp. baking powder
1	tsp. salt
½	tsp. baking soda
1½	cups sour cream

FROSTING

6	oz. white baking chips
¼	cup heavy whipping cream
2	tsp. vanilla extract
6	large egg whites, room temperature
1½	cups sugar
½	tsp. cream of tartar
½	tsp. salt
2	cups unsalted butter, cubed
	Blue, red and green liquid food coloring
4	oz. prepared fondant
2	candy eyes
	Optional: Sea creature candies and graham cracker crumbs

1. Preheat oven to 350°. Line bottoms of
3 greased and floured 9-in. round baking pans
with parchment; grease paper. In a large bowl,
cream butter and sugar until light and fluffy,
5-7 minutes. Add eggs, 1 at a time, beating
well after each addition. Combine the flour,
baking powder, salt and baking soda; add to
the creamed mixture alternately with sour
cream, beating well after each addition.
2. Transfer to prepared pans. Bake until edges
begin to brown, 25-30 minutes. Cool for 10
minutes before removing from pans to wire
racks to cool completely.
3. In a microwave, melt the baking chips
with the cream until smooth, stirring every
30 seconds. Stir in vanilla. Set aside to cool
slightly. Meanwhile, in heatproof bowl of
stand mixer, whisk egg whites, sugar, cream
of tartar and salt until blended. Place over
simmering water in a large saucepan over
medium heat. Whisking constantly, heat
mixture until a thermometer reads 160°,
8-10 minutes.

4. Remove from heat. With whisk attachment
of stand mixer, beat on high speed until
cooled to 90°, about 7 minutes. Gradually
beat in butter, a few tablespoons at a time,
on medium speed until smooth. Beat in
cooled baking chip mixture until blended.
5. Set aside ¼ cup frosting. Tint remaining
frosting desired shades of blue; spread blue
frosting between layers and over top and
sides of cake. Tint ½ oz. fondant red. Divide
remaining fondant in half. Tint 1 portion blue.
Leave other half white. On a work surface
dusted with confectioners' sugar, roll out blue
fondant to ⅛-in. thickness. Using a 3-in. round
cutter, cut out 1 circle; repeat with white
fondant. Using a sharp knife, cut mouth
opening, teeth and body shape on lower
portion of white circle. Place white fondant
cutout onto blue circle. Roll red fondant to
⅛-in. thickness; cut a small triangle and place
in mouth opening, under white fondant and
on top of blue fondant. If needed, brush
fondant lightly with water to help layers
adhere. With remaining rolled blue fondant,
cut a crescent moon shape for tail and a
triangle for fin. Secure fin and tail to body,
brushing edges lightly with water, if needed,
to help pieces adhere. Secure candy eyes to
body with a bit of reserved frosting. Place
fondant shark on side of cake by pressing
gently into frosting. Tint remaining reserved
frosting green. Using a leaf tip, pipe seaweed
on sides of cake. If desired, decorate cake with
sea creature candies and graham cracker
crumbs for sand. Refrigerate until serving.
Remove cake from refrigerator 30 minutes
before serving. Refrigerate leftovers.
1 piece: 777 cal., 46g fat (28g sat. fat), 150mg
chol., 503mg sod., 86g carb. (62g sugars, 1g
fiber), 8g pro.

DID YOU KNOW?

A mixture of sugar, water and
cream of tartar that has been
cooked to the soft-ball stage,
fondant is often used for decorative
purposes or as a candy center. It is
commonly rolled into a sheet and
draped over cakes or molded into
shapes. Food coloring and
flavoring are often added.

HOMEMADE SANDCASTLES

SANDY BEACH TRIFLE

My husband doesn't like chocolate desserts, so I created this trifle using vanilla flavors from the pudding and cookies. It is so easy to put together and can be made ahead. Everyone loves it!

—*JoAnn Wegrzyn, Kingsley, MI*

Prep: 25 min. + chilling • **Makes:** 10 servings

- 2 **cups cold 2% milk**
- 1 **pkg. (3.4 oz.) instant vanilla pudding mix**
- 1 **pkg. (8 oz.) cream cheese, softened**
- ¼ **cup butter, softened**
- ¾ **cup confectioners' sugar**
- 1 **carton (8 oz.) frozen whipped topping, thawed**
- 1 **pkg. (19.1 oz.) Golden Oreo cookies, finely crushed**

1. In a small bowl, whisk milk and pudding mix for 2 minutes. In a large bowl, beat cream cheese and butter until smooth. Beat in confectioners' sugar until light and fluffy. Gradually beat in prepared pudding. Fold in whipped topping.
2. Place 1⅔ cups crushed cookies in a 3-qt. trifle or glass bowl. Top with half the pudding mixture. Repeat layers. Top with remaining crushed cookies. Cover and refrigerate at least 4 hours or overnight.
1 cup: 550 cal., 28g fat (14g sat. fat), 39mg chol., 383mg sod., 66g carb. (44g sugars, 0 fiber), 5g pro.

STRAWBERRY CREAM DIP

After a card game one evening, our hostess served graham crackers spread with prepared strawberry cream cheese. The flavor combo was delicious. So I decided to make a similar blend using fresh berries. Guests appreciate this simple snack.

—*Carol Gaus, Elk Grove Village, IL*

Takes: 10 min. • **Makes:** 2 cups

- 1 **pkg. (8 oz.) cream cheese, softened**
- 2 **Tbsp. honey**
- 1 **tsp. vanilla extract**
- 1 **pint fresh strawberries, sliced Graham crackers**

In a large bowl, beat cream cheese, honey and vanilla until smooth. Add strawberries; beat for 1 minute. Serve with graham crackers.
2 Tbsp.: 82 cal., 5g fat (3g sat. fat), 16mg chol., 84mg sod., 6g carb. (0 fiber), 3g pro.

HOMEMADE SANDCASTLES

Here's the perfect centerpiece for a beach-themed party. Children can join in the fun of making this easy project.

—*Taste of Home Test Kitchen*

Takes: 20 min. • **Makes:** 1 sandcastle

- ⅓ **cup all-purpose flour**
- 2 **Tbsp. sugar**
- 1 **cup cold water**
- 6 **cups moist sand**
  Sandcastle molds of various shapes and sizes
  Nautical rope, rocks and seashells

1. In a saucepan, combine flour and sugar. Gradually add cold water; mix well. Cook and stir over low heat until mixture thickens to pudding consistency.
2. Place sand in a large pail; stir in flour mixture. When cool to the touch, mix together with your hands, adding more water if needed so the sand holds its shape. Firmly pack into molds. Invert onto a flat surface; remove molds.
3. Let dry completely before handling. Depending on the humidity, this may take a few days.
4. To create a centerpiece, weave rope between the sandcastles; fill in with sand, rocks and seashells. The sand mixture will keep for weeks when stored in an airtight container.

BONFIRE PARTY

Summer is almost over, but there's still a warm breeze kissing your cheek. After soaking up the final days of swimming, kayaking, hiking or lounging in a hammock, gather with family and friends around a crackling bonfire. The cozy comfort and delicious food will turn any outdoor evening into a memorable night.

FAVORITE
HOT CHOCOLATE

FAVORITE HOT CHOCOLATE

You need just a few basic ingredients to stir up this spirit-warming sipper. It's smooth and not too sweet, making it just right for a cozy night around a bonfire.
—*Flo Snodderly, North Vernon, IN*

Takes: 15 min. • **Makes:** 8 servings

- 1 **can (14 oz.) sweetened condensed milk**
- ½ **cup baking cocoa**
- 6½ **cups water**
- 2 **tsp. vanilla extract**
  Optional: Sweetened whipped cream, marshmallows, chocolate syrup and Pirouette cookies

1. Place milk and cocoa in a large saucepan; cook and stir over medium heat until blended. Gradually stir in water; heat through, stirring occasionally.
2. Remove from heat; stir in vanilla. Add toppings as desired.
1 cup: 177 cal., 5g fat (3g sat. fat), 17mg chol., 63mg sod., 30g carb. (27g sugars, 1g fiber), 5g pro.

JALAPENO SLIDERS WITH CRISPY ONIONS

My husband and I love spicy foods, and this recipe was an excellent step up from a typical burger. It has just the right amount of flavor and spice for us, but it can be adjusted to suit your family's tastes.
—*Christina Addison, Blanchester, OH*

Takes: 25 min. • **Makes:** 8 servings

- 1 **lb. ground beef**
- ½ **tsp. salt**
- ¼ **tsp. pepper**
- 1 **to 2 jalapeno pepper, seeded and thinly sliced**
- 2 **slices white American cheese, cut into 4 squares**
- 8 **slider buns, split and toasted**
- 1 **can (2.8 oz.) french-fried onions**

1. Shape beef into eight ½-in.-thick patties; sprinkle with salt and pepper. In a large skillet, cook sliders over medium heat 2-3 minutes. Turn and top with the peppers and cheese. Continue cooking until a thermometer reads 160°, 2-3 minutes.
2. Serve on toasted buns. Top sliders with french-fried onions.
1 slider: 292 cal., 15g fat (5g sat. fat), 54mg chol., 517mg sod., 23g carb. (2g sugars, 1g fiber), 14g pro.

Sparkler Station

Use a galvanized metal bucket to house sparklers that guests can grab at their convenience. Then get ready to light up the night!

VANILLA CHAI TEA

An aromatic chai is comfort in a cup. It's extra special with a dollop of fresh whipped cream and a sprinkling of ground allspice on top.
—*Taste of Home Test Kitchen*

Takes: 25 min. • **Makes:** 6 servings

- 8 **whole peppercorns**
- ½ **tsp. whole allspice**
- 2 **cardamom pods**
- 1 **cinnamon stick (3 in.)**
- 4 **whole cloves**
- 8 **tea bags**
- 1 **Tbsp. honey**
- 4 **cups boiling water**
- 2 **cups 2% milk**
- 1 **Tbsp. vanilla extract**
- ½ **cup heavy whipping cream**
- 1½ **tsp. confectioners' sugar**
  Ground allspice

1. Place the first 5 ingredients in a large bowl. With end of a wooden spoon handle, crush mixture until aromas are released. Add tea bags, honey and boiling water; steep, covered, 6 minutes.
2. In a small saucepan, heat milk. Strain tea into a heatproof pitcher; stir in the milk and vanilla extract.
3. In a small bowl, beat cream until it begins to thicken. Add confectioners' sugar; beat until soft peaks form. Top servings with whipped cream; sprinkle with allspice.
1 cup (with 2½ Tbsp. topping): 131 cal., 9g fat (6g sat. fat), 33mg chol., 48mg sod., 9g carb. (7g sugars, 0 fiber), 3g pro.

GRANDMA'S CLASSIC POTATO SALAD

When I asked my grandmother how old this recipe is, she told me that her mom used to make it when she was a little girl. It has definitely stood the test of time.
—*Kimberly Wallace, Dennison, OH*

Prep: 25 min. • **Cook:** 20 min. + chilling
Makes: 10 servings

- 6 medium potatoes, peeled and cubed
- ¼ cup all-purpose flour
- 1 Tbsp. sugar
- 1½ tsp. salt
- 1 tsp. ground mustard
- 1 tsp. pepper
- ¾ cup water
- 2 large eggs, beaten
- ¼ cup white vinegar
- 4 hard-boiled large eggs
- 2 celery ribs, chopped
- 1 medium onion, chopped
  Sliced green onions, optional

1. Place potatoes in a large saucepan and cover with water. Bring to a boil. Reduce heat; cover and cook until tender, 15-20 minutes. Drain and cool to room temperature.
2. Meanwhile, in a small heavy saucepan, combine flour, sugar, salt, mustard and pepper. Gradually stir in water until smooth. Cook and stir over medium-high heat until thickened and bubbly. Reduce heat; cook and stir 2 minutes longer.

3. Remove from the heat. Stir a small amount of hot mixture into eggs; return all to the pan, stirring constantly. Bring to a gentle boil; cook and stir 2 minutes longer. Remove from the heat and cool completely. Gently stir in white vinegar.
4. Chop and set aside 1 hard-boiled egg; chop the remaining hard-boiled eggs. In a large bowl, combine the potatoes, celery, onion and eggs; add dressing and stir until blended. Refrigerate potato salad until chilled. Garnish with reserved chopped egg and, if desired, sliced green onions.
¾ cup: 144 cal., 3g fat (1g sat. fat), 112mg chol., 402mg sod., 23g carb. (3g sugars, 2g fiber), 6g pro. **Diabetic exchanges:** 1½ starch, ½ fat.

MAC & CHEESE CUPS

I started making these for a close friend's daughter when she started eating solid food. She loves mac and cheese and could hold these in her tiny hands to feed herself. Now the adults like them more than the kids! They're always requested at potlucks.
—*Karen Lambert, Weaverville, NC*

Prep: 20 min. • **Bake:** 25 min.
Makes: 24 servings

- 1 lb. uncooked elbow macaroni
- 3 cups sharp cheddar cheese, finely shredded
- 5 Tbsp. butter, softened
- 3 large eggs
- 1 cup half-and-half cream
- ½ cup sour cream
- 1 tsp. salt
- ½ tsp. pepper

1. Preheat oven to 350°. Cook macaroni according to the package directions, drain. Transfer to a large bowl. Stir in cheese and butter until melted.
2. In another bowl, whisk the eggs, cream, sour cream, salt and pepper until blended. Add to macaroni mixture; stir until well blended. Spoon macaroni into 24 well-greased muffin cups. Bake until golden brown, 25-30 minutes.
1 piece: 178 cal., 10g fat (6g sat. fat), 50mg chol., 226mg sod., 15g carb. (1g sugars, 1g fiber), 7g pro.

WATERMELON & CUCUMBER SALSA

WATERMELON & CUCUMBER SALSA

The combo of watermelon and cucumber may sound unusual—it tastes anything but! Eat the salsa with chips, or serve it as a topper with hot dogs or chicken tacos for a refreshing change of pace.
—*Suzanne Curletto, Walnut Creek, CA*

Takes: 15 min. • **Makes:** 3 cups

- 1½ cups seeded chopped watermelon
- ¾ cup finely chopped cucumber
- ½ cup finely chopped sweet onion
- ¼ cup minced fresh cilantro
- 1 jalapeno pepper, seeded and minced
- 2 Tbsp. lime juice
- ¼ tsp. salt

In a small bowl, combine all ingredients; refrigerate until serving.
¼ cup: 10 cal., 0 fat (0 sat. fat), 0 chol., 50mg sod., 3g carb. (2g sugars, 0 fiber), 0 pro.
Diabetic exchanges: Free food.

Summer Night Snuggles

Pack blankets in a basket to easily tote to the party. Spread the blankets on the grass or beach (keeping a safe distance from the fire), or snuggle up in one if the night air gets chilly.

SPICY SOUTHWESTERN FRUIT SALAD

This colorful fruit salad is special enough for company or to take to a potluck dinner. It's easy to double the recipe or swap in different fruits depending on what your family prefers.
—*Paula Marchesi, Lenhartsville, PA*

Takes: 30 min. • **Makes:** 8 servings

- 1 cup cubed peeled mango
- 1 cup cubed peeled papaya
- 1 cup cubed peeled fresh peaches
- 1 cup fresh blueberries
- 1 medium ripe avocado, peeled and cubed
- 1 cup frozen corn, thawed
- ⅓ cup chopped dried apricots
- ⅓ cup flaked coconut
- ¼ cup minced fresh cilantro
- 1 cup corn chips, lightly crushed

CHIPOTLE-COCONUT DRESSING
- ¼ cup coconut milk
- 2 Tbsp. lime juice
- 1 Tbsp. cider vinegar
- 1 chipotle pepper in adobo sauce, chopped
- 2 garlic cloves, minced
- ¼ tsp. cayenne pepper
- ¼ tsp. brown sugar
  Optional: Additional corn chips or flaked coconut

In a large bowl, combine first 10 ingredients. In a small bowl, whisk the coconut milk, lime juice, vinegar, chipotle, garlic, cayenne and brown sugar. Drizzle over fruit mixture; toss to coat. Sprinkle with additional corn chips or coconut if desired. Serve immediately.
¾ cup: 161 cal., 7g fat (3g sat. fat), 0 chol., 65mg sod., 24g carb. (13g sugars, 4g fiber), 2g pro. **Diabetic exchanges:** 1 starch, 1 fat, ½ fruit.

SMOKED TURKEY MELTS WITH TOMATO-ARTICHOKE SPREAD

I've served this recipe at many potlucks and it always gets great reviews. The recipe can be doubled or tripled, depending on the number of people.
—*Jess Apfe, Berkeley, CA*

Prep: 30 min. • **Bake:** 15 min.
Makes: 12 servings

- ¾ cup oil-packed sun-dried tomatoes, drained
- ⅔ cup grated Parmesan cheese
- ½ cup water-packed artichoke hearts, chopped
- ¼ cup olive oil
- 3 Tbsp. chopped fresh basil

- 2 Tbsp. chopped fresh parsley
- 2 garlic cloves, halved
- 2 tsp. balsamic vinegar
- ⅛ tsp. salt
- ⅛ tsp. pepper

SANDWICHES
- 12 slices Italian bread (½ in. thick)
- 1 cup roasted sweet red peppers, drained and chopped
- 24 thin slices deli smoked turkey
- 1 small red onion, halved and thinly sliced
- 3 Tbsp. balsamic vinegar
- 12 slices part-skim mozzarella cheese

1. Preheat the oven to 450°. Place the first 10 ingredients in a food processor; process until mixture resembles a paste. Spread over 1 side of each bread slice. Layer with the red peppers, turkey and onion. Place on baking sheets; drizzle with balsamic vinegar. Cover loosely with foil.
2. Bake 10 minutes. Uncover and top with cheese. Bake until the cheese is melted, 3-5 minutes longer.
1 open-faced sandwich: 334 cal., 15g fat (5g sat. fat), 37mg chol., 957mg sod., 28g carb. (4g sugars, 2g fiber), 21g pro.

VEGGIE BACON SLAW

This crunchy salad is nutrient-dense and tasty, too. Mix and match with your favorite dried fruit and nuts or whatever you have on hand.
—*Jeanne Larson, Rancho Santa Margarita, CA*

Prep: 20 min. + chilling • **Makes:** 12 servings

- 4 cups shredded fresh Brussels sprouts
- 4 large carrots, peeled and shredded
- 1 lb. bacon strips, cooked and crumbled
- 8 green onions, chopped
- ⅔ cup dried cranberries
- 1 cup sliced almonds, toasted

DRESSING
- 1 cup plain Greek yogurt
- ½ cup reduced-fat mayonnaise
- ½ cup cider vinegar
- ⅓ cup honey
- ½ tsp. garlic powder
- ½ tsp. sea salt

In a large bowl, combine first 6 ingredients. In another bowl, whisk dressing ingredients until smooth; drizzle over salad and toss to coat. Refrigerate the slaw, covered, at least 2 hours before serving.
¾ cup: 269 cal., 16g fat (4g sat. fat), 22mg chol., 423mg sod., 25g carb. (18g sugars, 4g fiber), 9g pro.

CHEESE & PIMIENTO SPREAD

My mother made delicious pimiento cheese, but this is a spicy, modern variation of her recipe. Serve it stuffed in celery or spread on crackers or a sandwich.
—*Elizabeth Hester, Elizabethtown, NC*

Takes: 15 min. • **Makes:** 2¾ cups

- 12 oz. sharp white cheddar cheese
- 8 oz. reduced-fat cream cheese, softened
- 2 tsp. Worcestershire sauce
- 2 tsp. white vinegar
- ¼ tsp. white pepper
- ¼ tsp. garlic powder
- ¼ tsp. cayenne pepper
- 1 jar (4 oz.) diced pimientos, undrained
  Assorted crackers and vegetables

Shred cheese; transfer to a large bowl. Add cream cheese, Worcestershire sauce, vinegar, pepper, garlic powder and cayenne; beat on low speed until blended. Drain the pimientos, reserving 2 Tbsp. juice. Stir in pimientos and reserved juice. Serve with assorted crackers and vegetables.
2 Tbsp.: 90 cal., 7g fat (4g sat. fat), 23mg chol., 150mg sod., 1g carb. (1g sugars, 0 fiber), 5g pro.

Tin Can Lantern
Upcycle an empty tin can into a twinkling outdoor lantern. Using a drill or hammer and nails, drill or punch holes into the can. You can create a decorative design if you'd like. Place a votive candle inside for a warm glow. Be sure to place the can on a firesafe surface and do not leave a lit votive unattended.

CHEESE &
PIMIENTO
SPREAD

S'MORES CUPCAKES

Marshmallow frosting puts these cupcakes over the top. Chocolate bar pieces and graham cracker crumbs on top make them extra indulgent and even more like the real thing—but better!
—*Erin Rachwal, Hartland, WI*

Prep: 30 min. • **Bake:** 20 min. + cooling
Makes: 2 dozen

- ¾ cup water
- ¾ cup buttermilk
- 2 large eggs, room temperature
- 3 Tbsp. canola oil
- 1 tsp. vanilla extract
- 1½ cups all-purpose flour
- 1½ cups sugar
- ¾ cup baking cocoa
- 1½ tsp. baking soda
- ¾ tsp. salt
- ¾ tsp. baking powder

FROSTING
- 1½ cups butter, softened
- 2 cups confectioners' sugar
- ½ tsp. vanilla extract
- 2 jars (7 oz. each) marshmallow creme
- 2 Tbsp. graham cracker crumbs
- 2 milk chocolate candy bars (1.55 oz. each)

  Optional: Toasted marshmallows and graham cracker pieces

1. Preheat the oven to 350°. In a large bowl, beat the water, buttermilk, eggs, oil and vanilla until well blended. Combine the flour, sugar, cocoa, baking soda, salt and baking powder; gradually beat dry mixture into liquid mixture until blended.

2. Fill paper-lined muffin cups half full. Bake 16-20 minutes or until a toothpick comes out clean. Cool cupcakes in pans for 10 minutes before removing from pans to wire racks to cool completely.

3. For frosting, in a large bowl, beat butter until fluffy; beat in confectioners' sugar and vanilla until smooth. Add marshmallow creme; beat until light and fluffy. Spread or pipe the frosting over cupcakes. Sprinkle with cracker crumbs. Break each candy bar into 12 pieces; garnish cupcakes. If desired, top with toasted marshmallows and graham cracker pieces.

1 cupcake: 330 cal., 15g fat (8g sat. fat), 47mg chol., 298mg sod., 43g carb. (35g sugars, 1g fiber), 3g pro.

S'MORES CUPCAKES

S'more Bar

It's not summer without everyone's favorite treat—s'mores! Pack a tray with mason jars, a Thermos, cups and other accouterments to create an al fresco s'more or hot cocoa bar.

BUTTERSCOTCH PEANUT BUTTER SQUARES

These bars, which our family refers to as peanut butter brownies, are delicious. They slice and pack easily, making them ideal for road trips and bake sales. I always double the recipe because a single batch is never enough!
—*Debbie Johnson, Centertown, MO*

- -

Prep: 20 min. + cooling
Bake: 20 min. + cooling
Makes: 16 squares

- 1¼ cups all-purpose flour
- 1 tsp. baking powder
- ½ tsp. salt
- 1½ cups packed brown sugar
- ½ cup butter, cubed
- ½ cup chunky peanut butter
- 2 large eggs, room temperature, lightly beaten
- 1 tsp. vanilla extract

1. Preheat oven to 350°. In a small bowl, whisk flour, baking powder and salt.
2. In a large saucepan, combine brown sugar, butter and peanut butter; bring to a boil, stirring to blend. Remove from heat; cool slightly, about 10 minutes.
3. Stir in eggs and vanilla. Stir in flour mixture. Transfer to a greased 9-in. square baking pan. Bake until golden brown and a toothpick inserted in center comes out clean (do not overbake), 20-25 minutes. Cool completely in pan on a wire rack. Cut into squares. Store in an airtight container.

1 square: 222 cal., 10g fat (4g sat. fat), 39mg chol., 203mg sod., 30g carb. (21g sugars, 1g fiber), 4g pro.

OKTOBERFEST

Raise a stein to an Oktoberfest celebration that's filled with as much beer, food and fun as the annual two-week festival in Munich. Eat and drink in true Bavarian style with rustic, familiar German dishes, including sauerbraten, blaukraut and pork schnitzel. These recipes will show you how easy it is to bring *gemutlichkeit* to the table. Prost!

Currywurst (p. 240) **Chewy Soft Pretzels** (p. 237)
Obatzda (German Beer Cheese Dip) (p. 236)

OBATZDA (GERMAN BEER CHEESE DIP)

GERMAN RYE BREAD

We like this homemade rye so much that I seldom buy store-bought bread anymore. I've made it for our church bake sales for years and it always goes quickly.
—*Mary Ann Bonk, New Berlin, WI*

Prep: 30 min. + rising • **Bake:** 30 min.
Makes: 4 loaves (8 pieces each)

- 1 pkg. (¼ oz.) active dry yeast
- 4 cups warm water (110° to 115°), divided
- 2 cups rye flour
- 6 Tbsp. sugar
- 2 Tbsp. caraway seeds
- 2 tsp. salt
- 7 to 8 cups all-purpose flour
- 2 tsp. cornmeal

TOPPING
- 1 large egg, lightly beaten
- 4 tsp. caraway seeds

1. In a 4-qt. glass bowl, dissolve yeast in 2 cups warm water; whisk in rye flour until smooth. Cover loosely with a clean kitchen towel. Let stand in a warm place for about 4 hours or until batter falls about 1 in. and surface bubble activity is reduced. Stir in the sugar, caraway seeds, salt, 5 cups all-purpose flour and remaining water; mix well. Stir in enough remaining flour to form a firm dough. Turn onto a floured surface; knead until smooth and elastic, about 8 minutes. Cover and let rest for 15 minutes.

2. Divide dough into 4 portions. Cover and let rest for 15 minutes. Shape into 4 round loaves, about 6 in. each. Coat 2 baking sheets with cooking spray; sprinkle each with 1 tsp. cornmeal. Place loaves on pans. Cover and let rise until doubled, about 45 minutes.

3. With a sharp knife, make several slashes across the top of each loaf. Brush with egg. Sprinkle each loaf with 1 tsp. caraway seeds. Bake at 400° until browned, 30-35 minutes, rotating pans after 15 minutes. Cool loaves on wire racks.

1 piece: 136 cal., 1g fat (0 sat. fat), 7mg chol., 150mg sod., 29g carb. (0 sugars, 2g fiber), 4g pro. **Diabetic exchanges:** 2 starch.

OBATZDA (GERMAN BEER CHEESE DIP)

Obatzda, otherwise known as German beer cheese dip, is delicious and creamy. It's the perfect dip to make the night before a party.
—*Beate Trinkl, Einsbach, Germany*

Takes: 15 min. • **Makes:** 3½ cups

- 2 rounds (8 oz. each) Camembert cheese, rind on, sliced
- 1 pkg. (8 oz.) cream cheese, softened
- 1 medium onion, finely chopped
- 1 tsp. paprika
- ½ tsp. caraway seeds
- ¼ tsp. salt
- ⅛ tsp. pepper

In a small bowl, mash Camembert cheese with a fork to desired consistency. Beat in cream cheese, onion and seasonings. If desired, sprinkle with additional caraway seeds.

2 Tbsp.: 79 cal., 7g fat (4g sat. fat), 20mg chol., 183mg sod., 1g carb. (1g sugars, 0 fiber), 4g pro.

Small Bites

For quick nibbles, set out radishes, Cambozola and sausage, such as landjaeger, on a wooden platter.

CHEWY SOFT PRETZELS

These homemade pretzels never last long around our house. My kids love to make them, and eat them! I serve them to company with a variety of dips, such as pizza sauce, ranch dressing, spinach dip or hot mustard.
—*Elvira Martens, Aldergrove, BC*

Prep: 1 hour + rising • **Bake:** 15 min.
Makes: 1 dozen

- 1 pkg. (¼ oz.) active dry yeast
- 1½ cups warm water (110° to 115°)
- 1 Tbsp. sugar
- 2 tsp. salt
- 4 to 4¼ cups all-purpose flour
- 8 cups water
- ½ cup baking soda
- 1 large egg, lightly beaten
  Optional toppings: Kosher salt, sesame seeds, poppy seeds and grated Parmesan cheese

1. Dissolve yeast in warm water. In a large bowl, combine sugar, salt, yeast mixture and 2 cups flour; beat on medium speed until smooth. Stir in enough remaining flour to form a stiff dough.
2. Turn dough onto a floured surface; knead until smooth and elastic, about 5 minutes. Place in a greased bowl, turning once to grease the top. Cover and let rise in a warm place until doubled, about 1 hour.
3. Punch down dough; divide and shape into 12 balls. Roll each into a 22-in. rope; shape into a pretzel.

4. Preheat oven to 425°. Place water and baking soda in a large saucepan; bring to a boil. Place pretzels, 1 at a time, in boiling water for 30 seconds. Remove; drain on paper towels that have been lightly sprayed with cooking spray.
5. Place on greased baking sheets. Brush with egg; top as desired. Bake until golden brown, 12-14 minutes. Remove from pans to wire racks; serve warm.
1 pretzel: 164 cal., 1g fat (0 sat. fat), 16mg chol., 400mg sod., 33g carb. (1g sugars, 1g fiber), 5g pro.

OKTOBERFEST SOUP

I love Oktoberfest beer and food, and I'm also a big fan of soups. I was in a bar a few years ago during Oktoberfest, sampling the food, and I realized they didn't have a soup on the menu. I decided to make one inspired by the flavors of my favorite festival.
—*Tim Pietrowski, Middlsex, NJ*

Prep: 15 min. • **Cook:** 50 min.
Makes: 8 servings (2½ qt.)

- 1 lb. uncooked bratwurst links
- 3 Tbsp. water
- 2 Tbsp. olive oil
- 1 large onion, chopped
- 3 garlic cloves, minced
- 8 medium red potatoes (about 2 lbs.), cubed
- 1 carton (32 oz.) chicken stock
- 1 bottle (12 oz.) Oktoberfest beer or 1½ cups chicken stock
- 1 Tbsp. ground mustard
- 1 Tbsp. caraway seeds
- 1 tsp. salt
- ½ tsp. pepper
  Shredded Swiss cheese

1. Place bratwurst and water in a Dutch oven. Cover; cook over medium heat 10 minutes. Uncover; turn bratwurst and cook until browned and centers are no longer pink, 13-17 minutes longer. Remove and cool slightly. Cut into ¼-in.-thick slices; set aside. In the same pan, heat oil over medium heat. Cook and stir onion until tender, 5-7 minutes. Add garlic; cook 1 minute longer.
2. Stir in potatoes, chicken stock, beer, mustard, caraway seeds, salt and pepper. Bring to a boil; reduce heat. Simmer, uncovered, until potatoes are tender, 20-25 minutes. Add sliced bratwurst; heat through. Just before serving, sprinkle with cheese.
1¼ cups: 335 cal., 21g fat (6g sat. fat), 42mg chol., 1027mg sod., 24g carb. (3g sugars, 3g fiber), 13g pro.

GERMAN-STYLE GREEN BEANS

My grandmother often prepared her fresh green beans this way, and we preferred these to plain buttered beans. The recipe goes back to before the 1920s and was a favorite dish of our family when I was growing up.
—*Lois Gelzer, Standish, ME*

Takes: 30 min. • **Makes:** 6 servings

- 1½ lbs. fresh green beans, cut into 1-in. pieces
- 6 bacon strips
- 1 large onion, chopped
  Salt and pepper to taste

1. Place beans in a saucepan and cover with water; bring to a boil. Reduce heat; cover and cook for 15-20 minutes or until tender.
2. Meanwhile, in a skillet, cook bacon until crisp. Remove bacon and set aside. Saute onion in drippings until tender; remove with a slotted spoon. Drain beans; return to pan. Add onion, 1 Tbsp. drippings, salt and pepper; heat through. Crumble the bacon; add to the beans and toss. Serve immediately.
¾ cup: 166 cal., 13g fat (5g sat. fat), 15mg chol., 172mg sod., 9g carb. (4g sugars, 4g fiber), 4g pro.

Pretzel Display Stand

Are you "knots" for pretzels? If these salty snacks are a must at your Oktoberfest celebration, you'll want an easy way to display them so guests can grab one at their convenience. A copper pretzel stand like this one works beautifully. Or, for a clever DIY version, set up a colorful towel rack and hang the pretzels on clean metal shower curtain hooks.

GERMAN POTATO BALLS

With a few basic ingredients, my mother transformed russet potatoes into delightful dumplings. This authentic German side dish is so hearty and comforting. We love the dumplings covered in sauerbraten gravy.
—*Cathy Eland, Hightstown, NJ*

Prep: 50 min. + chilling • **Cook:** 15 min.
Makes: 10 servings

    3   lbs. russet potatoes
    2   large eggs
    1   cup all-purpose flour, divided
    ½   cup dry bread crumbs
    1   tsp. salt
    ¼   tsp. ground nutmeg
        Dash pepper
        Minced fresh parsley, optional

1. Place the potatoes in a saucepan and cover with water; bring to a boil. Reduce heat; cover and simmer for 30-35 minutes or until tender. Drain well. Refrigerate 2 hours or overnight.
2. Peel and grate potatoes. In a bowl, combine the eggs, ¾ cup flour, bread crumbs, salt, nutmeg and pepper. Add potatoes; mix with hands until well blended. Shape into 1½-in. balls; roll in remaining flour.
3. In a large kettle, bring salted water to a boil. Add the dumplings, a few at a time, to boiling water. Simmer, uncovered, until dumplings rise to the top; cook for 2 minutes longer. Remove dumplings with a slotted spoon to a serving bowl. Sprinkle with parsley if desired.
1 cup: 190 cal., 2g fat (0 sat. fat), 43mg chol., 304mg sod., 38g carb. (3g sugars, 3g fiber), 6g pro.

TEST KITCHEN TIP

When it comes to cooking potatoes, there are several simple ways to achieve tasty results. Regardless of the cooking method you choose, avoid using aluminum or iron pots as they can turn potatoes gray.

GERMAN SAUERBRATEN

Our family loves it when Mom prepares this wonderful old-world dish. The tender beef has a bold blend of mouthwatering seasonings. It smells so good while it's cooking, in the oven and tastes even better! Before starting this recipe, be advised the beef roast needs two days to marinate.

—*Cathy Eland, Highstown, NJ*

Prep: 10 min. + marinating • **Cook:** 3 hrs.
Makes: 14 servings

- 2 tsp. salt
- 1 tsp. ground ginger
- 1 beef top round roast (4 lbs.)
- 2½ cups water
- 2 cups cider vinegar
- ⅓ cup sugar
- 2 medium onions, sliced, divided
- 2 Tbsp. mixed pickling spices, divided
- 1 tsp. whole peppercorns, divided
- 8 whole cloves, divided
- 2 bay leaves, divided
- 2 Tbsp. vegetable oil
- 14 to 16 gingersnaps, crushed

1. In a small bowl, combine salt and ginger; rub over roast. Place in a deep glass bowl. In a large bowl, combine the water, vinegar and sugar. Pour half of the marinade into a large saucepan; add half of the onions, pickling spices, peppercorns, cloves and bay leaves. Bring to a boil. Pour over roast; turn to coat. Cover and refrigerate for 2 days, turning twice a day. Refrigerate remaining marinade.
2. Remove remaining marinade from the refrigerator and add the remaining onions, pickling spices, peppercorns, cloves and bay leaves. Cover and refrigerate.
3. Drain and discard marinade from roast; pat roast dry. In a Dutch oven over medium-high heat, brown the roast in oil on all sides. Pour 1 cup of reserved marinade with all of the onions and seasonings over roast (cover and refrigerate remaining marinade). Bring to a boil. Reduce the heat; cover and simmer for 3 hours or until meat is tender.
4. Strain cooking juices, discarding onions and seasonings. Add enough reserved marinade to the cooking juices to measure 3 cups. Pour into a large saucepan; bring to a boil. Add the gingersnaps; reduce heat and simmer until the gravy is thickened. Slice roast and serve with gravy.

4 oz. cooked beef with gravy: 233 cal., 7g fat (2g sat. fat), 72mg chol., 410mg sod., 11g carb. (6g sugars, 0 fiber), 30g pro.

GERMAN SAUERBRATEN

BLAUKRAUT

This dish is special to me because my mom used to make this for us when we were kids. It's an authentic German recipe and simple to make. The dish has become one of the most popular German sides in our restaurant, the Bavarian Inn, and our guests love it! Try it as a side dish with pork chops or your favorite German entree.

—*Dorothy Zehnder, Frankenmuth, MI*

Prep: 20 min. • **Cook:** 20 min.
Makes: 10 servings

- 6 oz. bacon strips, chopped
- 1 medium onion, chopped
- ¼ tsp. liquid smoke, optional
- 2 lbs. red cabbage (about 1 medium head), shredded
- 3¼ cups water
- 1½ cups white vinegar
- 1 medium apple, sliced
- 1 cup sugar
- 1¼ tsp. salt

1. In a Dutch oven, cook bacon over medium heat for 5 minutes. Add onion; cook and stir until tender, 6-8 minutes. If desired, stir in liquid smoke.
2. Add cabbage, water, vinegar, apple, sugar and salt. Bring to a boil; reduce heat. Simmer, covered, until cabbage is crisp-tender, about 20 minutes, stirring every 10 minutes. Serve with a slotted spoon.

½ cup: 189 cal., 7g fat (2g sat. fat), 11mg chol., 433mg sod., 30g carb. (26g sugars, 2g fiber), 4g pro.

Game time!

Oktoberfest is so much more than cold brews and brats! Amp up the fun factor with these traditional games and activities. Lederhosen optional.

HAMMERSCHLAGEN

In this classic German game, players take turns, using only one hand and the pointed end of a cross-peen hammer, as they attempt to hit their designated nail flush with the surface of a tree stump or log.

BEER STEIN RACE

Fast and steady wins the race! Set up a winding course for your pals to run, with steins in tow. Whoever finishes with the speediest time—and the most beer in their stein—wins!

CHICKEN DANCE

It's an Oktoberfest tradition! Shape both hands to mimic chicken beaks; open and close them to the beat. Next, bend your arms at the elbows and imitate a chicken trying to fly. Then place your hands behind you to look like tail feathers and shake. Finish off with four claps!

STEIN-HOLDING CONTEST

Have competitors hold a full 1-liter beer stein out in front of them with a straight arm. Prize goes to the last person standing.

PORK SCHNITZEL WITH DILL SAUCE

Schnitzel is one of my husband's favorites. It reminds him of his German roots, and I like that it's easy to make for a group.
—*Joyce Folker, Parowan, UT*

Prep: 20 min. • **Cook:** 20 min.
Makes: 6 servings

- ½ cup all-purpose flour
- 2 tsp. seasoned salt
- ½ tsp. pepper
- 2 large eggs
- ¼ cup 2% milk
- 1½ cups dry bread crumbs
- 2 tsp. paprika
- 6 pork sirloin cutlets (4 oz. each)
- 6 Tbsp. canola oil

DILL SAUCE
- 2 Tbsp. all-purpose flour
- 1½ cups chicken broth
- 1 cup sour cream
- ½ tsp. dill weed

1. In a shallow bowl, mix flour, seasoned salt and pepper. In a second shallow bowl, whisk eggs and milk until blended. In a third bowl, mix bread crumbs and paprika.
2. Pound pork cutlets with a meat mallet to ¼-in. thickness. Dip cutlets in flour mixture to coat both sides; shake off excess. Dip in egg mixture, then in crumb mixture, patting to help coating adhere.
3. In a large skillet, heat oil over medium heat. Add the pork in batches; cook 2-3 minutes on each side or until golden brown. Remove to a serving plate; keep warm. Wipe skillet clean if necessary.
4. In a small bowl, whisk flour and broth until smooth; add to same skillet. Bring to a boil, stirring constantly; cook and stir 2 minutes or until thickened.
5. Reduce heat to low. Stir in sour cream and dill weed; heat through (do not boil). Serve with pork.
1 serving: 451 cal., 24g fat (8g sat. fat), 115mg chol., 739mg sod., 23g carb. (3g sugars, 1g fiber), 31g pro.

CURRYWURST

When I lived in Berlin, Germany, many years ago, one of my favorite things to eat was currywurst and pomme frites. When I came back to the States, I created my own version, which is a pretty close to the original.
—*Julie Merriman, Seattle, WA*

Prep: 15 min. • **Cook:** 40 min.
Makes: 4 servings

- 1 lb. uncooked bratwurst links
- 3 Tbsp. water
- 1 Tbsp. olive oil
- 1 medium onion, finely chopped
- 2 cups ketchup
- ½ cup chicken broth
- ¼ cup packed brown sugar
- 4 Tbsp. red wine vinegar
- 2 Tbsp. curry powder
- 2 Tbsp. smoked paprika
  Hot cooked french fries

1. Place bratwurst and water in a skillet, cover and cook over medium heat for 10 minutes. Uncover; turn bratwurst and cook until browned and centers are no longer pink, 13-17 minutes longer. Remove and cool slightly. Cut into ½-in.-thick slices; set aside.
2. In the same skillet, heat olive oil over medium heat. Add onion; cook and stir until tender, 5-7 minutes. Add ketchup, chicken broth, brown sugar, vinegar, curry powder and paprika. Bring to a boil; reduce heat. Simmer, uncovered, until slightly thickened, 8-10 minutes, stirring occasionally. Add sliced bratwurst; heat through.
3. Serve sausage mixture with french fries; sprinkle with additional curry powder.
1 serving: 612 cal., 37g fat (12g sat. fat), 85mg chol., 2611mg sod., 56g carb. (47g sugars, 3g fiber), 17g pro.

DID YOU KNOW?

Lager Lineup

Beers from six Munich breweries are served at the festival in Germany—Hofbrau, Hacker-Pschorr, Paulaner, Spaten, Augustiner and Lowenbrau. All are available stateside. Score!

CURRYWURST

ALMOND PEAR TORTE

Pears and nutmeg complement each other in this creamy torte. Sprinkling slivered almonds on top adds a nice crunch.
—*Trisha Kruse, Eagle, ID*

Prep: 30 min. • **Bake:** 55 min. + cooling
Makes: 14 servings

- 1⅓ cups all-purpose flour
- ¾ cup butter, softened
- ½ cup sugar
- ½ cup ground almonds, toasted
- ¼ tsp. ground nutmeg

FILLING
- 2 pkg. (8 oz. each) cream cheese, softened
- ¼ cup packed brown sugar
- ¼ tsp. almond extract
- 2 large eggs

TOPPING
- ½ cup packed brown sugar
- ¼ tsp. ground nutmeg
- 3 cups thinly sliced peeled fresh pears
- ½ cup slivered almonds

1. In a small bowl, combine the flour, butter, sugar, almonds and nutmeg. Press onto the bottom of a greased 9-in. springform pan; set aside.

2. In a large bowl, beat the cream cheese, brown sugar and extract until smooth. Add eggs; beat on low speed just until combined. Pour over crust.

3. For topping, combine the brown sugar and nutmeg. Add pears; toss to coat. Arrange over top. Sprinkle with almonds.

4. Bake at 350° for 50-60 minutes or until the center is almost set. Cool on a wire rack for 10 minutes. Carefully run a knife around the edge of pan to loosen; cool 1 hour longer. Refrigerate leftovers.

1 piece: 388 cal., 26g fat (14g sat. fat), 92mg chol., 180mg sod., 36g carb. (23g sugars, 2g fiber), 6g pro.

GERMAN APPLE STRUDEL

This gorgeous strudel has just what you crave—thin layers of flaky crust and lots of juicy apples.
—*Darlene Brenden, Salem, OR*

Prep: 1 hour + standing • **Bake:** 45 min./batch
Makes: 2 strudels (8 pieces each)

- 3 cups all-purpose flour
- ½ cup canola oil, divided
- ¾ cup warm water (120°)
- 1 large egg, room temperature, lightly beaten

FILLING
- 1½ cups fresh bread crumbs
- 6 cups chopped peeled apples (about 6 medium)
- ½ cup raisins
- 1 cup sugar
- 1½ tsp. ground cinnamon
- ⅓ cup butter, melted
- 3 Tbsp. sour cream

1. Place flour in a mixer bowl; beat in ¼ cup oil (mixture will be slightly crumbly). In a small bowl, slowly whisk warm water into beaten egg; add to flour mixture, mixing well. Beat in the remaining oil until smooth. Transfer to a greased bowl, turning once to grease the top. Cover dough and let rest in a warm place for about 30 minutes.

2. Preheat oven to 350°. Spread the bread crumbs into an ungreased 15x10x1-in. baking pan. Bake for 10-15 minutes or until golden brown, stirring occasionally. Cool completely.

3. Tape a 30x15-in. sheet of parchment onto a work surface; dust lightly with flour. Divide dough in half; place 1 portion on parchment and roll to a very thin 24x15-in. rectangle. (Keep remaining dough covered.) Remove tape from parchment.

4. Sprinkle ¾ cup bread crumbs over dough rectangle to within 1 in. of edges. Starting 3 in. from a short side, sprinkle 3 cups apples and ¼ cup raisins over a 3-in.-wide section of dough. Mix sugar and cinnamon; sprinkle half of the mixture over fruit. Drizzle with half of the melted butter.

5. Roll up jelly-roll style, starting at the fruit-covered end and lifting with parchment; fold in sides of dough as you roll to contain filling. Using parchment, transfer the strudel to a 15x10x1-in. baking pan; trim parchment to fit pan.

6. Bake on lowest oven rack 45-55 minutes or until golden brown, brushing top with sour cream 2 times while baking. Repeat with the remaining ingredients.

7. Using parchment, transfer to a wire rack to cool. Serve warm or at room temperature.

1 piece: 285 cal., 12g fat (3g sat. fat), 24mg chol., 61mg sod., 42g carb. (20g sugars, 2g fiber), 4g pro.

⬆

To make fresh bread crumbs, tear bread into pieces and place in a food processor; pulse until fine crumbs form. Two to three bread slices will yield about 1½ cups crumbs.

GERMAN APPLE STRUDEL

GUGELHOPF

Bring a taste of the Old World to your table with this time-honored German pastry. It's sure to please everyone...even those who don't care for fruitcake. You can use dried cherries or raisins in place of the other dried fruits if you like.
—*Karen Deaver, Babylon, NY*

- -

Prep: 20 min. + rising • **Bake:** 30 min. + cooling
Makes: 12 servings

3½	tsp. active dry yeast
1	cup warm 2% milk (110° to 115°)
3	cups all-purpose flour
¾	cup sugar
½	cup butter, softened
4	tsp. grated orange zest
	Dash salt
4	large egg yolks
½	cup chopped dried apricots
½	cup dried cranberries
½	cup slivered almonds
	Confectioners' sugar

1. In a small bowl, dissolve yeast in warm milk. Place the flour, sugar, butter, orange zest and salt in a food processor; cover and process until blended. Add the egg yolks; cover and process just until moistened. While mixture is processing, gradually add milk mixture in a steady stream. Stir in the apricots, cranberries and almonds.

2. Transfer to a greased 9-in. decorative tube pan. Cover and let rise until doubled, about 1 hour. Bake at 375° until pastry is golden brown, 30-35 minutes. Cool 5 minutes before removing to a wire rack to cool completely. Sprinkle with confectioners' sugar.

1 piece: 324 cal., 12g fat (6g sat. fat), 83mg chol., 91mg sod., 48g carb. (21g sugars, 3g fiber), 6g pro.

GOOD WITCH, BAD WITCH

Invite friends to drop in for a magical Halloween party celebrating the witches of Oz. Hosting a bewitching bash inspired by the timeless classic needn't be a brain twister. Just follow the yellow brick road to fun with these enchanting pink and green foods, decorations and party favors. Everyone will be spellbound!

Cherry Lemon-Lime Punch (p. 246) **Good Witch Cake** (p. 252) **Bad Witch Cake** (p. 252) **Confetti Snack Mix** (p. 246) **Turkey, Gouda & Apple Tea Sandwiches** (p. 248)

CHERRY
LEMON-LIME
PUNCH

GARLIC DIP

I've been making this dip for years, and now my grown daughters fix it for their families. My mom makes it, too, and her motto is, "You can never have too much garlic!"
—*Jauneen Hosking, Waterford, WI*

- -

Takes: 5 min. • **Makes:** 1½ cups

- 1 pkg. (8 oz.) cream cheese, softened
- ½ cup sour cream
- 1 Tbsp. 2% milk
- 1½ tsp. Worcestershire sauce
- 3 garlic cloves, minced
- ¼ tsp. salt
- ⅛ tsp. pepper
- Fresh vegetables or pretzels

In a small bowl, beat the cream cheese, sour cream, milk, Worcestershire sauce, garlic, salt and pepper until blended. Serve the dip with vegetables or pretzels.
2 Tbsp.: 89 cal., 9g fat (5g sat. fat), 22mg chol., 120mg sod., 2g carb. (1g sugars, 0 fiber), 2g pro.

CONFETTI SNACK MIX

I've made this party mix for many years, and I usually double the recipe because it goes so fast. It makes a nice hostess gift or party favor when wrapped in a decorative container.
—*Jane Bray, Temple Terrace, FL*

- -

Takes: 10 min. • **Makes:** 7 cups

- 4 cups Golden Grahams
- 1 cup dry roasted peanuts
- 1 cup dried banana chips
- 1 cup raisins
- 1 cup milk chocolate M&M's

In a large bowl, combine all ingredients. Store in an airtight container.
¼ cup: 125 cal., 6g fat (3g sat. fat), 1mg chol., 98mg sod., 18g carb. (12g sugars, 1g fiber), 2g pro.

CHERRY LEMON-LIME PUNCH

I make an ice ring out of cherry soda pop to keep the punch cold and add extra color. The flavor always brings folks back for more.
—*Carol Van Sickle, Versailles, KY*

- -

Takes: 15 min.
Makes: 22 servings (5½ qt.)

- 8 cups cold water
- 1 can (12 oz.) frozen lemonade concentrate, thawed plus ¾ cup thawed lemonade concentrate
- 2 liters ginger ale, chilled
- 1 liter cherry lemon-lime soda, chilled
- Optional: Maraschino cherries and lemon wedges

In a large punch bowl, combine water and lemonade concentrate. Stir in ginger ale and lemon-lime soda. If desired, garnish with maraschino cherries and lemon wedges. Serve immediately.
1 cup: 102 cal., 0 fat (0 sat. fat), 0 chol., 13mg sod., 26g carb. (24g sugars, 0 fiber), 0 pro.

7-FRUIT SALAD

A tongue-tingling lime dressing complements the variety of fruit in this salad. It's always a hit.
—*Judi Cottrell, Grand Blanc, MI*

- -

Prep: 20 min. + chilling • **Makes:** 10 servings

- ½ cup lime juice
- ½ cup water
- ½ cup sugar
- 2 medium nectarines, thinly sliced
- 1 large firm banana, thinly sliced
- 1 pint blueberries
- 1 pint fresh strawberries, sliced
- 1½ cups watermelon balls
- 1 cup green grapes
- 1 kiwifruit, peeled and chopped

1. In a large bowl, combine the lime juice, water and sugar; stir until sugar is dissolved. Add nectarines and banana; toss to coat.
2. In a 2½-qt. glass bowl, combine the remaining fruits. Add nectarine mixture; stir gently. Cover and refrigerate for 1 hour. Serve with a slotted spoon.
1 cup: 116 cal., 1g fat (0 sat. fat), 0 chol., 2mg sod., 29g carb. (25g sugars, 3g fiber), 1g pro.

CONFETTI
SNACK MIX

TURKEY, GOUDA & APPLE TEA SANDWICHES

These fun mini sandwiches are a tasty addition to any gathering. The cranberry mayo lends a unique flavor twist, and the apples add a nice crunch. Serve them with frilled toothpicks for extra flair.
—Taste of Home *Test Kitchen*

Takes: 25 min. • **Makes:** 4 dozen

⅔ cup reduced-fat mayonnaise
2 Tbsp. whole-berry cranberry sauce
24 very thin slices wheat or white bread, crusts removed
12 slices deli turkey
2 medium apples, thinly sliced
12 thin slices smoked Gouda cheese
4 cups fresh baby spinach

1. Place mayonnaise and cranberry sauce in a small food processor. Cover and process until blended. Spread over each bread slice.
2. Layer the deli turkey, apple slices, cheese and spinach over each of 12 bread slices; top with the remaining bread. Cut each sandwich into quarters.

1 tea sandwich: 258 cal., 12g fat (4g sat. fat), 48mg chol., 456mg sod., 22g carb. (5g sugars, 1g fiber), 16g pro.

Make ahead: Cranberry spread can be prepared a day in advance; cover and store in the refrigerator.

To switch up the flavors, replace the deli turkey with deli chicken or use smoked cheddar or mozzarella in place of the Gouda.

APPLE-NUT BLUE CHEESE TARTLETS

These tasty appetizers have loads of blue cheese flavor. They look and taste gourmet, but they're easy to make. The phyllo shells and filling can be made in advance—just fill the cups and warm in the oven before serving.
—*Trisha Kruse, Eagle, ID*

Prep: 25 min. • **Bake:** 10 min.
Makes: 15 appetizers

- 2 tsp. butter
- 1 large apple, peeled and finely chopped
- 1 medium onion, finely chopped
- 1 cup crumbled blue cheese
- 4 Tbsp. finely chopped walnuts, toasted, divided
- ½ tsp. salt
- 1 pkg. (1.9 oz.) frozen miniature phyllo tart shells

1. Preheat oven to 350°. In a small nonstick skillet, melt butter over medium-high heat. Add apple and onion; cook and stir until tender, 3-5 minutes. Remove from the heat; stir in blue cheese, 3 Tbsp. walnuts and salt. Spoon a rounded tablespoon of mixture into each tart shell.

2. Place tarts on an ungreased baking sheet. Bake for 5 minutes. Sprinkle with remaining walnuts; bake until tarts are lightly browned, 2-3 minutes longer.

Freeze option: Freeze cooled pastries in a freezer container, separating layers with waxed paper. To use, reheat pastries on a baking sheet in a preheated 350° oven until they are crisp and heated through.

1 tartlet: 76 cal., 5g fat (2g sat. fat), 7mg chol., 200mg sod., 5g carb. (2g sugars, 0 fiber), 3g pro. **Diabetic exchanges:** 1 fat, ½ starch.

SPIRAL PASTA SALAD WITH MARJORAM VINAIGRETTE

I like to use home-grown herbs in my recipes. Marjoram, which I think is underused, gets well-deserved attention in this fresh-tasting pasta salad.
—*Sue Gronholz, Beaver Dam, WI*

Takes: 25 min. • **Makes:** 12 servings

- 1 pkg. (12 oz.) spiral pasta
- 3 plum tomatoes, seeded and chopped
- 1 medium green pepper, chopped
- 1 small onion, thinly sliced
- 1 can (2¼ oz.) sliced ripe olives, drained

MARJORAM VINAIGRETTE

- 3 Tbsp. white wine vinegar
- 2 Tbsp. honey
- 1 Tbsp. minced fresh marjoram or 1 tsp. dried marjoram
- 1½ tsp. minced fresh basil or ½ tsp. dried basil
- 1 tsp. Dijon mustard
- ¾ tsp. salt
- ⅛ tsp. pepper
- ½ cup olive oil

1. Cook the pasta according to the package directions; drain and rinse in cold water. In a large bowl, combine pasta, tomatoes, green pepper, onion and olives.

2. In a small bowl, combine vinegar, honey, marjoram, basil, mustard, salt and pepper. Gradually whisk in oil. Pour over pasta mixture and toss to coat. Cover salad and refrigerate until serving.

1 cup: 212 cal., 10g fat (1g sat. fat), 0 chol., 208mg sod., 27g carb. (5g sugars, 1g fiber), 4g pro. **Diabetic exchanges:** 2 fat, 1½ starch.

SPRITZ
COOKIES

SPRITZ COOKIES

Here's a sure standout on your treat tray. Use cranberry-flavored gelatin for pink cookies and lime-flavored gelatin for green cookies.
—*Kristen Rahn, Burnsville, MN*

Prep: 30 min. • **Bake:** 10 min./batch + cooling
Makes: 5 dozen

- ½ cup butter, softened
- ½ cup butter-flavored shortening
- ½ cup sugar
- ¼ cup cranberry or lime gelatin powder (about 4 oz.)
- 1 large egg, room temperature
- 1 tsp. vanilla extract
- 2 cups all-purpose flour
- ½ tsp. baking powder
- ¼ tsp. salt
  Colored coarse sugar, optional

1. Preheat oven to 375°. In a large bowl, cream butter, shortening, sugar and gelatin until light and fluffy, 5-7 minutes. Beat in egg and vanilla. Combine the flour, baking powder and salt; gradually add to creamed mixture and mix well.
2. Using a cookie press fitted with the disk of your choice, press dough 2 in. apart onto ungreased baking sheets. If desired, sprinkle with coarse sugar.
3. Bake until set (do not brown), 6-8 minutes. Remove to wire racks to cool completely.
1 cookie: 58 cal., 3g fat (1g sat. fat), 8mg chol., 27mg sod., 6g carb. (3g sugars, 0 fiber), 1g pro.

TEST KITCHEN TIP

You may want to chill the dough before putting it in the cookie press. Not all recipes require this step, but sometimes the dough is too soft to use right after mixing. A half-hour in the refrigerator, covered, helps firm it up a bit before you put it into the cookie press. Don't fret if your shapes turn out a little sloppy; you can always roll it back up and put it into the press again.

Up, Up and Away

Guests will be over the rainbow when they're greeted with a stunning balloon arch. Place the arch over your buffet table or use it as a fun backdrop for photos. Creating a balloon arch is surprisingly easy. Purchase a kit or look for DIY tutorials online.

OLD-TIME POPCORN BALLS

Our family loves popcorn. These old-time popcorn balls are great anytime, but they're especially fun to pass out to trick-or-treaters or to use as spooky party favors. They always look appealing when covered in a clear wrap and tied with a festive ribbon.
—*LaReine Stevens, Ypsilanti, MI*

Takes: 30 min. • **Makes:** 8 servings

- 2 qt. popped popcorn
- ½ cup molasses
- ½ cup sugar
- ⅓ cup water
- 1 Tbsp. white vinegar
- 1 Tbsp. butter
- ¼ tsp. baking soda

1. Place popped popcorn in a large bowl and set aside. In a large heavy saucepan, combine molasses, sugar, water, vinegar and butter. Cook, without stirring, over medium heat until the mixture reaches 235° on a candy thermometer (soft-ball stage). Add baking soda and stir well.
2. Remove from heat and immediately pour over popcorn, stirring gently with a wooden spoon until well coated. When cool enough to handle, quickly shape popcorn mixture into 3-in. balls, dipping hands in cool water to prevent the syrup from sticking.
1 popcorn ball: 170 cal., 5g fat (1g sat. fat), 4mg chol., 159mg sod., 33g carb. (24g sugars, 1g fiber), 1g pro.

PEAR TEA SANDWICHES

Both good witches and bad witches will enjoy the ingredients in these delightfully different tea sandwiches. They're an enticing mix of creamy, crunchy and sweet.
—*Laurie Bock, Lynden, WA*

Takes: 30 min. • **Makes:** 8 servings

- 1 cup dried pears
- ¼ cup spreadable cream cheese
- 2 Tbsp. maple syrup
- ⅔ cup chopped walnuts, toasted
- 8 slices cinnamon-raisin bread, toasted and crusts removed

1. Place pears in a small bowl. Cover with boiling water; let stand for 5 minutes. Drain. Cool slightly; chop pears.
2. In a small bowl, combine cream cheese and syrup. Stir in pears and nuts.
3. Spread over 4 slices of toast; top with remaining toast. Cut each sandwich into 2 triangles.
1 triangle: 230 cal., 9g fat (2g sat. fat), 8mg chol., 97mg sod., 36g carb. (18g sugars, 4g fiber), 6g pro.

GOOD WITCH CAKE

All wishes will be granted when you serve this glitzy pink cake inspired by Glinda the Good Witch. It's a magical dessert for all types of soirees—a Halloween party, birthday party, princess party or a baby shower.
—Taste of Home *Test Kitchen*

Prep: 1¼ hours • **Bake:** 40 min. + cooling
Makes: 16 servings

- ¾ cup butter, softened
- 2½ cups packed brown sugar
- 4 large eggs, room temperature
- 6 oz. semisweet chocolate, melted and cooled
- 3 tsp. vanilla extract
- 3 cups all-purpose flour
- 3 tsp. baking soda
- ½ tsp. salt
- 1½ cups sour cream
- 1½ cups water

FROSTING
- 1¼ cups butter, softened
- 10 cups confectioners' sugar
- 2 tsp. vanilla extract
- ¼ tsp. salt
- ½ to ⅔ cup 2% milk
- 4 oz. yellow candy coating disks
    Pink gel food coloring
    Optional: Edible gold spray paint, edible gold paint and edible gold glitter
    Assorted sprinkles, pink sanding sugar, gold and pink pearls

1. Preheat oven to 350°. Line the bottoms of 3 greased 8-in. round baking pans with parchment; grease parchment. In a large bowl, cream butter and brown sugar until light and fluffy, 5-7 minutes. Add eggs, 1 at a time, beating well after each addition. Beat in melted chocolate and vanilla. Combine flour, baking soda and salt; add to creamed mixture alternately with sour cream, beating well after each addition. Gradually beat in water.

2. Pour batter into prepared pans. Bake until a toothpick inserted in the center comes out clean, 40-45 minutes. Cool for 10 minutes before removing from pans to wire racks to cool completely.

3. For frosting, in a large bowl, beat the butter until smooth. Gradually beat in confectioners' sugar, vanilla, salt and enough milk to reach desired consistency; remove 1½ cups frosting and set aside. Tint remaining frosting with the pink gel food coloring until desired color is reached; tint reserved frosting a lighter shade of pink.

4. If cake layers have rounded tops, trim with a serrated knife to make level. Place 1 cake layer on a serving plate; spread with ⅔ cup frosting. Repeat layers. Top with remaining cake layer. Frost top and sides of cake.

5. For decoration, place melted candy coating in piping bag fitted with a small round tip; pipe star shapes onto waxed paper. Let stand until set. If desired, coat star shapes with edible gold spray paint or edible gold paint; sprinkle with edible gold glitter. Top the cake with assorted sprinkles. Place light pink frosting in piping bag fitted with large star tip; pipe onto top of cake. Just before serving, gently stand 1 star on top of cake. Adhere the remaining stars to sides of cake by gently pressing into the frosting.

1 piece: 881 cal., 35g fat (22g sat. fat), 114mg chol., 578mg sod., 135g carb. (115g sugars, 1g fiber), 6g pro.

BAD WITCH CAKE

Satisfy an itch for dessert with this mean and green cake. Not only will it delight partygoers, you'll forget all about those ruby slippers.
—Taste of Home *Test Kitchen*

Prep: 1¼ hours • **Bake:** 40 min. + cooling
Makes: 16 servings

- ¾ cup butter, softened
- 2½ cups packed brown sugar
- 4 large eggs, room temperature
- 6 oz. semisweet chocolate, melted and cooled
- 3 tsp. vanilla extract
- 3 cups all-purpose flour
- 3 tsp. baking soda
- 1 tsp. salt
- 1½ cups sour cream
- 1½ cups water

FROSTING
- 1¼ cups butter, softened
- 10 cups confectioners' sugar
- 3 tsp. vanilla extract
- ¼ tsp. salt
- ½ to ⅔ cup 2% milk
    Green and black gel food coloring
- 4 oz. black candy coating disks, melted
    Assorted black sprinkles, sanding sugar and pearls

1. Preheat oven to 350°. Line bottoms of 3 greased 8-in. round baking pans with parchment; grease parchment. In a large bowl, cream butter and brown sugar until light and fluffy, 5-7 minutes. Add eggs, 1 at a time, beating well after each addition. Beat in melted chocolate and vanilla. Combine flour, baking soda and salt; add to creamed mixture alternately with sour cream, beating well after each addition. Gradually beat in water.

2. Pour into the prepared pans. Bake until a toothpick inserted in the center comes out clean, 40-45 minutes. Cool for 10 minutes before carefully removing from pans to wire racks to cool completely.

3. For the frosting, in a large bowl, beat the butter until smooth. Gradually beat in the confectioners' sugar, vanilla, salt and enough milk to reach desired consistency; remove 1½ cups frosting and set aside. Tint remaining frosting with green gel food coloring until desired color is reached. Tint the reserved frosting with black food coloring.

4. If cake layers have rounded tops, trim with a serrated knife to make level. Place 1 cake layer on a serving plate; spread with ⅔ cup frosting. Repeat layers. Top with remaining cake layer. Frost top and sides of cake.

5. For decoration, place melted candy coating in piping bag fitted with a small round tip; pipe witch hat shapes onto waxed paper. Let stand until set. Top cake with assorted sprinkles. Place black frosting in piping bag fitted with large star tip; pipe onto top of cake. Just before serving, gently stand 1 witch hat on top of cake. Adhere remaining witch hats and black pearls to sides of cake by gently pressing into frosting.

1 piece: 882 cal., 35g fat (22g sat. fat), 114mg chol., 504mg sod., 135g carb. (115g sugars, 1g fiber), 6g pro.

If I Only Had a Treat...

If you're hot on the heels for the perfect party favor, try one of these cute ideas. Whether pretty in pink or gruesome in green, these take-home treats—nail polish, hairbands, and candy—are sure to melt hearts (not witches). Get creative with the vessels, too. Serve pink presents in clear plastic bubbles and green goodies in black cauldrons.

BAD WITCH
CAKE

GOOD WITCH
CAKE

RECIPE INDEX

TIMELINES, PARTY PLANNING TIPS & MORE

SHARE YOUR MOST-LOVED RECIPES

Do you have a cherished recipe or a special tradition that has become part of your family's holiday? Are homemade gifts and crafts included in your celebrations? We want to hear from you. Visit *tasteofhome.com/submit* to submit a recipe, craft or other idea for editorial consideration.

P. 25

P. 235

P. 215

P. 88